The Nature of Risk

The Nature of Risk

◆•◆•◆•◆•◆•◆•◆

Stock Market Survival
and the Meaning of Life

Justin Mamis

▲▼▼

Addison-Wesley Publishing Company
Reading, Massachusetts · Menlo Park, California · New York
Don Mills, Ontario · Wokingham, England · Amsterdam · Bonn
Sydney · Singapore · Tokyo · Madrid · San Juan
Paris · Seoul · Milan · Mexico City · Taipei

Library of Congress Cataloging-in-Publication Data

Mamis, Justin, 1929–
    The nature of risk : stock market survival and the meaning of life
/ Justin Mamis.
        p. cm.
    ISBN 0-201-57770-4
    ISBN 0-201-62235-1 (pbk.)
    1. Stocks. 2. Speculation. 3. Risk. 4. Risk-taking (Psychology)
I. Title.
HG6041.M339 1991
332.63′22—dc20   91–14143
                                                                CIP

Cover design by Alwyn R. Velasquez
Text design by Joyce C. Weston
Set in 11-point Trump by Shepard Poorman

1 2 3 4 5 6 7 8 9-MU-9796959493
First printing, August 1991
First paperback printing, February 1993

To all my children—
Toby, Lisa, Josh, Noah

"Do as I say,
not as I do."

Contents

Preface

IF anyone had ever suggested—in my college days—that I would develop an obsession with, and career in, the stock market, I'd have socked him or her in the nose. But my scribblings in the margins of my old college professor's philosophy textbook (see chapter 20) reveal that I was even then trying to understand how and why we act as we do. (Actually, at age 20 I was convinced that I already knew.) It turns out that I've written a book that seems true to my life's span: a discussion of "the power to extend a partially given whole," to use Professor Blanshard's phrase, using the stock market to make comments about our daily life, and using our daily behavior to discuss ways to confront safely and successfully the risk in the stock market.

The stock market has a form and structure of its own to which we bring all sorts of human attitudes and emotions. "Avoid reading acquired meanings," Professor Blanshard warns, "into the experiences we start with." Wall Street is a place vastly more complex than it was in my youth—whoever realized we'd have to understand monetary policy, currencies, geopolitics, and the like?—but it is still, over and over, a testing of ourselves.

◇◆◇◆◇ One writing difficulty must be addressed here: the stylistic problem of "he or she," which often seems awkward and/or unnatural. I've agreed with myself to make several subtle distinctions: (1) Finding "he or she" awkward to the rhythm of writing, I have used that solution as often as I appropriately could, but only when it sounded comfortable to my writer's ear. (2) In many instances, the example, derived from my own experience, is naturally oriented to "he" rather than to "she," and then I've kept the masculine point of view. (3) Further, some examples are rooted in a stock market that until very recently was primarily masculine. There are still virtually no women traders, either as retail customers who talk to their brokers all the time, or as professionals who sit "upstairs" or stand on the trading room floor all day long, hoping for an edge. But women portfolio managers are growing in number, and are acquiring all of the job's stress, so that the term *portfolio manager*, or *money manager*, actually has validity representing both "he and she."

❖❖❖❖ Several people have helped me immeasurably, in particular my current associate, Amy Goldstein, and my former associate, Helene Meisler, who has carried her knowledge off to her own greener pastures, but continues to be helpful. Both are proof that the stock market stuff discussed herein is understandable *and* applicable. Stan Fishkin gave me a needed boost at a needed time, while Susan Schulman provided a great deal of initial encouragement. I'm a lot better at saying than doing, so I don't make zillions—that's Gerry Levine, who furnished the Kierkegaardian vision of how to get past the constant anxiety to the reward. Noah wrote his own stories over my files, and yet somehow they remained intact—as well as more fun to read. My wife, Susan, as my broker, has consistently displayed an ability to pick stocks, and an uncanny sense of when to sell them, thus helping me stay in touch with the world of the boardroom, brokers, and clients. She also understands me— which is the greatest help of all.

❖❖❖❖ I have developed a habit of seeing the stock market in other aspects of life, and here not only want to credit but to thank those whose writings I have referred to. Reading "Boggs

Bills" (chapter 8) was a delight as well as being thought-provoking, but then everything I've ever read of Lawrence Weschler's has been a treat. The *New Yorker* article by Jeff Coplon about Leonard Rogozin's horse-racing career (chapter 9) was a revelation to an old track cashier ($10 window; win, place, and show; previous races and previous days) in itself. Most of all, *Adam's Task*, by Vicki Hearne, changed my way of perceiving more than any book I've read in the past decade, and there is an underlying tenor to some of my sentences and feelings that she would recognize. I thank her for the contribution to my head and recommend *Adam's Task* to all: when reading it, simply substitute stock market (and, often, children) for her descriptions of animal behavior and human training, and you'll see what I mean.

Finally, I want to thank the stock market itself. Although it has no more socially redeeming value than pornography, it is never boring (even on dull days), often fascinating (even when aggravating), and occasionally challenging enough to redeem it socially. I wish for all of us enough stimulation from the market, as our equivalent of Picasso's brush and Casals's bow, to keep us going into a similarly lively old age.

The Nature of Risk

· ·

· 1 ·

The Future Is the Risk

TH E first word parents want a baby to understand and respond to is not *Mama* or *Daddy*—it's *No*. How is anyone going to learn to venture, to take a risk, when "No" resounds?

Parents and baby may exchange smiles, but as soon as the baby wants to take a risk—that is, do something venturesome—the infant hears: "Don't touch that," "Watch out," "Be careful." From infancy's earliest days, taking a risk becomes a negative concept. Parents know all about the dangers of the world. There's the hot stove, the steep stairway, the electrical outlet. Infants believe they can crawl across the entire universe, unaware of the edge of the bed. Have you ever noticed the surprised look on a mother's face when she realizes that the baby actually saw the danger ahead and paused on the edge, without her having to yell "No"? Mothers and fathers don't trust their supposedly bright baby to have any intuitive sense at all. "Watch out." "Be careful." "Don't" becomes a family motto.

Parents become consumed with anxiety about the terrifying risks their baby is taking, an anxiety absorbed in turn from their parents, from the news, from experience itself. Wanting the best for our children, we begin by trying to protect them from harm, from hurt, from loss, from risk itself.

Have you ever seen an infant, about to take a wobbly step or creep around the corner, turn back to look at his parents for reassurance—asking not only if it is safe to proceed, but also, is it permitted?—before he'll venture forth. "Don't" becomes, as we get older, "Look before you leap." The anxiety that breeds such phrases—however well intentioned—translates into an anxiety about every potential action. We worry about potential harm, potential hurt, potential loss, just as our parents worried on our behalf when we were too little to know any better. Taking a risk may mean divorcing; getting fired; or having to face parents', teachers', or a spouse's wrath. It also includes the way we view the stock market: an anxiety about the potential loss of money. "Don't." "Be careful." "Look before you invest."

Of course, as we toddle ahead into life, we are forced to, or are taught to, overcome certain anxieties. Our parents leave us behind to go out to dinner by themselves; we scream in terror, but they go, and they come back, and we've survived. Gradually, we scream because we don't want them to go, not because we're terrified; the lurking learned insecurity makes us want to control what happens next. The *uncertainty* of the next moment, the next hour, the next event, becomes the anxiety. What will happen? *The future is at risk.* Off we go to school, hand held, but are then compelled to go inside by ourselves where there are new "Don't"s and more "Be careful"s; one of the lessons of the school system (and later, of course, the army) is that the future is less at risk if you do what you are told.

Eventually, having been filled with all the warnings about crossing the street, we are permitted to walk home from school alone and learn to proceed so easily that it seems as if we are no longer anxious at all. Caution becomes rational, sensible. Somewhere deep inside, what is still a risk—crossing the street—has become natural. We step off the curb with scarcely a second thought because we have learned how to deal with that risk by looking both ways even when the light is on our side. *Deal with* it, not *eliminate* it. There are those who dart across recklessly between cars or, at the other extreme, the person, perhaps elderly, who steps off the curb, falters, gets out into the lane, takes two steps more, two steps back, finally retreats to the curb. That is, there are those who take risk to the extreme of trying to ignore or defy it, and those who have become so intimidated that any risk at all confuses and paralyzes.

◇◆◇◆◇ Everything is risky. Our childhood experiences, from the outset, are contained. What our parents have done is to have fed us, along with mother's milk, a steady strain of negative comments about how to proceed. They strapped us into walkers, they put gates on the stairways, they snatched dirt out of our mouths. Kids become scared of dogs simply because, as they come near, a voice calls shrilly: "Be careful, he may bite." No one ever suggests to a toddler: "Why don't you go see what's around that corner?" An infant knows no risk; all is ahead. Parents know all is risk, and try to protect. The child learns what the parents teach, and a world that starts out full of possibilities becomes full of limits and danger.

Nor does this sense of danger disappear as we gain experience. To the contrary, a new risk develops: ego risk. It was okay to risk taking a tentative first step, and then to fall, because, presumably, one's parents provided a safe environment. But if they laughed, or scoffed, and somehow made the toddler feel that failure—instead of renewed adventure—then the first ego-risk jolt has occurred. Why do we marvel at that folk saying that states if you fall off a horse you should get right back on? because it seems so daring, so full of risk, to try again so soon. Wouldn't you be embarrassed to fall off again? then people might say, "What a dope, didn't you know enough to walk?"

We come into adolescence with fear of failure as a new risk: the opposite sex won't like you; the teachers don't believe in you; how are you ever going to be an adult unless you do what your parents say and take no risks? Stage fright, or its equivalent, is everywhere, and everywhere understood: the less you expose yourself, the less danger of failing.

You can see this in sports very clearly. "Choking" under pressure separates the second stringer from the star. The difference between the top tennis players in the world, and the next rung down, Billie Jean King once said, is not the strokes—at that level, strokes are approximately the same—but in the mental attitude. The top players play to win; the others play the game so as not to lose.

When it gets to be match point, some players become tentative and hit the ball carefully. Often this kind of player is so fearful of losing that he actually double-faults at match point. The sense of ego risk does him in. In contrast, the top players continue to drive the ball from the first point to the last; when behind, they try to serve an ace. And by playing past the anxiety of the risk, they win. Even on a club level, tennis players will tell you anecdotes of how they were behind 5–0; deciding they were going to lose anyhow, they simply started to hit the ball; that ease, with nothing at risk anymore, took them to 5–5, whereupon the ego risk returned. As soon as they might win, the caution returned and produced the tentativeness that caused them to lose.

We know, of course, of the people who boast of their stock market winnings—and never say a word about the stocks they have losses in. They may believe that it is a loss on paper, and hence not a real loss, but it isn't a mirage to their ego—that's what they are protecting. (They boast about profits on paper, don't they? as if those are real.) Will you think less of them? Will their spouses refuse to go to bed with them if they have a big loss in their portfolio, if they aren't perfect? Ego risk, whether in sports, business, or the stock market, causes hesitation, faltering, and, therefore, failure.

As we get older, risk of loss becomes focused on not being able to take care of oneself. Retirement appears to be an extremely risky venture. For the sake of security, many people take, and stay in, jobs that produce pensions. In effect, they give up the best years of their lives to bureaucratic jobs so as not to face what they think of as the perils of old age. Ego risk is not as much a factor as self-risk. "Look before you leap" becomes "I can't take a chance anymore."

◆◆◆◆◆ Such language innately defines risk as negative. I've taken the risk of defining the word without first looking it up in the dictionary. Now as I open the pages (Webster's Collegiate, 5th edition), here is what I find: "Hazard; peril; exposure to loss or injury." I'm right, then. Imagine: peril! There's nothing positive about risk. "Exposure to loss or injury." No wonder parents worry. In the dictionary, the word *risk* invariably refers to danger.

We grow up in such a pervasive atmosphere of caution that it becomes astounding when we read about, or see, someone who actually does take risks willingly, skillfully, successfully. The venture capitalist, the entrepreneur, the firefighter, the batter with two strikes on him in the last of the ninth, the person who leaves a vice-presidency at age 42 to go to law school or to farm—all those who risk money, security, and the possibility of failure are so unusual nowadays that they have become folk heroes. And even more astonishing: there actually are a few people who never consider risk at all; they just do.

Were they never told "No"? Were they never limited as to where they might crawl? or what they might read? or what they might believe? Or was it the reverse? so restricted that they broke free, using defiance as a form of defense. How does one become able to venture forward without anxiety? *How does one use risk positively?*

◆◆◆◆ We are not talking here about foolhardiness, or defiance that smacks of self-destruction. Someone else can analyze the person who searches out the extreme risk of hang gliding or parachute jumping as a Sunday afternoon sport because anything less doesn't satisfy, or who, knowing the risk, believes he alone is the one who can stick a needle in his arm and not get hooked.

Children without parental "Don't"s are less likely to understand danger, as if the word is not in the language of their growing up. Such acts as holding onto the back of a bus moving up Broadway, leaping between subway cars, or a casual, even effortless, use of drugs express, it seems to us, both anger and defiance—but in part might be a language lack, too. The very notion of danger to street kids may be incomprehensible in the sense in which a suburban goody-goody has been brought up to understand it. When *all* is risk, as war is, or the street, or cancer, there is *no* future. "What the hell" derives from that sense, in contrast to a more standard "The future is at risk" so "Be careful." Thus it is *fear of the future* that risk magnifies.

There are degrees of risk to which that dictionary word *peril* clearly apply, risk beyond what can be measured and turned into a positive—and yet someone somewhere will take that kind of chance. Russian roulette is an extreme of risk, an "exposure to loss" that suits reality as well as the dictionary.

Foolhardiness, defiance, sheer gambling, and other extremes aside, *if there are ways to learn to evaluate what a risk is, and whether it is worth taking, and, indeed, whether it is actually less risky than not taking it—turning the notion of risk into a positive—it may be that we can translate such answers into our own too-often too scared, too anxious behavior.* If we can learn not to choke up on match point, but rather to stroke positively, then we can learn not to choke when buying and selling stocks. *Here we have a "security"—already there is a built-in semantic implication of anti–risk-taking—that needs to be challenged. What is there about risk that can be used to produce better stock market performance?*

◇◆◇◆◇ Let's examine one daily life situation—crossing the street—to see what the risks are: When risk is examined in terms of the moment-to-moment decisions—stepping off the curb being an assumption of risk with all the dictionary negatives of hazard, peril, exposure to danger, but also with a positive: to get successfully to the other side—*risk* is at its core *making a choice.* It is a form of binary Yes/No, for Maybe merely postpones choice.

Crossing the street involves an absolute danger: a car coming can hit you and knock you down, injuring or killing you. Therefore we have learned certain safety rules: Cross at the intersection, with the light in your favor, and not in the middle of the block. We also know that some drunken driver, or crazy cabbie, could go careening through the red light and clobber us.

So we are taught to look both ways before crossing. If we follow these rules we ought never to get hit by a car while crossing the street.

But then, getting a little bolder, we come to believe that if we follow the second rule—looking both ways—we can safely cross in the middle of the block. It's a bit more of a risk, because we don't have the protection of the traffic light, but still okay. And suppose we are in a hurry. Can we simply rush across—looking as we leap? The need to get to the other side impels us. But why? to save 30 seconds we forget all we've been taught. Suddenly, going against our own best judgment, we rush out into the street even as traffic is coming—"sure" we can get across ahead of that onrushing truck. But suppose we slip, or stumble on a pothole? That moment's risk, for the sake of saving 30 seconds, does us in.

Clearly, then, we can either take what we know about proceeding safely and turn it into an assumable "safe" risk, or, in a moment of thoughtlessness, actually take an unnecessary risk. In these days of terrorists and hijackings, you frequently hear the expression "Everything's a risk—I could get hit crossing the street." But we can reduce the risk of crossing the street. It is within our control, even when trying to beat the truck, to determine the degree of risk; the timing—do we need to run?—and sense of how far away the truck is can be measured visually and through past experience. Comparing crossing the street to activities that are beyond our control is an apples versus oranges kind of comparison.

Although infinitely more complex, *the stock market is more like crossing the street.* (Those professorial types who throw up their hands and claim the market is unpredictable simply don't understand the nature of market risk.) We can learn all manner of careful things to do. The more careful, the slower we have to proceed—get to the intersection, wait for the light to change, look both ways while pausing for that last taxi to sneak through, and then proceed to a very carefully defined goal: nothing more than getting to the other side safely. We could still get clobbered by something unexpected—perhaps an angle we have failed to consider, a car emerging that we missed, or even, as may more often be the case, being so unsure, too tentative despite our precautions, that we move too slowly; as the light changes back, we become trapped in an untenable position.

There is no perfect, risk-free way to cross the street. There are varying degrees of risk, up to and including the foolhardy. But if we do it right under the prevailing circumstances—how heavy is the traffic? how far to the other side?—we can succeed even if we ignore the parental warning of crossing only at the light. It may not be important enough to take that added chance, but that, too, is something that must be factored in: *how important is the risk?*

· 2 ·

The Nature of Risk

HE R E is how a typical broker tries to reduce risk. He decides that you should own, and might be willing to buy if he talked you into it, a certain stock. But maybe it'll go down after you buy it and he'll be embarrassed. So he wants to reduce that risk as much as possible, both to his ego and to your wallet. The way he does that is by trying as best he can to be sure. There is nothing more sure than seeing the stock go up instead of down. If, while he is watching, XYZ goes down from 42 to 41³/₈, he gets timid. Maybe something's wrong. Maybe he should look for a different stock to recommend. Oh my! here it is at 40³/₄. That's not so good.

Obviously, it's a better price, but a much greater risk, isn't it? because "the sureness" has gone out of it. He's glad he waited . . . but now here it comes rallying back up. He puts his hand on the phone to call you. It's back to 41³/₄; there's a tick at ⁷/₈; the quote on the floor becomes 41³/₄ bid, offered at 42. Oh boy, look at it. Going up is much better action. Now he feels the confidence flowing back through his veins and into the phone line. He can call you, because the rising price is verifying, vindicating, his judgment. Let's buy it. Well, not yet. Maybe it'll get stuck here at 42 the way it did before. So he waits for a few more ticks, wanting to make sure all over again. Someone sells a block at the old high, and it dips back to 41³/₄; he takes his hand off the phone. Then the buyer, in one quick gobble, eats up all the stock offered at 42.

Because there is so little stock offered above that problem price, it skips ahead very quickly through a vacuum to $42\frac{1}{2}$. He's "sure" the stock is a winner now, so he calls you. As he gets you on the phone, there it is on the tape in a whole string at $42\frac{3}{4}$. What could be better proof that the stock is strong— because it actually *is* strong right before his eyes. The risk has gone out of the recommendation because it is proven "right." So you tell him to buy it, and then when the report comes back from the floor of the stock exchange at $42\frac{7}{8}$, you wonder how come you paid the high for the day again. (The broker blames the specialist.)

The need to be sure, as the way to reduce risk, has actually *increased* your risk.

That is, it has added to your price risk because you have now paid a higher price. If the stock backs off, for whatever reason, perhaps merely because of the arrival of a long-overdue market correction, you are more vulnerable because of having paid the higher price. The very thing that made you "sure" now makes you uncomfortable. You shrug, and mutter, "How can you ever know?"

Life is like that: the choice that turns into the gamble, the hesitancy, the deciding.

Terrible things happen every day: hijackings, crazed gunmen firing in malls, cancer and heart attacks, car accidents, gang wars hitting innocent children. But always risk is characterized by: "I could get clobbered just walking across the street." Risk has become associated with randomness. In the same way, investors in the stock market will mutter that market swings really can't be predicted. Who knows whether, or when, the market is going up or down? An increasing number of professionals (people who manage billions of dollars of other people's money) believe that because they aren't capable of anticipating when and/or whether the market will go up or down, it can't be done. Because they concentrate on what truly *can't* be known for sure, because analyzing the market will never be perfect, they opt for randomness. Thus after every "unexpected" slide, we have an ever-increasing trend toward indexing portfolios. Any choice becomes fatalistic, accompanied by that shrug of "You can't know," so why try? investors view the stock market in much the same way that they worry about terrorism but fly wherever their business requires them to go.

Similarly, any experienced broker knows that when a customer buys a stock that goes down, he shrugs; he learns to live with it on the same "time heals" theory we use to reassure widows. "Who knows what the market is going to do?" the victimized investor apologizes to his broker, and explains to his wife. (This is a particularly male response.) He says: "They did it to me again!" But if the stock he bought goes up, and you tell him to sell it, and then it keeps going up, he blames you vehemently; you cost him all that profit. His own loss is acceptable, as part of the randomness of life; but someone else's money he wants, greedily, as if it will keep him alive forever.

Of course, that's only hindsight; at the time the stock was sold he was worried about the timing of his order, the choice of stock, and whether to limit the price or make it a market order—the market's much more intense equivalent of what might happen the moment he set foot off the curb. Because the future can't be known perfectly, any choice becomes risky. If you can't know for sure, you might as well rely on luck and fate, exchanging responsibility for a belief in randomness. It's a "no sweat" way of making decisions, the market equivalent of "I could get hit crossing the street."

The fact is that some things truly are random. You really could get hit crossing the street, not because you crossed the street but because the drunken driver weaving around the corner straight at you *cannot be foreseen.* But you *can* stop and look both ways before you cross. You can wait for the light to change, cross at the intersection instead of in the middle of the block, run across instead of walk, beware of those taxicabs racing through even after the light has changed. And if you do, it isn't so random, is it?

But don't forget that even though you can make decisions

that will actually reduce risk, you may *yearn*, too, *for some speculative excitement* in your life. You and I may not understand those folks who hang glide, or mountain climb, or who bet on a long shot because it has a cute name. But the yearning is there to take a chance on something, so Mr. Staid Investor wants to buy a collapsing stock because "it's down so far already there's no risk," or it's an erstwhile famous name, or it's year-end time for such cats and dogs to bounce, or someone on television names a couple of $8 stocks to buy. What he really wants is a winner for his speculative ego—the "I'm more than my wife thinks I am" part of him, using the stock market for an affair, and insisting he is so much the master of his own fate that he'll sell it if it doesn't work out (although, of course, he doesn't, can't quite bring himself to give it up even though he knows he should; some men even end up murdering their wives for what began, in the same speculative way, as a one-night stand).

(Here we discuss "Mr." Investor not only because we understand and relate to him, but also because the above instance is particularly male. Like the latest statistics showing an increasing number of women having heart attacks as they assume the role of businesswoman, we suspect that women's investment approaches will become more "manly"—*not* a positive. As this is being written, we are into a generation of women only now learning about investing, and assuming the responsibility of choices. Thus, for now, a woman's ego remains on the side of nurturing funds, of perceiving risk outside the home as danger, *not* fun; and, still, of taking advice passively and deferentially. There are very few speculators. But among the ever-increasing number of female portfolio managers are the first two or three who have begun managing money aggressively: using options, selling short, and so on.)

The fascinating thing about the stock market—the factor that keeps us all involved—is that its risks are *not* random. Those who complain that "you can't know" are just lazy, or ignorant, or inexperienced. Others "know" it can be fathomed, and keep trying even as they accuse it of being random; they are unwilling to blame themselves for mistakes. Still others grasp that the market is anticipatory, yet are unable to perceive that their own actions are always coincident, instead. We aren't talking about randomness at all, but something demonstrably predictable—even though not perfectly so. Some people have, the psychiatrists tell us, a subconscious will to lose; others defiantly believe they can beat the odds; some—kids taking drugs, for example—get so caught up with the consensus opinion of their peers that they never even confront the risk. There is some sort of risk in every choice, even in not making one, and it may very well turn out that the greater risk was taken along the apparently safer path.

The value of technical analysis in the stock market is to reduce risk. It is especially helpful in guiding you to believe what otherwise seems unacceptable. By extension, therefore, it is *most helpful* at identifying significant market turns, both for the market and for individual stocks. The action of individual stocks *cumulatively* becomes the most important indicator of market direction, and all our internal indicators are but reliable ways of summarizing that individual stock action. (Sentiment indicators are attempts to identify the consensus so as to be grouchily contrarian.) Stock charts and the indicators are like doctors' advice: exercise, diet, reduce stress, and so on. They are a means of establishing imperfect but relatively objective ways to understand market risks and market choices.

I'd prefer to be a purist—shut the door and look only at the charts, using John Magee's dictum of reading the newspaper only when it is yellow—but stock market life isn't like that. Decisions—real decisions—are made by those who know what they are doing and why, and with the power of money behind those decisions. They are the lords of the playing field, while the technician is but the observer and reporter of their (collective) behavior. Experience over the years tells me that (1) in a crunch—confusion, chaos, crisis—being pure helps: (a) put blinders on in trying to understand the market's behavior; (b) try to be on the side of the New York Stock Exchange (NYSE) specialist; and (c) constantly ask oneself: what is the least expected thing the market could do? (Such guidelines would have helped immeasurably at such otherwise bewildering times as October 19 and 20, 1987, and January 15 and 16, 1991.)

At other times, however, (2) recognize that all significant (that is, affecting the price) buying and selling stems from some form or other of fundamentals. Chief among these, perhaps in order of importance, are (a) corporate management; (b) the reliability of corporate information; and then (c) whatever information—book value, cash flow, even earnings and dividends—a particular investor values. Fundamentals, therefore, are derived *apart from* the market, whereas technical factors are rooted in the market itself. We would argue that fundamental forecasts are based on judgments as to how the company is likely to do in the future applied subjectively to future price in the marketplace, whereas a technical forecast is based on the potential validity of those judgments as revealed by objective data already in that marketplace.

In both cases, however, the *willingness* to forecast is vital. There's really nothing you can do about the inherent risk of being in the stock market at all—and little you can do about the ongoing risk that, because the market is constantly changing, no sooner do we act than we may perceive something significantly different occurring. The future is not guaranteed. And all choices have a possibility of failure.

But that's as true of daily life as it is of the stock market. Crossing the street symbolizes the sense of risk that every little act involves as we cross *into the future*. It expresses our ability to look both ways, to be careful or careless, to be in control of our own destiny and yet vulnerable to what others, including crazy people, might do.

We have to understand that all stock market decisions—each and every one, including doing nothing—involve risk. Some people believe they can minimize their risk by relying on the cop-out "risk/reward ratio" cliché: "Ten points potential reward compared to 5 points potential downside" becomes "okay to trade" without even the slightest consideration of what the chances are that the stock will actually move in the undesired direction. *It is the risk itself that needs to be analyzable, not the potential reward.* The stock might already have moved extensively; the reason might already be known; support underneath might be flimsy; the stock hasn't moved yet even though the market is already up a lot; and so on. Not until we grasp the extent of and the kind of risk should we consider the degree of reward. Hope has never kept a stock up when it is doing things wrong.

Reducing risk, as the typical broker never learns, begins with taking a risk *before* we know enough to make it safe. It requires anticipating because the market itself is anticipatory. A willingness to act on that anticipation is what puts us in, or takes us out, at a better price. Such forecasting is *not* crystal-ball stuff. Consider the January 15, 1991, Persian Gulf war deadline: everyone knows something is going to happen; everyone believes that the outbreak of hostilities will produce selling—presenting, they also believe, an opportunity to buy at better prices. Accordingly, a lot of selling takes place in anticipation of that future "down" news; the Dow Jones Industrial Average falls 200 points. Just as it wasn't hard to anticipate that anxious selling was going to take place beforehand, it was equally easy to anticipate that the consensus waiting to buy wasn't going to be rewarded with an additional "down" because the 200 points down had *already* occurred; the Dow leapt over 100 points on the very news it was supposed to go down on. Those who'd sold, those who were waiting to buy, were left behind—worse, got emotionally involved and in a panic rushed to buy at much higher prices. So why did they take the greater risk of waiting to actually know more? what made them feel it was less of a risk? is it really fate? the "How can you ever know what the market is going to do?" syndrome. Is it a neurotic desire to lose? is it trying to get something without risk?

What happened in that real-time market example is similar to our literal individual stock example: buying at a lower price was exchanged for knowing more. Or, to put that another way, when the stock is down and you don't know anything about it, you have an "information" risk but the "price" risk is considerably less. When you know more, you have reduced your discomfort level—less "information" risk, but increased "price" risk, more market vulnerability. Because fundamental market analysts require information (as do reporters), it is virtually impossible for them to accept the apparent mysticism of technical analysis. "Sureness," to a technician, is a function of stock action; to fundamentalists, it is a function of news and available balance sheet and earnings information as if the analysis itself is a form of news. That's why people will always buy news; and it is why good news comes out at tops!

Meanwhile, the person who, let's say, bought at 40¾—taking a much bigger risk because the stock was then falling—now has a better price. He can sit there and say: "Let it fluctuate back down if it has to." He is less apt to panic out near a correction low. The insecurity of his purchase decision—watching the stock decline while he has little or no information about it—has somehow produced a less risky "price" position.

Because the market anticipates, the more you know, the later it is. The later it is, the greater the risk. There is no safety to buying on positive information (or shorting on bad news). Thus *all information has a negative bias* against the price trend.

Let's begin with a stock that is falling severely. As we approach the bottom, virtually all the information is negative: price falling, corporate news gloomy, no buyers, selling pressure on the "just get me out of that piece of junk" basis. We all know, as a cliché, that "bad news comes out at bottoms" and someone might venture to guess at the bottom when the first prominent piece of bad news is announced. But the chart itself tells you nothing yet, with the potential exception of identifying where important support has occurred in the past (but with no guarantee that such support is going to hold this time in the face of such apparently dire news). The price risk has *lessened* because of the decline to a third or more off the peak level—but there is still price risk remaining because you have absolutely no idea beyond *sheer guessing* how close to the ultimate low you are.

And you also have, obviously, information risk—you don't

know anything at all about the stock that would warrant buying it, but, instead, you know only the scary "bad" news items. The best bottoms form on extremes of negative information—typically, both shoes drop, plus the kitchen sink—so you may not have learned the worst yet. In addition to this information risk, you still really do have price risk, too, because there is no sign on the tape or on the chart that the stock has stopped going down. Third, you also have a time risk because you know—as a chartist—that even if you are lucky enough to catch the bottom eighth, the stock would then need months and months to form a sufficient base, during which time all sorts of things could happen: you could get scared out by the market, it could make a new low, and so on. *"Time risk" is always present for those who try to bottom-fish.* In other words, what turns out to be the literal bottom—in hindsight—is a *high risk* place to buy a stock.

There is still a dearth of positive information. The decline has scared investors, and the reasons for the decline have become clear, causing research departments to sharply lower earnings estimates and reduce expectations. In an example of "locking the barn door," wire house ratings at this juncture often go to a 3-3 rating, and sometimes even 3-4, so negative is the news outlook. For example, Travelers was selling at 40 at the outset of 1990; the top that had formed looks like an umbrella! By June it was down to 32 and still falling—long before the Middle East crisis. Four months later—by this time Travelers was 20, which certainly looks as if "someone" already knew "something"—there was a not-so-surprising dividend cut and the stock plunged to under 14 in two days. That panic, in a supposedly conservative, well-known, large company, was followed by a feeble attempt to hold. Fascinatingly, as soon as Travelers had plunged 6 points in two days, several money managers phoned to ask if they could buy the stock now that it was down so far; such bottom-fishing accounted for the struggle to hold. But there was no proof in the stock's action; TIC closed at its low and kept sinking. The market's message was that there was still more bad news to come.

But note (see Chart 1) what happened after the stock fell further, to a lower low at $11\frac{1}{2}$, as the company was releasing its third-quarter report. Indeed, the report itself made such awful reading in the morning newspaper that it even scared me: more losses reported, more reserves likely in the quarters ahead, no way to raise needed cash, and a write-off of everything, including the proverbial kitchen sink (amounting to taking a $4.93 per share loss). But *despite* the news, or because the news was finally in the public domain—few were left to sell (compared to the buyers who showed up) so that TIC opened unchanged, and actually kept going up to close at $12\frac{3}{8}$. The news caused the Merrill Lynch analyst *only then* to change its previously favorable rating to a 4—okay to sell—but what did the market know? The fundamental information was entirely negative; no money manager called to ask if the stock was then okay to buy; they'd been frightened away. And the only positive was a subtle market clue that the stock didn't want to go down anymore. In the course of the next five trading days, had you bought on the dire news, you'd have had a 3-point (about 30 percent) gain. Three weeks later TIC dipped one last time back to $12\frac{1}{2}$, on even less selling pressure. This successful test almost always occurs after the onslaught, so that what you have, in sequence, is the ability to hold on awful news, followed by market action of *no new low*. Because this is the *confirming* moment of what has come before, such a test is a low-risk time to buy, even though you have no information as to why in the world the stock would go up. Travelers then headed almost straight up to over 20.

Thus what we have is information risk—buying the stock is scary because we haven't the vaguest idea why the stock should have such an enticing base. The fundamentals are against it; the uncertainty about the company is enormous; but someone has been buying it sufficiently to create a base of sufficient magnitude. We don't know what that someone, or someones, know but by believing the chart, and buying purely because of the base formation, we *assume* (in both senses of the word) the information risk, and thereby have reduced our price risk: the stock has shown its ability to bottom.

Chart 1
TRAVELERS

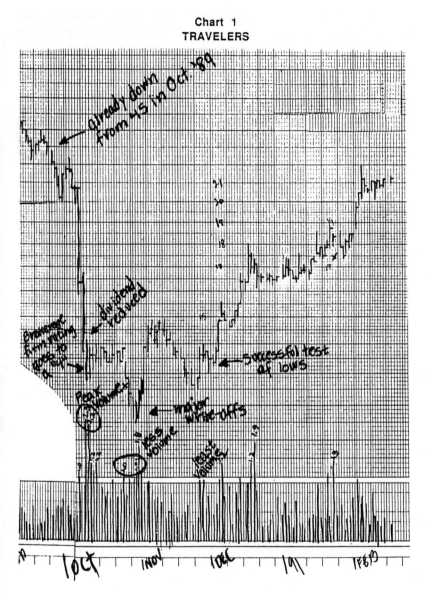

Unfortunately, in this imperfect market world there are nuances. Two things can go wrong: (1) The stock can spoil the base by breaking down to a lower low. (We read the chart wrong, or got prematurely too eager, or there was additional bad news forthcoming.) In this case the price risk helps to keep our loss to a minimum; having bought relatively low, if subsequent trading proves us wrong, selling produces a small rather than a catastrophic loss. Or (2) the apparent break eventually proves to be the "head" of what will turn out to be a much bigger head and shoulders bottom. In this case we survive our price risk, but now have to assume a considerable time cost; it's going to take a lot longer before the stock turns around and moves higher.

But no one ever said it was going to be easy, and only your mother demands that you be perfect.

· 3 ·

Information Versus Price

LET us put aside for the moment such decision-affecting factors as emotion, experience, confidence, style, upbringing, and the condition of the playing field of the market itself. Our concern in this chapter is the way confusion and contradictions between information and price affect an investor's perception of risk.

Initially, price is a minor consideration. Price is simple: there it is, on the tape, in the newspaper, and, by extension, on the chart (which is, after all, just a graphic representation of the prices at which transactions take place). Price varies only in relation to time, and whether one sells to the bid, or buys on the offer. Price is an objective known; its validity cannot be denied, and when it changes that change is publicly known, from the open outcry required on the stock exchange floor to its appearance in the newspaper tables. But such minute, moment-to-moment changes are significant for longer-term decisions only in their accretion, as shifting grains of sand make a beach; a rough idea of price is a sufficient tool. So the relationships between various pieces of information can be lopsidedly skewed toward corporate and economic (and even noneconomic, emotion-generating) information, the stuff of press releases, analyst reports, and testimony before Congress versus only price and volume. And this is skewed even further by the need of reporters, brokers, analysts, and advisers to have a constant and current stream of "news" to talk about; price becomes an aside, a one-liner. If the answer to "What's happening, baby?" is only "the market was up 14 points today," all else becomes commentary on "Why?"—everything, that is, that as news is already known. "More buyers than sellers," although most accurate, isn't even considered a humorous explanation.

◆◆◆◆ One of the major changes that has taken place in this modern era is the instant availability of information. I can remember the days when a broker would jump up out of his chair whenever he heard a bell go off on the Dow Jones news ticker—the "broad" tape. The bell was to alert subscribers to the service that "hot" news was being printed. A dutiful nearby broker would race over to the machine and squint at the words. Perhaps a dividend was being raised, or cut; perhaps IBM's earnings were being announced; perhaps the world was coming to an end (three bells).

In those days financial news itself was slow-moving, much of it derived from press releases, word of which was spread around even while the Dow Jones clerk was typing the material for the machine. Many current items of interest would have seemed like gossip, then, or too trivial, merely momentary tidbits for traders, and the business of brokerage house analysts in raising or lowering their numbers was done through mailed reports because such research was not expected to have immediate impact.

But nowadays an adolescent need for instant gratification has taken over. There's an immediate, almost automatic response to the news of the moment. Every media outlet gears itself for the forthcoming economic number-of-the-day, trying to provide a 15-second scoop and thereby *make* news. Put out a buy or a sell recommendation and the whole country, indeed the whole world, seems to know about it instantaneously, and responds as rapidly, so that stocks pop or drop on such items. (Often, people at other firms know what I've said before brokers in my own firm have received the memo.) Such instantaneous decisions have little, or nothing, to do with the price, but are, like everyone rushing to one side of the ship at once, thereby over-doing it, a response almost entirely to the news itself, although such "news" may actually be nothing more than one man's opinion. The rush to act ahead of everyone else—to try to beat the system—presumes that others will also buy (or sell) on the "news," taking the price up (or down), so that whatever the price happens to be at the moment is not as important as that there will be movement.

Thus the instant availability and dissemination of "news" is not as much of a good thing as it is supposed to be. It has altered reaction time, and therefore has increased volatility. It has reduced liquidity; everyone knows together, and wants to buy or sell together, so there frequently is an at least temporarily lopsided order flow. It has become much harder to get paid—to profit—for being smarter and more discerning than everyone else. (The Security and Exchange Commission's [SEC's] misguided requirement that what a company tells one analyst it must tell all, even if what he has learned is due to his own diligence, has led to a consensus of number-crunchers, increased secrecy, and a desire for inside information.)

This has produced an interesting revelation about the minds of portfolio managers and traders: in the old days, no one knew what was going to happen that day (except, of course, as a carryover from the way the market had closed the day before). Before the next morning's opening, floor brokers for various firms would comb the floor, gossiping with specialists, trying to gauge the flow of orders. Moments before the opening bell would ring, these brokers would dash to their phones and rather breathlessly tell "upstairs" that there were "buyers" or "sellers." Sometimes this would be qualified: "buyers in IBM," or "heavy sellers." But it was all anyone got to know before the opening, and, coming at the last second, was of little use, except to give those "upstairs" the feeling that, ah, now they weren't adrift; they knew something, at least. Then the market would open, and they would say to themselves, "See, there really were sellers"; and then they'd feel better that it wasn't all a mystery.

Those in the business, be they retail brokers or institutional portfolio managers, used to approach the day's opening of trading with an unstated feeling of anxiety: what *was* going to happen? Tension was always in the air because of the unknown quality of what lay ahead. But now, ah, now we know "everything." Instead of milking the cows, you can learn before dawn about the entire global scope of things. In the East, at 6 A.M., one can switch from the gory late-night movies to hear, on cable news channels and all-news radio stations, a version of "Live from Tokyo," as the announcer talks directly to an American working for one of the firms in Japan. In addition to a "live update" about the Tokyo stock market, we get what's happening to the currency and bond markets, overnight economic news from that side of the world, plus the Hang Seng index from Hong Kong, a phrase about Singapore, and a line about the Sydney Exchange. And then it's on to London.

At 6:30 A.M., and again at 7:30, one cable news channel provides two somewhat different half-hour shows of business news, while other channels strive to compete. The Tokyo action is recapped, in case you were too busy feeding the chickens, Germany has become vital information, and London is dealt with more extensively, for trading there is still going on, so we get updates as the programs progress. Such shows will also give you the prices at which a few big-name American stocks are trading in London at that hour—IBM down an eighth, as if that really matters—and occasionally, when there is added interest because of overnight "news," the announcer, using overseas trading in the Amex's Major Market Index (XMI), will inform us that "brokers say that means the U.S. market will open up (or down) 50 points." Fifteen minutes before the NYSE opens, that same XMI contract begins trading to add to the apparent advance info (it actually "speaks" of the emotional content in the Street). The more we know, the more we know what to expect. In addition, experts are interviewed as to what they think the market is going to do, and although they might try to present, in those 90 seconds allotted to them, an overview, the interviewer demands to know what is going to happen right now, this coming day.

In considering this modern-age behavior, note the extensive degree to which information and opinion are *current*; whatever is happening, whatever is becoming known, at that instant, is given extraordinary emphasis—even though the stock market itself is an *anticipatory* mechanism, and even though the news, like most news, is going to be ephemeral. Of course, reporters, anchormen, and daily commentators are forced, by the nature of their business, to be oriented toward the momentary items of the day; what else would they have to write or talk about? The root cause for why the market went up that day—"more buyers than sellers"—cannot be seriously cited on the evening news. The notion that the market, except when news is genuinely unexpected, will have already dealt with it—"It's in the market" is the phrase—is untranslatable into the news media. Yet *this* is where price, seemingly of lesser importance, becomes more important. *Information must always be related to the degree to which it is known.*

The classic example of how the market—which does not read newspapers or press releases, or tune in the news—can anticipate, *as if* it knows, is the so-called silver panic of March 1980. In January, stock charts began to show so much toppiness and vulnerability that I was short, but getting increasingly uncomfortable with losing positions because there was no decline. Then, abruptly, the market started to slide; in six weeks the Dow was down 20 percent, culminating in a late tape as prices collapsed on the "news" that the Hunt brothers had been trying to corner the silver market. (The panic actually spread from the widespread belief that their default was going to bring Bache and other brokerage firms down the next morning.)

No one, including the market itself, *knew* about the Hunts when the tops were forming. So the market was anticipating what it didn't even know—just that stocks had become overextended and vulnerable. In 1980 it knew *something* was going to be wrong, and *that* was enough to know. It doesn't have the word *recession* in its vocabulary, only *distribution* and *vulnerability.* Indeed, what culminates in a bear market, or creates a top, is not the known news that investors rely on for selling or buying decisions. What the market is anticipating is forthcoming direction, which turns out, of course, to be related to eventually known human reasons.

A similar example on a smaller scale than the 1980 quick crash is the attention paid to the "number du jour"—that is, the economic figure that, when announced, is supposed to have a significant impact on the market. In the 1960s, brokers hung around the office after the close on Thursday afternoons to learn what the Fed's weekly report said about M1. More recently, the monthly trade figures became the key, and when interest in that petered out, the unemployment figures took over the "must know" role. Radio and TV stations now break into their news at 8:31 A.M. to report such items as the Producer Price Index, Industrial Production, and whatever else comes along that previously had been relegated to whenever the business minute came along.

And yet such numbers are consistently easy to forecast, because the market really does anticipate . . . in its own way— that is, it reports, perversely, on what market players are anticipating. What does the market know? when it is not privy to Washingtonian leaks. But when prices have been rising beforehand, the market "says" the news announcement is likely to be "surprisingly" negative. Who's left to buy? When prices are already up, we have only vulnerability left. And if the market's been falling, the number du jour is often better than expected; and even if it is as bad as expected, with prices already down, few sellers are left and buyers can step forward. The same principle applies to worries about Treasury bond auctions: the more advance anxiety has affected behavior, the more the market is set up for a successful auction. Does someone know? someones? Collectively, the market anticipates by its own action beforehand. It has so consistently declined significantly ahead of every recession that the one exception, in 1962, has come to be known as the bear market when everyone expected a recession that never came. Obviously, if you think a recession is coming, you sell. *That* selling is what creates the top and causes the market's anticipatory decline. And it is why the bottom typically forms at about the time the recession is over; those who have been "out" begin to buy for the recovery, which the market, by rising, therefore anticipates. In 1974 some individual stocks had already started going up during the summer, so that the major secular bottom—replete with positive indicator signals—had formed in the fourth quarter, precisely when the government officially announced a recession.

◈◈◈◈ Nowadays what is known comes not only from those proliferating news sources at dawn, but also from the information machines on office desks. The typical broker or portfolio manager has never given much thought to the degree to which his anxiety has been assuaged by early morning news about what markets are already doing around the world. *Bad news or not, he knows*, and that's preferable to entering not just the lion's den, but the lion's maw itself, as he walks into his office. And there he learns more, if he wants to know: the activity in U.S. Treasury bond futures contracts—not even the bonds themselves but a speculative surrogate, as traded the evening before in Chicago—is now posted on his market monitor. Indeed, bond trading opens before the stock market does, with its message, and then, 15 minutes ahead, the XMI contracts begin to trade, just to get a jump on the stock market itself. Thus how the market is going to open, what it is going to do, and why are now readily discernible. Our hero can call out to his secretary that "the market's going up," and when it does he can show her on his machine how smart he was.

Of course, that is all momentary information, and of little use. The one who profits is not the one who learns in the morning, and then acts on that knowledge, but the person who anticipated such opening action the afternoon before. If he has bought near the close, and all the overnight "news" points to a higher opening, thereby exciting those who believe they "know" something significant, he can sell to our hero's excited buy order as the market opens higher in New York. One of the problems—indeed, the major problem—with those amateur traders who plug in all their software at night to try to get computer-generated signals as to what to do the next morning is that they end up buying from (or selling to) the professionals *who have already taken the risk* the night before and who, by doing so, have created the very inputs that produce computerized signals (especially on oscillator-type indicators) that evening. A little knowledge, as they say, is a dangerous thing.

◇◆◇◆◇ But the same thing is true of information of more than momentary significance, be it forthcoming earnings reports, new product development, takeover activity, or whatever. *Information serves to relieve anxiety.* The more one knows, the more readily one is willing to act (or the more comfortable one becomes about not acting). But, you might ask, "How can information that has already become widely and immediately disseminated in this era of instant communication affect the market?" The belief that investors immediately react to and adjust to what becomes known is the basis for the academic argument denying that the market can be forecast; calling it an "efficient" market, they insist that all known information is reflected in the stock price, with buyers and sellers instantly at the ready to adjust any price that gets out of line.

The reason that such arbitraging of information doesn't work is that you can ascribe to the market all sorts of human characteristics—perversity, spitefulness, seemingly being out to punish even the innocent—but efficiency is not one of them. "The market" is the sum total not only of what everyone knows, but how each of those everyones responds to that knowledge. Being subject to judgment and, less consciously (but often more influentially), emotions is what makes the game of playing the market so frustratingly fascinating. If we were to tell, let's say, five active market players that XYZ was going to be taken over, one would jump up and call his broker to buy; one, before he'd act, would try to determine who he knew that could confirm the rumor; one would sit down with research material—be it charts (was the price up already? were there volume clues?) or corporate details (how much is XYZ's breakup value?); a fourth, disbelieving, would be too scared to do anything at that moment, but is the patsy who abruptly, when a much higher price gives apparent validity to the story, decides he can't stand missing the action anymore; and the fifth might very well react by deciding to take advantage of the rumor by unloading his shares to the excited believers. Not only are these reactions differing *and* sequential, there is the varying size of their orders to weigh as well. By the time the market has "efficiently" adjusted, the next tick and the next are already taking place.

To cite another example of how the market is sequential in its pursuit of the efficient: "Why is Digital down $2^7/_8$?" The answer comes back, "A brokerage firm slashed its earnings estimate in half this morning. . . . " To begin with, the time it takes salesmen to call their clients with the "news" one by one, and for those clients to disseminate that information within their firms, keeps the decline sequential; meanwhile, other investors are hearing it through the grapevine. But some clients knew the day before that the analyst was about to cut his estimate; that's why the stock became weak late that day. And still others, over a period of several days beforehand, had become aware that the analyst was working on a negative DEC report, because he may have commented casually about it at morning sales meetings, or groused about it by the watercooler, and he almost certainly answered questions about the stock in cautionary terms as he did his marketing tours and phone calls. But perhaps his budding beliefs were not enough, so that at least some of those money managers didn't believe, didn't act, until they saw the market's big down reaction. *Belief is as sequential as the inefficient spread of information.*

Indeed, sequential patterns can even combine with *instant* dissemination of actual corporate news. In the old days, a salesman would call a client to tell of the firm's recommendation to sell DEC. The client would respond, "I'll bring it up at next Thursday's policy meeting." As the speed of market reaction increased, he began to reply, "I'll think about it and let you know," "I'll discuss it with my partner when he comes back from lunch." And then: "I'll think about it and call you back." And now, the knee-jerk reaction is "Sell at the market; I'll tell my partner when he comes back from the men's room." Because of the spread of instant communication, it appears that no one can afford to wait. The salesman's call has become news in itself.

When the company announces its "surprise" disappointing earnings, the flood of sell orders can cause the specialist on the NYSE floor to halt trading or delay the opening. Many of the sellers, remember, are those who knew, or suspected, what was coming, but couldn't bring themselves to act until the actual announcement; their emotional response makes the selling look all the more moblike. By delaying the opening, the specialist's action is supposed to help him balance the flood of sell orders at some lower reopening price where he can find enough buy orders to make a match, thus taking care of the problem all at once. But some holders will calculate that if they also throw in their sell order, it will further unbalance the situation, so that the opening price will be even lower; they decide to wait for the inevitable rebound. I was in an office in Boston once when this actually happened to Digital Equipment, and I overheard the whispered (and aghast) remark "We've got 500,000 shares to sell; the stock'll open 3 points worse, so we can't sell right now." They waited, and eventually, as the stock steadily fell thereafter, got out at much lower prices along the way down. Hence the classic rebound has become increasingly skimpy—as so many in the same boat try to salvage something by selling up a bit. Obviously, that leaves so many shares in the hands of people who want out that if they don't succeed on the rebound (too greedy for an extra eight, or not enough buyers around), they dump—each holder in dawning sequence. This causes the stock to break below its so-called cleanup price, which causes at least some of those who had bought the apparent "bargain" on the reopening to flee, too, taking a small loss while they can. This sequence of a second leg down leads to an increased conviction that the next time such "news" surprises—sell; indeed, the next time a salesman calls—sell. Such almost automatic reactions have by now caused great gaps in price: 7, 8, even 10 points down. In this manner, the sequential behavior remains—no matter how instantly everyone knows everything.

It's worth noting that there was one time when the clean-out lower reopening proved genuinely climactic. Indeed, it worked as it is supposed all around the stock exchange floor. One of the great turns of all time came not on Monday, October 19, 1987—the day of the crash—but on the next day. Stocks opened higher on Tuesday, and then plunged again. By 11 A.M., NYSE specialists began shutting down trading in stock after stock as sell orders poured in. So many major stocks were halted that it was possible—even at that moment of hushed hysteria—to remind oneself of the specialist's function: to match all the sell orders at whatever lower price was necessary to arouse sufficient buyers (including using his own capital), and only then to reopen trading. On October 20, *that* process truly represented the clean-out of just about everyone in the world who wanted to get out—orders from Switzerland; margin calls; panicky brokers panicking their clients to get out—which meant that a vacuum of sellers would be left overhead so that *any* buyer who came in thereafter would take the stock price up. (Sequentially, plenty of buyers showed up, muttering "If I'd known it was going to open 'down there' I'd have bought some.") I explained this in a hastily written memo just before lunchtime that day and described it to a packed room full of portfolio managers at lunch. But there was a shell-shocked look on every face. I've often wondered if anyone left that lunch and went back to his or her office to start buying—for *that halt in trading represented the crash bottom;* with no sellers left, stocks rallied as soon as they reopened.

Obviously, an almost infinite variety of responses to rumors or real information or real-but-only-opinion "news" items are possible, some based on experience, some on emotion, some on gambling, and so on. There is still plenty of whispered info, and a sort of sophisticated sharing of "hot tips," which gradually filter out into the mainstream, but even that information is then subject to a host of individual factors that affect the stock's price action over a period of time. The degree to which the dissemination of information penetrates like osmosis into the marketplace is hard to pinpoint—*except by price action itself.*

The market climate itself is one of the major factors affecting a stock's price action. In the later stages of a bear market—and, indeed, immediately after the turn—pessimism is so great that few believe anything positive; accordingly, when we see stocks start to hold in the face of further bad news, it is the market telling us the underlying trend is changing. Similarly, after prices have gone up so far and for so long that it seems they're never going to come down again, any piece of information, any outlandish rumor or story, will be seized on as gospel. Along the way, information has grown on investors the way we grow: imperceptibly but constantly; the bigger we get, the more confident we become that we are in control; and the older we get, the more stubborn that we're right. So, too, the more information about a stock or about the market, the more confident we are, so confident, it seems, that even speculative phrases (hot tips, rumors, and the like) become accepted as actual information to rely on when playing the game.

◇◆◇◆◇ But someone must know something; someone must be willing—why?—to take the other side of the trade. Sometimes news is so glaring that it proves to be culminating. And sometimes that combination tells us that we can join in. *The single best time to buy a stock*—you can put this in your will for your grandchildren to rely on—*is when, given bad news, the stock refuses to go down any more.* So, as we trace the shifting relationship of price to information, let's start at that point.

I prefer not to use the name of a company, even the textbook classic of Widget, Inc., because any name brings with it connotations of size, industry, familiarity, that distort what we are trying to point out. So let's just call our example by its ticker symbol XYZ, a company that has been falling in price because of falling business. Actually, business hasn't been so good anywhere (so the market's downtrend is also a negative), but XYZ has been affected more and sooner than most other companies. Virtually all the information is negative, but some are tempted to guess at the bottom, thinking that the price has come down

Chart 2
"XYZ"

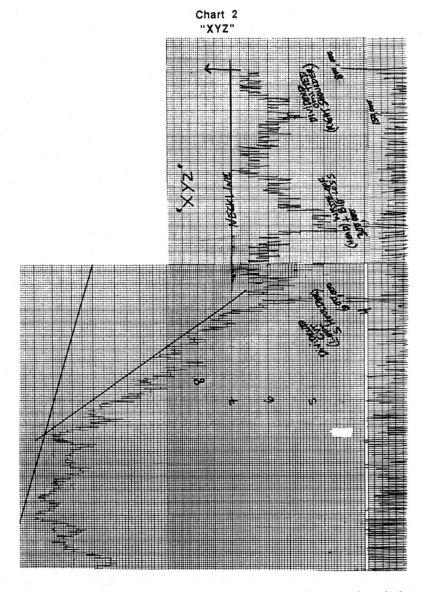

far enough already, and perhaps even remembering the cliché
that "bad news comes out at bottoms." The latter months
of 1974 are a great example: Watergate revelations abound,

president resigns, Franklin National Bank collapse—the biggest up to that point in U.S. history—occurs, new-car sales are down 34 percent and housing starts at an eight-year low . . . all the while the Dow was bottoming at 577 after a five-year bear cycle and as it began its journey to 3000. But if you'd guessed at the bottom in June, when the bad news began to accelerate, you'd have been 250 points too early. Bottom-fishers are themselves, in their optimism, an indication that the end is still in the future; the question from portfolio managers has got to change from "Is it okay to buy Citicorp here?" to "Is it too late to sell Citicorp here?" Bottoming information has to be an outpouring of bad news that seems as if it is never going to end. Although the price risk has lessened because of the considerable decline already (XYZ has dropped from 20 to single digits, let's say), at least some price risk remains because there's no way to tell beyond sheer guesswork how close to the ultimate low the stock price is.

Let's say that at this juncture the company's board of directors finally votes to cut the dividend in half to conserve capital. The stock's price decline accelerates to 5 on the news, on heavy unloading by those pained holders who are finally forced to surrender their hope of survival. Most of this selling comes from those who played ostrich, telling themselves that "it's only a paper loss," and "I'll sell when I get even." The announcement causes an emotional disgorging that is met by guessing at the bottom by bargain hunters.

Someone has to buy, to help make the chart—let them, with *their* money. Sometimes long-term charts indicate where important support has occurred in the past, but even then there's no guarantee that such support is going to hold this time in the face of such apparently dire news. It's much too soon for the stock's "old" chart to help; XYZ needs to rebuild, to start over. The first positive feelings aren't "buy," but are no more than beginning to observe that downside momentum is lessening. *"Time risk" is always present for those who are over anxious to bottom-fish.* What does eventually turn out to be the bottom eighth—in hindsight—*is a high-risk place to buy a stock.*

Over the next several weeks, though, abetted by bargain hunters guessing at the bottom, there is a modest fluctuation back up toward 7 until, as the company is about to report its earnings, the price turns downward again. Either someone knows the report is going to make dreadful reading, or can readily assume that it will, based on previous announcements and simple deductive analysis. Indeed, the news is even worse than expected: XYZ reports not only a loss, but a massive write-off, too. The price immediately drops to a new low at 4³/₈, although, oddly, this decline isn't as sharp or as deep as the first, nor does it occur on anywhere near as much volume because so many holders had already dumped aggressively on the dividend cut. Some of this "late" selling actually comes from the premature bargain hunters who've gotten scared by the magnitude of this latest news. It's easier for them to take a loss than those who've held XYZ down from 20.

With lots of bad news now out of the way ("it's already in the stock price" is another way to put it), a fresh batch of bottom-fishers arrives. While the earlier players are likely to be traders trying to catch an extremely oversold swing back up, the second batch is more apt to be investment-oriented, with longer time horizons in mind. Their attitude is apt to be "There's a long-term bottom in here somewhere, so paying a point or so too much doesn't matter." They may be early from the technician's point of view, but do, of course, help make the stock chart, so there follows a modest fluctuation back up to, let's say, near 7 again. Remaining holders who missed getting out on the previous bounce but are now so scared or discouraged enter sell orders when they see the stock back up to where it got stuck before, as do some traders who have actually made a neat percentage profit on this bounce! That stems the rebound once again, as if 7 has become an inevitable end; then the stock drifts aimlessly. Who cares about XYZ? especially because the market is no great shakes either, until another seemingly foreseeable news announcement is made: XYZ is totally eliminating its dividend, coupled with an announcement explaining how awful things are going to remain. Whoops! negligent (lazy? dumb?)

portfolio managers who run the sort of pension funds (often state-regulated and bureaucratically managed) that are forbidden by law to own nondividend paying stocks now must sell, so on this final piece of bad news the stock opens at 5½, dips to 5⅛, and then seems to disappear from the tape.

For the marketplace is able to absorb those sellers. There are so few holders left who want to sell, while many recent buyers can afford to hold on, and might even be buying more as part of a planned long-term accumulation. Volume is much lower than on either of the previous news-induced sell-offs; the selling pressure doesn't last very long—sometimes only 15 minutes—and thus—whoops, again—XYZ actually bounces back to close unchanged or even up an eighth. *We have learned from this action that there are no more sellers left to respond to bad news.* We weren't so brilliant as to buy at the bottom eighth, nor did we have to guess stressfully along the way how low was low enough, but this time, although still on the sidelines, *we now actually know something*, not about the company but *about the price*. We know that the stock doesn't want to go down any more, even on worsening news.

Of course, what we know relates to the marketplace and to a price where there are no sellers left to sell; it just happens to consistently coincide with when company information is at its worst, and interest in the company's stock has turned to distaste. *At the bottom, there is maximum negative, and no positive, information, but the price risk is minimal.*

◆·◆·◆·◆ Why can't the stock do as it had twice done before: meander back up in a standard stock market fluctuation, and then renew its slide? Suppose bankruptcy lies ahead. Nothing's guaranteed, but when bad news meets with little or no response—*after* a substantial decline has already taken place—the message is that selling has been exhausted. Anyone who wanted to sell, who could be driven, or scared, into selling, has sold; he has literally given up on XYZ. That's what we learn when the stock does not make a lower low on the bad news, but, instead, absorbs the last bit of selling and turns around. Maybe those buyers actually do know something about the company that we don't know—its valuation, for example, or its survivability—but we don't need to know. If you sketch this sequence out on a scrap of paper, you'll see that it resembles the chartist's head and shoulders bottom pattern (some people feel more comfortable calling it a reverse, or inverse, head and shoulders), with the "head" as the low, and with this final *but failing* attempt to keep the downtrend intact serving as the pattern's right shoulder. Typically, although there is considerably less trading activity, there is more hysteria and negativism, and, often, actual anger, as the right shoulder forms, because everyone now not only believes the worst but believes it is going to go on indefinitely. The emotional content of a right-shoulder bottom is one of hatred and aversion; the technical content is one of low volume and disinterest. *The price risk—because selling is exhausted—has been taken out of the stock, even though we have total information risk.*

But why should we buy XYZ at that juncture? How do we know that bankruptcy will not, indeed, happen? We don't. All we know is bad news. If we are to buy at all it is because we recognize the positive price turn and the evident exhaustion of sellers, and presume, therefore, that the chance of the stock going any lower is far less than the chance that XYZ is turning from down to up. It may be that what we are identifying is only temporary, that some weeks or months later a minimal rise is followed by deteriorating price action, which once again will be warning of *renewed* price risk. But that's a different game at a different time; it does happen, but it is rare. Here we want to reiterate that *at the moment of maximum information risk, the price risk is minimal.*

◆·◆·◆·◆ Let's proceed from that low through a typical cycle, beginning with the obvious question: Who stepped forward at that time to buy the stock from the remnants of selling? who was willing to assume that risk? A few may have done intense research: calling the company officers, talking to suppliers and distributors and competitors, and so on, trying to determine the possibility of a genuine rebound in earnings. Others will note that the stock has started to show up on its preprogrammed computerized "value" screens; someone may believe the chairman's professions of hope for the future. We don't know precisely who, nor do we need to know why, because the evidence of that decision is enough. (The market aphorism is that "the stock moved from weak to strong hands." The buyers are stronger than the remaining sellers, like the victors of a tug-of-war, because they begin to drive the price up.) But we can speculate that the buyer(s) might be more than just the specialist on the floor, who is required to buy if there's no one else around to do so; he could stem the decline, but wouldn't chase it on an uptick. So it might be someone whose brother-in-law has a friend who plays golf with the chairman of XYZ and is told "to get in on a good thing"; someone else may live next door to the company treasurer or have a daughter who dates an accountant handling the books. Or it might be the executives of XYZ themselves, who have decided that they'd seen all the bad news, had cleaned up the balance sheet with the write-off, were going to use the money saved from paying out dividends to turn things around, and maybe they even have a notion that a new order or two or new product is coming along.

More likely, one portfolio manager, having made money in XYZ in the past, and knowing the company well, has decided that the "value"—however calculated, and whatever might be meant by that magic word *value*—was so great, relative to the stock price, that he felt compelled to start accumulating shares. Another, also paying attention and not distracted by previously having taken a big loss in the stock, might be able to come up with all those "insider" reasons via his own analysis; a third, knowing not the company but the nature of markets, and thus having a contrarian style, would realize that once all the bad news (or all he could conceive of) was out of the way he could take a position in the stock (and wanted to do so because of the underlying quality of the company, or its industry's future in the business cycle). You and I still don't know about a potential bankruptcy, but we do know that someone(s) is voting with real money that it isn't going to happen. At least some of those emerging buyers probably don't know very much more than we could glean, except that "the price is right." They are willing to take the information risk because there is minimal price risk.

Can't a brokerage firm's analyst produce the same sort of possibility? in his heart, perhaps, although not for the record. He's a company analyst first and foremost, not a stock predictor, and at this juncture, like so many others, has become consumed by the bad news, and prejudiced by the way he has been let down: "his" company is now worth so much less. Besides, even if he felt some hope, there is still such a dearth of information that he would have nothing to write about; he is virtually compelled to keep his mouth shut. Meanwhile, the chart shows that the downside momentum has been stemmed, and then that a bottom has begun to form; the behavioral pattern of sellers and buyers during this phase is creating the chart pattern that tells us of the reduced risk. But "begun" is not quite enough. At this juncture, I would speak of such clues to portfolio managers, and half-jokingly suggest, "If you want to help make the chart . . . " Buying the stock remains scary because there's no comfortable reason why one should act: the known fundamentals are against it, the analyst is still angry, and the uncertainty about the company's future continues.

Nevertheless, in the course of the next several weeks and perhaps months, other portfolio managers also begin to nibble on XYZ shares. They are encouraged because the stock price has begun to hold (such buying helps create a self-fulfilling prophecy); they talk to the company's management and find out things are getting no worse; they may have made their own stylistic decision to begin accumulating out-of-favor companies; the market itself may have begun to improve. Whatever their reasons, we can see this action in the pattern of a base forming on the chart itself. There's a lid on the stock as some traders take a profit "up," in company with a few others who've sweated out the entire decline and now, fearful that the bottom is going to drop out, seize on the price lift to sell. But there is also a bid underneath, as buyers continue their accumulation.

Call this the base-building period, during which there may be nuances of positive information available to the more assiduous digger, while the price risk has not changed all that much from the lows. As the stock finally forms a significant base, the best kind of answer we can get from a fundamental analyst is "It's two quarters away." Such a comment suggests that the analyst senses a change ahead (remember the anticipatory nature of the market), but lacks the actual information needed. Those who buy during this period *assume* (again, in both meanings of the word) the information risk, because there is lessened price risk now that the stock has shown its ability to bottom.

As time passes, more and more information becomes available. The market climate has begun to improve as well, and XYZ's shares participate in a general rebound. Let's say that at this stage XYZ has risen to 6½ but not yet broken out above the lid on the chart (the "neckline"—around 7 in our example—of the reverse head and shoulders that has formed during the basing). At this point, the chart has become an "almost"—basing is sufficient to support a new bull move, measuring to the neighborhood of 10, but won't be officially complete until that upside breakout takes place. Meanwhile, analysts who cover the company for their brokerage firms are still (accurately) reporting "No sign of an upturn yet," because the actual signs at the company are unreliable, meager, dangerous to build a bullish case on even though the analysts themselves feel better about XYZ's prospects. They aren't about to put that feeling into print; a feeling lasts two sentences, while they get paid for 20-page analytical reports!

The stock market, though, is anticipatory. A *few* more investors—it doesn't take many out of the entire universe of brokers and portfolio managers—develop the same feeling and thus more confidence about an eventual corporate turnaround that the analyst also senses. (Often, direct contact with an analyst from one firm or another during a marketing trip will provide a read-between-the-lines insight. In answer to a question at a lunch in Chicago or in a conference room in Richmond, the analyst might say, "The worst may be over, but . . . " or "I'm beginning to see some improvement" or even "I'm starting to do some work on it.") Many of these portfolio managers will also only watch, not act, because they, too, want to see some actual results so as to be "sure" before exposing themselves. But one or two will *take the information risk, so long as the price risk is relatively low.*

This low-keyed, almost drifting, or lurching, behavior may make it appear as if the stock is going nowhere, but the chart will begin to show higher lows depicting a gradual closing-in on the overhead breakout point. It will become possible to say that "*if* the stock . . . " and then to change that language to "*when* . . . " because the action speaks of an impending upside breakout. Note how a form of faith grows even though there is still nothing literally proven. Among many remaining anxieties, you can now build a positive case that you never dreamed of two or three months earlier, even though it is still filled with ifs and maybes and supposes. You're afraid—simultaneously and alternately—that the sequence of higher lows won't hold and that you won't own the stock when it breaks out. Then: one day your broker will phone to tell you how smart you are for having *talked* about XYZ—it's up a full point to 7³⁄₄ on 800,000 shares—but because you only talked and didn't buy you'll howl in anger/frustration because you'll realize you should have bought beforehand, and hadn't needed to be so scared after all. "Woulda, coulda, shoulda," you'll mutter.

The moment of such a breakout is often dramatic: typically, a round number helps—or at least a neat ¹⁄₂—but odd eighths don't matter in such a world. We want it to be done in a grand, not a trickling, manner. Helping the drama is that there usually is a big block of stock offered at that round number, sort of like soldiers guarding the gate. The stock may trade at 6³⁄₄, or 6⁷⁄₈ and back to ³⁄₄, and you may begin to sense an increasing itchiness. (Remember: *you* are watching now with a prejudicial point of view; you *know* that the chart says crossing 7 would be a major breakout across the neckline of a head and shoulders bottom. That makes you bullish, whether or not you already own the stock yet.) In almost every instance, the stock does *not* then trade as if snipers are picking off a few shares at 7 from time to time; rather, someone comes along and takes the whole damn block at once, and whoosh. . . . Because 7 actually was—now proven—such an important number, there is a vacuum of sellers just overhead and late-arriving buyers now have to reach up for more shares. The stock rushes through $1/8$ and $1/4$ and $3/8$ like an express through the now-open gate, and doesn't find enough sellers to meet the demand until it gets to $7^1/2$. Maybe you have to be obsessive about the stock market game to feel this, but it does feel, for those few moments, damned exciting.

There is usually a straightforward and momentary pullback toward the breakout point, but now the stock advances, although there'll be setbacks along the way as economic encouragement mingles with words of anxiety. The slogan that "a bull market climbs a wall of worry" is as true of individual stocks as it is of the averages. Many other investors insist on knowing more; they want reliable, actually announced information before they'll bet their money; possibilities are not enough, hunches and tendencies are insufficient. So it isn't until two, perhaps three, quarters later (just as the analyst foretold with the "It's two quarters away" remark), when the company is finally reporting a literal turnaround in earnings, that they are willing to buy, each deciding at a different hour, on a different day, in overlapping sequence. By this time, all sorts of positive information is readily available—it's a matter of degree of enthusiasm, rather than whether or not—but the stock price has already risen considerably. And the buying that ensues, now that it reflects confidence, takes the price even higher. *The more information that becomes available the greater the price risk because the stock has already risen.*

Ultimately, investors—and tagalong analysts—become enthusiastic about XYZ. Business is booming; the dividend has been restored; estimates of future earnings are scaled up with every positive report; the good news entices those who haven't gotten in yet, but now they look to buy on minor dips. Their bids help the stock to hold sell-offs fed by profit-taking from those who bought early, so that people say, "See how strong XYZ is; they can't put it down." Eventually, just about everyone who wants to own XYZ has bought.

Then look what happens to the stock price: it starts first to struggle, then to cease going up. A booming quarterly earnings gain excites the analysts, causing them to raise estimates once again, but on the floor of the stock exchange, shares of XYZ fail to make a new high. (And maybe the DJIA has itself made a new high, so that XYZ's failure contributes to a failing indicator reading.) Indeed, to keep this theoretical example symmetrical, we may even find that on an announced dividend increase the stock, after opening higher, actually declines by the close of trading that day on what is cavalierly dismissed as mere profit-taking. Well, it actually *is* "mere" profit-taking. The news that holders have been waiting for is now "in" the stock. Indeed, many such holders have become increasingly interested in taking their by-now big profits, and already have planned to sell once the good news is announced. What's more, it may be easy to see, if one is not mesmerized by the news itself, that from that moment on year-to-year comparisons are no longer going to make good reading. From our point of view, what has happened is that *the buyers have become exhausted . . .* simultaneously with an increase in sellers. Those who bought low can sell high. *Thus at the point of maximum positive information we also have maximum price risk.*

And, you see, at that point of maximum price risk, *no one knows anything negative about the company.* The company president is glowing in his annual report; analysts are busily writing about how great everything is. But someone is selling. I may have exaggerated the situation at the bottom a bit, because on the buy side, as the stock begins to base, a few people do know something. Valuation work (such fundamental tools as price to cash or price to book) has some validity at that juncture. Those who use such screens too often fall for an alluring name the moment it shows up on the screen, forgetting that the market demands excesses. But it is the excesses that work—the best buys are those of a stock that stays on the screen for weeks and weeks—long enough to be forgotten, ignored, derided—while the chart base forms. But this is bottoming stuff. At a top, it seems that no one knows anything negative, even though enough selling is taking place to cause that top to form on the chart. Who is that someone?

Consider the action in Intel in 1990. The worst that could have been said as INTC kept rising would have been "it's losing momentum." In mid-July the stock leapt to an all-time high of 52 following a marvelous earnings report. That very day, the *Wall Street Journal* in its "Heard on the Street" column reported that they "couldn't find a bear" among analysts and portfolio managers—at the very high! Volume began to pick up immediately thereafter—on the downside, as selling multiplied. If there was no negative news to know, what might one of those sellers have said? "Why be greedy," perhaps, or "What more good news can there be?"

One of my favorite anecdotes is that of the portfolio manager who sold his shares in Warner Communications at the very top in 1981. At that time, the chief investment officer of a major insurance company actually stood up and shook his fist at me across a conference table because I had stated that the chart of WCI showed a huge top. "Do you know what the earnings are going to be?" he bellowed. "No," I replied, rather meekly, backing away, "I only know that a top has formed and the stock should be sold."

After the stock had plummeted from over 60 to under 20, I went around the country using that as an example of how no one ever knows anything about the negative news, and yet the WCI chart showed that a mysterious someone(s) knew enough to sell enough shares to make a clearly visible top—not a simple spike, but a top that had formed over time in the face, evidently, of what was being touted as big bullish news still to come. "What did such sellers know," I would ask, "that the analysts following the company didn't know?"

Eventually, in Boston, the reply came: "I'll tell you why I sold my Warner Communications stock at the top." A portfolio manager explained that he'd come home one night for dinner and there was no dinner on the table. Nor was there any sign that dinner was even being planned. When he found his wife, he went on, she was in the den playing with her Atari cartridges. The portfolio manager decided that if a middle-aged suburban housewife was into Atari, then there was no one left to buy the product. Its business had peaked, he concluded, so he sold, as simply as that.

Other such anecdotes from other money managers then came pouring forth. One manager had sold an auto stock near its good-news top because as he was out walking the dog he strolled past the neighborhood dealer's lot and noticed that it was overstocked. Another sold shares of a retailer because he'd gone into the store on a Sunday afternoon before Christmas and it was empty. An analyst wrote a brilliant report recommending sale of a company, he told me, because after he'd left the office of the company's chief financial officer, where he'd been assured that everything was marvelous, he happened to notice cartons of the company's product stacked up in the hallways because the warehouses were already full of unsold goods. Or, said another, his teenage daughter had told him, "Oh Dad, no one buys those sneakers anymore."

Such anecdotes are random, not in the mainstream of what is generally thought about as corporate information. Brokerage house researchers pore over book value, yield on equity, and other flora and fauna of the Wall Street jungle, dependent on *annual* reports and company press releases for information that by its very nature has to be not only late but as "positive" as possible. Some may sell on a hunch, others to take profits, still others because they don't like the market climate anymore, and a few, it must be noted, because they have a fundamental valuation approach (measuring "overpriced" in some way or another—price to dividend, perhaps, or price to earnings) that provides them with the discipline to act, for all such selling is done when there is minimal negative information available, yet maximum price risk after such a prolonged rise. Then the downward spiral develops: as more and more negative information becomes available, the price falls and the price risk—the vulnerability—gradually lessens. Finally, the cycle is complete as XYZ reaches the point of maximum negative information and minimal price risk.

◇◆◇◆◇ The next question is: *How do we bring ourselves to act—to take the price risk—when we lack the comfort of information?*

· 4 ·

Fear or Confidence

WHAT is it that we want to know?

Something comforting, something that will take the risk out of life, out of investing. In other words, "Tell us what is going to happen in the future."

◇·◇·◇·◇ One of the experiences I persistently have with investor clients—and salesmen, reporters, TV interviewers, and so on—is that they invariably want to know what is unknowable. And, as a corollary, they don't want to know, or disbelieve, or wish they could believe but don't trust, what is actually known. It seems that *what is known is never enough.*

Thus, to put life in terms of the market, the "important" questions become: "Where is the Dow going to be . . . next week? six months from now? at year end?" Or "How much time is it going to take to get to 3600? to 1700?" (These are more difficult questions, I might point out, than "Should I major in ancient philosophy or in accounting?" or "Is he going to be bald and potbellied before he reaches 40?" The questions of life tend to be asked afterward: "Why me?")

But if you say, "The chart patterns of most cyclical stocks show lower highs," or "The diminishing number of new highs, while the DJIA has made its new high, is warning of a market top," they'll blink, or freeze. Even those who supposedly understand the negative message of such comments nevertheless—

thinking, "not now, not yet"—will demand to know the unknowable before they'll believe a word of what you are saying. Or, believing, will still *need to know more* before acting. They ask, "How soon will it happen, how far down will it go, how long will it last?"—otherwise, the message won't be considered significant enough. Providing a guesstimate makes them feel like they are being patted on the back. They won't act until they become comforted by "targets" of time and space—in the way men and women are comforted by being told the marriage will be "till death do us part." That the "answers" might be wrong, in life or the stock market, doesn't matter; it is the sense that, ah, now one knows "enough." Just as the couple about to be married will hear nothing of divorce statistics, investors really don't want to know that they're going to have to take a loss.

The demand to know more so as to be convinced before acting is especially true of negative/sell comments. While investors typically are too scared at bottoms to act on favorable words, they are usually able to hear them; the customary response is "Oh, do you really think so?" or even "Maybe I should, it's cheap enough" even though they remain paralyzed by the bad news and falling Dow. In contrast, no one wants to let in negative remarks. The same is also true about life choices: who lets in what the doctor is saying when it is serious? but hears instead the anxiety-placating words along the way, "You'll be okay tomorrow." Many people "know" what they ought to do about an illness, but despite the danger can't bring themselves to act (the lump in the breast being an obvious example). Often, one mishears, or doesn't hear, but even when what the doctor is saying sinks in, they demand to know *why* did this happen to me, *how long* has it been developing, rather than *what's* happening now, and *what* needs to be done about it.

An example of this is "tape reading." Of course, no one "reads" the tape anymore; it is becoming a lost art. Those who were good at it are retiring or already retired. Many brokerage offices constructed or remodeled in the 1980s do not even have a tape streaming across the front wall. Only old-timers remember the clacking electric price boards. Those who sit in front of their boxy "quotation machines" are so mesmerized by the rap-idly blinking shifts on the monitor portion of their screen that even if, for old times' sake, they have a few lines of the tape at the top of the video display screen their eyes can't keep still long enough to "read" it.

What's wrong with this loss of an old-fashioned virtue, re-placed by computers, is discussed in greater detail subsequently. Here my point is that few believe in the art of "tape reading" because there is a continuing sense, while watching, that the tape provides *insufficient* information, even though it is spe-cific, even though it is reporting on an actual transaction, even though you usually can perceive whether a seller or a buyer initiated the transaction. Of course, there is the abstract absence of knowing *why* someone is buying or selling. But in the literal sense, one invariably feels a need, a compulsion, to wait to see one more tick, and then another—after all, the tape is steadily streaming past with such information. Poised to go out to lunch, a broker will pause in the doorway to watch one more tick, as if the *next one* will—at last—tell him what he needs to know . . . sort of the way, in the burlesque houses of our youth, we would wait and watch for one more dancer to come out from backstage as if that next dancer would finally reveal the truth. What *is* known—the previous tick, the one now known—is never enough.

So let's return to the question "What is it we want to know?" Why is the literal action considered insufficient even though it is *caused* by the decisions of buyers and sellers? Since that mes-sage represents a cumulative decision of those who might very well know "why," shouldn't it be useful? Surely such buyers and sellers are not behaving frivolously; there's money at stake. How come they know "something"—enough of a "some-thing," that is, to cause them to act? Yet for the risk-nervous observer, literal, real, even dramatic action is deemed insuffi-cient to be convincing. More information is needed: what does the analyst say? what does the company say? as if it's our body, let's get a second opinion. The stock is down (or up) 3½ points on over a million shares, and they still can't accept the action until they learn "why." Or, at the other extreme, the stock goes down an eighth day after day, is down even on days when the DJIA is rallying. Yet, in the absence of understanding "why," hope persists that what is being seen is somehow wrong, or that even though it is right it is only temporary, or, even though the fever persists, it isn't serious.

Every so often, a portfolio manager nervously swirling around in his swivel chair will ask what I think of a particular stock. My "It's acting terrible" is responded to with a sigh: "I know, I know, I'm losing sleep about it; I don't know what to do." To a delicate suggestion that he could pick up the phone to his order room and say, "Sell," even if only to get a good night's sleep again, the money manager invariably replies: "I'm trying to find out what's wrong." He does not want to deal with what he already knows he must deal with; it isn't even the end of the hope for that stock that's at stake, but rather more the strain of actually having to stop swiveling and act. What kind of a risk is that which is substituted for the real risk? Doing something becomes a risk in itself. In these days of minuscule commission rates for institutions, and thus no consequential cost of getting out, and 5,000 other stocks to choose from, where is the virtue in denying a problem so as not to have to act? Why is "the lump in the breast" so often dealt with by not dealing with it? This is not such an incongruous comparison, because money, too, seems to be a "body" of ours, and its "paper" loss, its eating away, a form of cancer. Having to act requires accepting a reality we prefer not to face.

Thus while there is a need for "more" information, there are certain things we *don't* want to know. In a sense, they are too risky to know. In real life, some women, feeling that lump, won't go to a doctor precisely because they don't want to be told what they already know, because "learning" from the doctor will make the information more real. In similar style, that portfolio manager didn't need me to confirm his own observations, but wanted me to offer hope instead. Readily available stock market information may suffer from being too real: the investor with a tiny loss continues to call his broker every day to get some hope that the cut is healing; gradually, though, as discouragement sets in, he begins merely to look the price up in the next morning's newspaper; when the loss has bled him so much that he really doesn't want to know the price, he'll only look the stock up in *Barron's* over the weekend during a time-out in the football game . . . until finally he begins to forget that he owns the stock at all and doesn't even bother to open his monthly brokerage statement. And yet, through it all, he "knows" the price is down, and also knows that if he wants to heal himself from the pain he need do nothing more than tell his broker to sell. Hope becomes a very powerful piece of "information."

(But on the buy side, hope seems not to exist. Hesitation stems from the terror of being exposed as wrong. The very man who might hesitate to buy General Motors winds up taking a speculative plunge that stems from an "Oh, what the hell, you only live once" attitude. Or, as a compromise, other investors, like buying a lottery ticket, proceed on the notion that whatever the broker wants to do is okay.)

Behavior of this type takes "information" and by denying what is objectively known thereby increases the risk. Avoidance of the reality of otherwise available information can be translated into preferring to learn information that one knows in advance is *not* going to be forthcoming—a higher price, a benign biopsy. Thus the ostrich-avoidance is cousin to wanting more information. Both increase risk.

◇•◇•◇•◇ That lump, or in a man's case, undeniable blood in the urine, may be far down the evolutionary process of information gathering. We get "tape reading" bits and pieces of information in real life—a "tick" of someone's smile as phony or felt is a simple example. I *knew* months beforehand that something had changed in my body—just because it was my own body—but even though these "ticks" were passed on, to the doctor the information wasn't sufficient to act on . . . sort of like saying, "That stock's not acting the way it should so I think we ought to sell just to be safe," and having the broker reply, "Well, yes, we'll watch it and if it gets any worse, *then* we'll sell." At this reaction by the professional, I became more passive, more accepting of the "downticks," yet more uncomfortable. Some men, I'm sure, would have urinated in the middle of the night and thus perhaps didn't notice; others would tell themselves, "I'll call the doctor if it happens again"; still others would try to ignore the evident "loss." We absorb these "ticks" in the same manner that we let the tape stream by our eyes (or used to, when there was a tape); sometimes the information registers, sometimes we know and yet don't know, sometimes we really weren't watching, sometimes we actually have a clear realization and then don't do anything about it.

Thus it does not seem to be folly or arrogance to relate the moment-to-moment action of both daily life and the stock market. Imagine, for example, that the day's "tape reading" begins as your car pulls out onto the expressway. Are you driving well, or not? you didn't see that car and had to swerve, reacted in time but more slowly than you had confidence you always would? does getting older then occur to you? worry you? When you pause on your way into the office, do you snap at the luncheonette clerk, or growl at the slow pace of the line of people getting coffee ahead of you? Do you realize that each morning lately you've gone up in the elevator irritably, blaming it on not having had your coffee yet? even though it might be more deeply rooted. Or does the proverbial "light bulb" pop on in your head, as you wonder what that budding anger means? Is it how you left your spouse? or what lies ahead at work? You sneeze three times; your shirttail is out; and when you march toward your cubicle your secretary ducks. While your own "tape reading" misses these little ticks—too distracted, or too busy denying, or sure it won't last—would an objective observer note the beginning of a downtrend and only half-jokingly whisper to your secretary: "Sell that guy short"? In sum, because *knowing can lead to a change*, ignoring what is known around us—be it behavior on the tape or in our behavior—increases our risk.

Lest this sound too negative, consider the upbeat side of romance. A man in love, whistling down the street, suddenly realizes that women who never would have given him a glance were he despondent are now noticing him. Women who come to a party feeling great about themselves have more suitors surrounding them than if their lover has just kicked them out of the house. Both man and woman—I guarantee it—could make a better stock trade at that moment than at any other time in the ticker-tape flow of their lives. If we are trying to deal with how we proceed through life in terms of the risks we take, then we can perhaps also understand the moment-to-moment sense of risk in the marketplace. And perhaps we can ultimately conclude that *many of us "play" the market as a proxy for life risks too great to take, for the speculative excitement our lives don't contain.* As a way to lose, playing the market that way parallels the way a balding accountant falls for a chorus girl.

The actual action as it occurs on the floor of the Exchange (or via telephone and computers, nowadays), is composed of minute changes—in price, in tick, in volume. The "tape" is the shorthand record of every transaction. "Who bought 20,000 shares of Bessie?" is not announced, but that *someone* "bought" rather than sold is knowable because we can observe that the "tick" on the tape printed at a higher price than the previous different price. Our eye/mind having been caught, we begin to see BS more frequently. From those momentary tidbits, equivalent to the flashing of an ankle in Victorian times, we can "read" that "the stock trades well." A number of prints of differing size (volume) persist at that same "up" price, and then—lo and behold!—there's another block bought another eighth of a point higher. Some will have missed the sequence, concentrating on other stocks or merely drifting through the day; others will notice, but not care—Bessie's not their kind of stock, meaning "not their kind of risk." A few might mutter to themselves or, nudging a neighboring tape watcher, "See that Bessie? acts like something may be going on there"; a something may be the hot tip he wished he had, or maybe that a buyer who, having done his investment homework, has decided to buy 100,000 shares. One investor, in one office somewhere in the entire United States, might believe enough—perhaps having already been intrigued by the chart—to react to "feeling" turned on by the ticks on the tape by actually entering an order. The order is the way he assumes the risk that what he's seen will lead to a reward. And then, of course, there are those who saw, but who reacted by wanting to know more; didn't take the risk, didn't make a buck, but later are able to boast that they spotted Bessie dancing across the tape back when it was only 7.

◇◆◇◆◇ You can't watch the tape? of course not, it's no way for a grown-up to spend a sunny day. But all such action adds up to a line on a chart that can be constructed of the day's high, low, closing price, and volume—a chart that is nothing but a graphic representation of the day's action. (And this action can further be summed up, of course, on a weekly or even monthly basis.) Such a simple daily "bar" chart is composed of minute changes. While individual minute changes are insufficient to base a decision on, over a period of time the chart can develop into a pattern that "says" something, but that is, nevertheless, everchanging: *that's why there is no one moment, or point, at which one can make an obvious decision. That's why, therefore, one always wants to know one more thing.*

Why, then, if something like "tape reading," or the chart form of such "reading," works, is it discounted and so often attacked? *Because it is the wrong kind of information.* There is no comfort to it, since, being the market, it *is* the changeable market. Technical analysis is *based on* the past—literal, knowable, printed-in-the-newspaper information available simultaneously to all—but is *accused of* being based on the future. Such information is supposed to cure our anxieties, but it doesn't. One attacks not what it can do, but what one wishes it could do. It doesn't know why; it doesn't understand; it is merely "reading" the market's language, and that's not enough. Since, in its everchanging way, it isn't, can't be, perfect, it is accused of being akin to tea leaves and crystal balls (which have, as it happens, no past whatsoever).

◇•◇•◇•◇   There is, I read in Vicki Hearne's *Adam's Task* (Alfred A. Knopf, New York, 1986), a phenomenon known as the "clever Hans" fallacy, named after a "clever" horse who was able to answer questions in an uncanny fashion. How could he "know"? Well, of course, he didn't, not really; what he was apparently "reading," with breathtaking accuracy, was *minute* changes in the body of the person asking the question: the angles of eyebrows, breathing, and so on. Thus Hans gave "answers" but ended up being a fallacy because he didn't understand the questions; he "merely" read body language. And yet his answers were right!

So, too, with technical analysis. If the technician is not analyzing the actual company, the real subject of investing, but is "merely" reading the stock market's body language, then the hell with his successes.

That suspicion, that denial, shows in its own way how important the question "What information do we really want?" actually is to risk-taking. *What we already know is never enough. We always want one more piece of information.* Some traders believe they can't even go to the bathroom for fear they'll miss the moment of *the* message, as if that famous "little birdie" who's going to tell them is making a tour of trading rooms. Even in this moment-to-moment way, the need to know what is going to happen next—what the *next* piece of information is going to be—becomes very powerful. We are back to the anxiety about the future again. Knowing what the future will bring is the "sure" way to reduce risk. Stopping in at the local gypsy's on our way to our broker's may help calm us down more than being told the information that is already known, especially when that information is presented in the form of the market's language and not that of the gypsy.

As a result, even if I announce at the outset of a speech about the stock market that I don't know, and, furthermore, don't believe it is important to know, what the averages are going to do by, say, year end (as if the market keeps a calendar, too), invariably someone in the audience will ask: "I know you said you didn't know, but could you at least hazard a guess as to where you think the Dow will be, can you put a number on it, can you estimate how long it will take to get there?" Can I predict how long it will take to get to a target I don't even know?

Well, yes, sometimes such answers, although truly not important to know, are possible. Those willing to believe a chart can identify where resistance is, where support is; you can "measure" a chart pattern and, often, the two answers will be approximately the same, thus confirming a potential target. "How long?" is more abstract, especially since market moves have less consistency than a decade ago. Occasionally, by estimating how long it ought to take for, say, a certain indicator to turn from bullish to bearish, or how many weeks on the chart it would take for the stock to trade sideways to get to its trend line, one can proffer a length of time. *But so what?*

Such aspects (resistance, let's say, or support, to use two simple concepts), *being knowable*, are, or ought to be, among the primary tools for decision making. But because what we are doing is "reading" the market's language rather than "understanding" why, it is accused of being insufficient. The investor wants to know more, so if I then say, surrendering to the audience, that it "looks like" 2200 is a "good" target, that's what gets heard. Few leave the meeting saying, "Justin says the basing on the charts is big enough to justify buying oil service stocks in here." They say, "Justin says the market is going to 2200." So they've transferred the risk-taking substance from what is meant to reduce risk (the support levels in the individual stocks one might actually buy), the positive look to the market as expressed by "It wants to go up," to a useless abstraction because they need to know, before they can bring themselves to act, "why" the market should go up to 2200. Obviously, if it were widely understood that the market was going to 2200 because it "belonged" at 2200, everyone would know and would have bought and it would be there already. *The doubt demands the answer to "why."* But we know why Justin thinks so: the bases are there; several indicators are speaking: *that*'s knowable. The knowledge reduces risk, actually telling us what to do in practical terms, but it is the kind of knowledge that doesn't relieve anxieties so no one is willing to take the risk.

Investors always want to know the future stated as an article of faith, before they can act. (And maybe that phrase "an article of faith" is as true as it is for religion, where one needs to hear about the future—heaven or hell, the soul surviving or dust, punishment or rewards—before one will believe.) The need for the wrong kind of information is their undoing because that which they long to know will only become manifest *at*, in this example, 2200. Thus the question really is not what information do we want, but *what information should we want so as to reduce risk?*

Oh, but you may say, Why shouldn't I find out whether the company's business is actually improving? why shouldn't I wait for the analyst, who after all talks to the company president, to tell me what the future earnings are going to leap to? If the market's future, and the stock's, is so difficult to determine, then one ought to at least know why, and what, is happening to the company—"comfort" information.

This translates into a belief that once this information becomes known, the stock price will be affected. The price will go up, more people will know, and then the price will go up some more. The quest then turns toward knowing corporate information *first*, before others. But this presumes two things: that the initial buyers have literal knowledge available to them, rather than relying on experienced suppositions and observations; and second, that, assuming literal knowledge (which includes, if that little birdie tells you, inside information), you'll be among the first to be told. Does the person who bought first (helping to make the chart) know something, and should we follow what he does, or should we wait until we learn what he knows? (We, as chartists, wait long enough to be convinced—never "sure"— that others are buying in agreement with the first buyer as to price and value, but never wait so long as until everyone gets to know sure stuff.)

Some portfolio managers manage money on the principle that because it is all risk their main goal is not to be so smart but to avoid blame. That translates into the slogan "I can't afford to let them go up without me" (or I'll get fired), "but we can all go down together" (it was the market's fault, how can they blame me for owning IBM and GM, so they won't fire me even if my portfolio is disastersville). Such managers often select already weak stocks that to their minds shouldn't go down any more as a sneaky way of limiting risk. This is merely a different form of "comforting" information.

But what does one do if the evident information is in conflict with the performance of the stock? Often, the fundamental analyst insists that business is still bad (or good), that earnings are going to be down (or terrific) for the next quarter or two, and so on. So who is buying (or selling), and why? Isn't it because the "real," the unknown, the future, information is different from what is already known? Lest you suspect the charts are perfect, it should be noted that when a stock with a seemingly positive chart does not go up when it should (that is, when the market is rallying), the message is that the sellers know more than the buyers. Information has a life of its own that we can't freeze once we're satisfied. The difference between a technician's lingo and a fundamentalist's is that while the fundamentalist deals with the news itself, and not the market's anticipatory nature, a technician cares about *how* the market responds to the news, not what the news is.

Human nature willingly—naively?—accepts what is known, is comforted by it, convinced of whatever the news happens to be: of good news at a top and of bad news at a bottom. And, it must be repeatedly said, this is abetted by the media reporting of such news, as if the market is a war zone. What shows up on TV seems to be exactly what is happening, and we have been conditioned to believe its importance.

If so, then why is money—that is, the ability of buyers or sellers to give the stock its dominant behavior—voting that something different is actually taking place? When that money is big enough, insistent enough, not to be dismissed, can't it be presumed to "know" something more than is yet in the news? *especially* because the market, as a discounting mechanism, is anticipating the next piece of information. That piece of information may be only that something different is going to take place. It may even be wrong: rumor that turns out to be no more than that, or earnings forecast by the nation's leading analyst that so often proves to be wrong. By waiting to find out what that next "something" literally might be, *one assumes an additional price risk!*

A simple real-life example: In the midst of considerable euphoria, breadth (as measured by the cumulative advance/decline line) reached a post-1987 Crash peak (with the Dow at 2752) on September 1, 1989. It was, to begin with, significant that

Chart 3
CUMULATIVE ADVANCE/DECLINE LINE
August 1989—October 1990

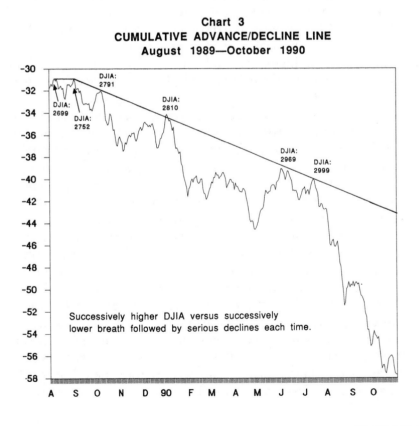

although the DJIA was then edging into new all-time high territory, that day's breadth reading was conspicuously less than its
mid-1987 level. And from then on, it was downhill, sometimes
in greased fashion. On the first trading day of 1990, the DJIA
made another new all-time (at 2810) high, which was glaringly
unconfirmed: fewer new highs and a breadth reading considerably worse than in August.

By themselves those negative divergences signaled trouble to
come: a 300-point three-week plunge immediately followed.
And then, most telling, a similar failure developed in mid-July
1990, when for two days in a row—eerie stuff!—the Dow
closed at 2999.75. But look what the market was "saying": the
advance/decline line was 15 percent worse than it had been on
January 2, which in turn had been worse, by about 10 percent,
from the September 1989 peak reading. Similarly, the number
of new highs registered at 102, compared to 110 and 111 at
those two previous peaks, and also was noticeably less than the
number of new highs that had been achieved just a few days
earlier. Yet, despite the evident underlying deterioration, it was
not until Iraq's invasion of Kuwait on August 2, 1990, that
investors discovered a "real" reason for selling—nearly 200
Dow points lower. For most investors, the invasion became the
"How could you know?" excuse for not having been prepared.

Mysteriously, without having a doctorate in global politics,
or understanding Middle East madnesses, the market *did know
something*—for nearly a year it had been topping out (with
breadth peaking on September 1, 1989), had already had several
sharp strokes. But each such sell-off seemed excusable as only
temporary; an easy explanation as to "why" wasn't there until
hindsight was able to blame the Iraqis instead of recognizing
what the market had already been warning about: weakness.
Tops are not made in a day. It takes time, it takes distribution,
and deterioration. The decline had already begun when the invasion was launched. The interesting, albeit academic, question
is, If the market had *already* declined, say, 20 percent, would
prices have collapsed just the same, on the war news? or would
it have been far less vulnerable? (The market was at a high when

Eisenhower had his heart attack—and plummeted; his ileitis attack came at the end of a long slide, so prices opened down and immediately rallied.) Was 1990's actual August–October slide due anyhow, whatever the reason? because, of course, the market, however it seemed to know "something," didn't know even as much as the CIA did. In mid-July it was announcing its own vulnerability; two days before bombs started falling in mid-January, it was announcing its oversoldness, so we got a big rally that was immediately considered "aberrant behavior" by analysts and the press alike.

Is it too painful to relate this to waiting for the malignancy to materialize in a bigger lump, or in a bright-red flow of urine not once or twice but too often, finally, to be ignored? The ongoing change in information is what frightens us. The additional risk of waiting is similarly true, and may be clearer to grasp, when it concerns the market itself. Why shouldn't one wait to be *sure* that the DJIA, or the individual stock itself, actually can begin to rise? Obviously, then, the cost of waiting is the higher price—that is, a greater price risk. Similarly, if one waits to learn why the stock is going down, one has to decide about selling at a worse price and under considerable emotional pressure as the price gets even worse. So then one decides to wait for a rebound to get out, which violates a "rule" I first wrote about in *Tape Reader* days: "In bear markets, the price you get today is likely to be better than the price you'll get on the next rally." Although it seems safer, more conservative, so as to reduce the information risk, waiting costs, leaves the money/body more vulnerable to loss.

◆◆◆◆ But suppose while I wait for that additional information the price has *not* advanced? The stock looked like it wanted to go up, ought to have gone up, but didn't. What's wrong? Why hasn't it? Is the market so nice and polite that it will wait for you? won't budge until the information you need to know becomes available, and, what's more, known to you a few minutes earlier than to anyone else so you can act? When something is wrong (note that "wrong" means not doing what it is "expected to do"), you are getting a different, but equally vital, piece of *market* information; you are assuming a different risk. It's a sort of "If your wife is supposed to love you, why isn't she hugging you" problem. When a stock isn't trading in conformity with what is known—good news, but more selling than buying; bad news, but the stock doesn't go down any more—isn't that a warning that something is apt to be "wrong" with the current price? In these circumstances, the available information is skewed by market action; he who hesitates needs different information because he is unwilling to believe what the market is saying. *When the market is doing something different from what it is supposed to, it is doubly significant.* And you can substitute your own "body" for "market" in that rule. It is you who takes the risk!

◆•◆•◆•◆ The problem may be that the investor is seeking the wrong information. It smacks of the way teenagers confuse sex with love. They don't have the experience to realize that the youthful passion they feel doesn't automatically translate into love, nor a short-term spurt into a long-term attachment. The information seems so powerful that it has to be worth investing in, so they get married. How can they know that the inputs they are receiving are the wrong pieces of information, when it feels so right? In their dating games, they keep searching for the passion that will be sufficient information to base a marriage on, when they ought to be asking other kinds of questions about the "ticks" of moment-to-moment being with each other. (In the stock market, such questions might begin with: Does everyone else know? does the stock action already reflect this information? And, does it matter?)

There is a gut problem with the abstraction of investing that investors are not aware of. The nature of risk becomes entwined not only with information but with ourselves. Because the market, as a proxy for life, is continuous, we wait and wait for further information before buying or selling. But as an abstraction it is hard to pin down. There is no given moment when the price reaches stasis, and can be counted on to stay there. Nor is there any given moment when *all* the information in *all* its sorting out is surely available. Buyers and sellers—in extent, desire, and timing—change all the time as the available information, and its emotional effect, change. It is a never-ending search for the idealized "efficient" market.

Accordingly, in its third version, the question isn't "What information do we need to take a risk?" nor even "What information should we want?" but rather, *"Since this is the information available, how do we use this information so as to reduce risk?"*

· 5 ·

The Stock Market as Life

THE stock market is as moment-to-moment within a long-term trend as life is. People think: I'm buying this house to live in while the babies grow up and go off to college; I'm marrying this person "till death do us part"—long-term investments but moment-to-moment decisions. How much do we know— surely not enough—about the value of the house? about our future spouse's parents and their potential impact on the marital "investment"? We get caught up in emotions, and believe our feelings represent our judgment about the long-term values. Thus there is a distinction between the religion of long-term beliefs, hopes, and expectations, and the secular short-term practice of our moment-to-moment behavior.

Although we might be convinced that the decisions we make have that long-term basis, they stem from the moment. Oh, sure, you'd like to marry that boy or girl, or one similar, because you want to be married long-term—but decisions are not like that. Those who wait until they've crossed 40, like a break-out, to overcome their fear—shy, or too busy, are the explanations—make their major investment decision to join the crowd before it's too "late," believing they have finally gathered enough information about marriage to proceed more safely. Others, as they emerge from adolescence, discover passion, which can seem so much like love that the next thing they know they're married. Life's decisions have an auction fever: you're buying as an investment, but standing up in the audience waving your hand for attention, desperate, at that moment, to buy at an even higher price.

Similarly, so-called long-term investors make buy or sell decisions for moment-to-moment reasons. A portfolio manager may contemplate buying a stock but has decided to wait until he or she gathers more information; along comes a short-term rise sparked by news—the Fed cuts the discount rate, for example—and the money manager can't stand being patient any longer, bangs on the phone to get the trader's attention, and buys right then and there into the excitement, up 2 points. On the sell side, stocks get tossed out emotionally—even though they were originally bought to be held for a "three-year time horizon"—just because the market looked awful that morning while it was selling off. The portfolio manager can't endure seeing—literally seeing at that moment—the money disappear. *Watching the market every moment can turn any longer-term investor into a hypochondriac.*

◇◆◇◆◇ The clichés of daily life are those of routine, discouragement, tiredness; of the rat race; of a cold, the IRS. People are always complaining that there should be more good news, when there isn't. Americans are often described as basically optimistic, when in reality it is that they are perpetually hopeful. Guys even root for dreadful teams for years—keep buying season tickets in the hope that eventually they'll own seats for the Super Bowl or World Series. And better than being a sports fan—because you can actually participate—and even better than gambling—because it is socially acceptable—playing the stock market becomes a way out of an otherwise mundane and stressful environment. It has glamour, plus the chance of improving one's lot without being an overt bet. There's an excitement to it, along with the illusion that a successful investment is almost within reach, if one only knew how to tap it. The market seems to represent hope itself. And yet, among professionals, even those who function on the stock exchange floor, a frequently heard stock market expression is "No one ever said it was going to be easy."

When even the good news of a rising market is stressful—might not last longer than yesterday; it's rising, but we don't own the right stocks; and so on—no wonder we long for some security. Indeed, the market often does look easy . . . in hindsight. Tops are made as everyone rushes to buy what has been profitable already. At that point, to the astonishment of those who've missed it, the cliché becomes: "The easy money has already been made." But while it is happening no one realizes it; investors are caught up in the classic "wall of worry" instead. *It never can be easy because the rule of the market is that you have to act before you know enough. Because it is a process, there is no one moment, or single point, at which one can make an obvious "sure" decision.*

◈◈◈◈ A useful simile for the stock market might be that of the tide, waves, and a beach. The tide comes in and goes out in cyclical fashion; the waves come in and go out like market fluctuations, but in differing fashions—crashing, gentle, white-capped, mild. Each wave, each tide, affects the grains of sand on the beach, shifting them here and there; there may be a period of erosion, a period of rebuilding, but in a different place. Those shifting grains of sand make up the ("long-term") beach, just as constantly shifting but minute changes in price, tick by tick, make up the stock market. A sudden violent ("short-term") storm can rip the beach up and change its shape, and even though we were warned by the weatherman, he did forecast such a "storm in the late afternoon," so we thought we could enjoy a picnic lunch first. We should have come the day before, when it was beautiful, but we missed the chance. And yet the weatherman was not wrong; he may have underestimated the severity, may have missed the precise timing, but there was the warning for us to believe or not. Disappointed, late—because we missed the better weather yesterday—and even though we see the storm clouds gathering in the distance, we may stay on the beach, trying to squeeze out another minute's swimming as a profit before the disrupting storm strikes. And besides, how do we know the storm is really going to come? it might blow over, just our luck it won't. . . . Hindsight reminds us of how much we knew, and yet still we got drenched in the parking lot.

◇·◇·◇·◇ Thus it is not just information that becomes the key to taking a market risk; it is also necessary to understand such information in terms of our relationship to that knowledge. "What do we know?" "How do we know it?" and "What is our reaction to that information?"—as well as "What do we need/wish/want to know?"—are all questions that affect the decisions we make every day.

Some of that is trivial, routine, habit. We "decide" what clothes to wear to work and in what sequence to put the garments on, but never pause to wonder if that routine might be best for us. Everything, so to speak, is laid out for us. And thus we might panic in preparing for a job interview because the getting-dressed risk of what had been easy to "decide" abruptly increases. The choice has become important instead of routine, and suddenly we feel as if we don't have enough information to make the decision. What *is* a suitable interview suit? how do we want to present ourselves? *The anxiety of making a mistake overpowers the ability to make a "free" choice.* When a decision *is* required, the way we take information in, and how we use it, affects that decision.

Our self's style goes back deep into childhood. Our neuroses can often be defined as safety nets, with our choices designed (albeit subconsciously) to protect against risk. Consider once again how we cross the street: each of us differently, depending on such information as oncoming traffic, distance to the crosswalk, the presence of a nearby policeman, and need for haste, but also affected by how our father crossed the street even as he held our hand. Have you ever found yourself hastening to get across a street because the light is changing even though you were in no particular hurry to get to the other side? That can become a New York City style even if you grew up on a farm, and you might then, in Sidney or Peoria, rush across streets unnecessarily. Would you realize in midcrossing that your style of behavior relative to the information at hand is no longer helping you make an informed and objective decision about the risk involved?

Are we behaving like a chicken crossing the road? knowing where we want to go—to the other side—but that's all. Suppose we're driving down an unfamiliar highway, in the dark, in the rain, looking for the right exit sign. "Was that it?" we mutter to our spouse in the passenger seat. "Did it say 'Route 28 next exit?' it came up on me so fast I'm not sure I saw right, but there'll be another sign; is this the exit? why isn't there another sign right here? should I get off? oops, I guess that really was it. Why didn't *you* tell me?" Note our experience even as we fumbled; our intuition, even as we didn't act on it, or even trust it; our hasty decision, even though we could have proceeded more carefully; our knowledge that the exit was near, even though we missed the opportunity. And, finally, notice how we turned the error into a chance to blame someone else.

These are humdrum examples, to be sure, but you can extend them into those more serious matters of destiny, such as the purchase of a new house; whether, approaching the altar, we really should go through with the marriage ceremony; or even, whether to buy or sell that stock. Surely, at least some of the seduction and intrigue, of both marriage and stock, comes from trying to please our own neuroses, and to protect against risk. The manner in which we let information in, our ability to understand it, to deal with it, and perhaps even distort it, all start with who we are, as developed from that moment of beginning, on our hands and knees, to explore the world.

Yet that person we've become can also go haywire. Aren't there times when we are incoherent in our own lives—days when we are absentminded or under the weather, weeks when something like a pending divorce or IRS audit affects the mind's ability to think clearly of other things (even though we insist we're okay); mornings when we can't seem to get untracked and afternoons when something, perhaps only tiredness, is disturbing our ability to concentrate or to perceive, like the last run of the day down the ski slope. Such impediments affect not merely judgment but understanding, as does, obviously, prejudice, stubbornness, and—when it comes to the stock market—the fear of being embarrassed by a mistake. And, of course, there are some people who claim to have no interest in the market, and so don't even understand the risk-taking nature of the decisions they've made about their savings so as to avoid the market itself. Others refuse to understand stocks because the market seems so frightening to them (the way girls are supposedly poor at math), or are so wishy-washy or imprecise as to be incapable of doing well buying and selling, while still others insist they understand but are constantly having emotional reactions that conflict with or suppress what they know and hence increase their risk. *But we must remember that there are times when the market, or life itself, is incoherent, unclear, and/or conflicting; times when it isn't us, it's it.*

◈◈◈◈ Thus the risk that we are about to take via our next decision is not a simple choice of "do it or not," of "yes or no." Before deciding, we need to know why what we know is never enough, a question that, in turn, leads to *what kind of information do we believe, or trust?* and, is it us, or the market?

At first glance, a battered woman's need to believe comes to mind: "I know he loves me, even though he beats me." Our market need to know is similar: "I know, I know, so how come, no matter how convinced I am, what I know is never enough to save me from being bruised?" Thus a second glance perceives that the need to know more stems from the insecurity that what is already known isn't true enough. "Maybe he beats me *because* he loves me." Information becomes a challenge of survival. "Why don't I know?" is then a problem of insecurity, of which being self-deceived is perhaps the most serious subconscious trait. The anxiety-ridden don't quite believe what they already know; the wrenching conflict between avoidance and the need to know more stems from fear—how wide across is that chasm I've got to leap?

The stock market itself makes matters worse. "I wouldn't believe a hot tip if God himself told me, unless I saw it on the tape." What becomes known to you and me can almost automatically be assumed to be late information. Who's going to call us first? Because of that, even "true" information may already have been acted on by insiders so that the market usefulness of that information is nil, despite the validity. Ah, but suppose the accountant who lives next door whispers in your ear that a deal is in the making. You—mere you—know what the big boys know, but you still have to know value, likely market response, and what to buy and when, presuming your neighbor has actually seen the signed papers. Risk the house on a once-in-a-lifetime leak? how much (more) do you need to know to go that far? Too often, even "true" information turns out to be inaccurate in market terms: there is the example of a succession of leaks, from $300 per share all the way down as the UAL buyout "deal" kept collapsing; you could have been promised any number of times that the price was truly the price that was being talked about, but never have been sure that the deal would go through. And MCA flipped and flopped all over the price map as many got excited about presumed 1987 values, so that although you could have been guaranteed that a deal would get signed—as it did—the price you dreamed of would have been a mirage, the call options you bought expiring near worthless. You know, and yet you wind up taking a risk anyhow.

◈◈◈ These are all the dangers of risk: the leap-even-though-you-looked dangers of everyday life. Is there a difference between market information and life information? Our only use of market information is to achieve a measurable gain, or to protect against loss, so that the risk is monetary (and thus we must, in subsequent chapters, get into ways to reduce that monetary risk). But money risk permeates both itself *and* daily life. Life information needs to be observable, factual, dependable, enduring . . . but it usually isn't, of course; it consists of the same kind of blurred or contradictory "facts" as the stock market, is colored by prejudices in the reading of the information itself, can't be counted on, keeps changing. Even medical tests that supposedly offer factual results invariably have statistical qualifications. Doctors can't tell you for sure. Ditto for brokers, juries, the Supreme Court, and mothers-in-law. *The risk can never be cured by knowing enough.*

We need, we crave, trust and belief from others, and their acceptance, even though they may really "not know us." But when information is insufficient we need the trust and belief in ourselves, and the inner acceptance that we'll be okay anyhow. We need the discipline to accept whatever is available. We need the experience to understand all the ifs, ands, and buts, and yet still confront the risk, and make the decision. Setting ourselves free from the quest for information, oddly enough, *is what reduces risk even as it appears from the freedom itself that risk is being scarily increased.*

Oh my, freedom; *that's* dangerous.

· 6 ·

The Emotions of Risk

THERE is an emotional content to risk, and to our reaction to risk, that includes all the obvious clichés of guilt, anxiety, stress, and so on, calling for a psychiatrist's sort of analysis to understand. We are not here writing about them as neuroses but as standard behavior (with personal variations) at the moment of (and the moment before) the risk. *Under pressure, emotions determine our action.*

Let's start with the overconfidence of youth. "I can drink and drive." "I know what I'm doing, Dad." "I can pass this test without studying." Such absolutism versus risk can even lead to beginner's luck, and hence even more overconfidence—before the proverbial fall. At the peak of the market in the summer of 1987, a pretty young woman got into the elevator with three almost equally handsome young men who looked and acted as if they each had Harvard MBAs. "I don't know what's so hard about the stock market," she bubbled, "I haven't had a losing trade yet." While I cringed, they laughed with her; it was their moment, and probably their top eighth. So we can begin with the blitheness of ignorance, the emotion of insouciance.

But those who survive—by the end of 1990, they had probably lost their jobs—are rewarded with the benefit of experience. In a version of the old joke about the adolescent who thinks his father is an old fogie, and then years later is surprised at how much the old man has learned, growing up introduces fear.

Although a gradual awareness of mortality introduces some physical fear, it is a far more internal danger: there is now a chance of losing. The stock market, like life, is not a perfect game; no one goes undefeated for longer than a season. Fear causes an increasing loss of confidence: you are going to lose.

◇◆◇◆◇ Obviously, if *risk* is defined as "peril," "danger of losing," then the first emotion that comes to mind is fear. *Fear is long-term, an underlying pervasive emotion, like the underlying primary trend of a bear market. It doesn't go away until it changes.*

Fear takes over consideration of what to do and how to do it. Even when, as it turns out in hindsight, everything has become all right, as in the case of a new bull market, fear dominates. Remember the Wall Street expression that "a bull market climbs a wall of worry." No one believes because there isn't enough information to help assuage the fear. They keep offering their shares for sale, convinced that the rise is just a selling opportunity. Recall the denials of the big rally that followed the outbreak of war in mid-January 1991. All those who had claimed to be waiting to buy "down 200 points" immediately attacked the rise: "Six reasons not to buy," wrote one market columnist, while the *New York Times* published successive articles about all the unsolved economic problems that would remain. One TV interviewer asked me what stocks I would short.

This is a form of the tried-and-true theory that "stocks move in the direction of the specialist's book." Even though the marketplace has changed so much over the years that specialist books on the floor of the exchange are virtually devoid of orders, the principle works anytime it can be applied. In order to buy, there has to be something available to buy, especially for big buyers—mutual funds, pension plans, and the like. Thus a requirement for a rising market is sufficient stock offered for sale (by the fearful) at limited prices overhead, so that the market actually "climbs" another eighth or quarter each time buyers take those overhead offerings. But if there are few offerings, of necessity they have to sit back on the bid side instead, waiting for someone to sell to them. Then their limited price orders are entered below the market, so that when someone wants to sell, prices fall in their direction.

During an underlying bear trend, fear in sheep's clothing is called hope. Oversold rebounds produce periods of confidence. It's like the relief of couples who have scary spats followed by passionate reconciliations; "We're okay, after all," they think. Such hope masks what they're beginning to fear; the quarrels return; something *is* wrong. Finally, there is enough information available—lowered expectations, write-offs—to overcome the hope; things are getting worse, and going to be even worse tomorrow. Divorce is called for. That leads to "selling," bitterly, when they could have gotten out on the upside had they faced the bearish realities instead of hoping.

In the stock market, fear returns, *usually when it matters most*, when one can't afford to be paralyzed. "Oh my God," fear speaks, "something terrible could, might, will, just my luck, happen to me. I'll be embarrassed, I'll be wrong, I'll be hurt, I'll lose. I'd better not." All the ramifications of what might lie ahead if one steps off that curb into the world fill the mind (and the lesser consciousnesses) like commercial jingles that keep repeating, can't be shaken away, interfering with any other thoughts and reactions trying to surface. *Fear is the emotional extension of the negative definitions of risk.*

Fear breeds another emotion: anxiety. *Anxiety is the operative portion of fear.* It is anxiety that actually paralyzes. "Choking" is the sports world's expression. With fear as the underlying trend, anxiety locks your elbow as you are about to serve at match point; anxiety causes you to step back onto the curb, even though the light confronting the truck is red; anxiety causes you to put in a limited price order under the market when you really want to own the stock. While hope keeps you from selling into a bear market rally, anxiety makes it appear that selling is called for, even at the bottom of a bear market, when one should be thinking instead of buying.

Anxiety gets in the way of taking a risk. You become convinced that if you step out boldly into the street, the truck is going to clobber you—even though you can see that it is coming up to a red light, you can hear the squeal of the air brakes being applied, and see the perceptible slowing. Fear sets you up; anxiety paralyzes you at curbside, where you are vulnerable to even a tricycle coming along to knock you to your knees.

◈◈◈◈ Because of that dictionary definition of *risk* as peril, fear and anxiety come instantly to mind. But at major market peaks, *greed* takes over: "Just this once, I can get away with it," thinks even the experienced investor who understands how late in the trend it is. Greed, as an avid desire for money, has a blinding "just gotta have it" sense to it, as if the investor, any investor, is having a form of midlife crisis of wanting, needing, being entitled to. Just as a midlife crisis makes it seem that the risk is masked, greed blindly proceeds as if there is no risk at that moment, overpowering choice because of our need. We color what we believe is objective.

Envy is the operative portion of greed. Whereas anxiety paralyzes, envy causes one to act—"I want some of that, too"—the "that" being the success others are having in the market. There is now plenty of information available to prove that everything's all right. The financial pages describe how easy it is to be successful—rising prices in the stock market day after day join with benign corporate earnings reports, positive gross national product (GNP) numbers, maybe even peace. And what negatives may lurk—often, by this time, the Fed has started to tighten—are of little or no concern when there's "pie in the sky" to be divvied up.

As this envy gets out of hand, it leads to *doing the wrong thing.* Envy turns the anxiety of love into acts spoiling the love. Envy in the marketplace—the torture of knowing that friends and neighbors (or so they say in the locker room) are making oodles of money—brings out the buy orders at the wrong (invariably late) time because it has taken a prolonged and increasingly obvious rise before this emotion can surface in full flower. The desire to possess in an absolute way is, in the stock market, called greed.

Trying to grab a piece of that pie is the other extreme from denial of loss. It is the risk of "denial of risk." And from such greed is born stubbornness. Of course those stocks bought at the top are still going to produce profits—this little downturn is just a correction. As the risk of a bear market increases, the person who has been seduced into buying near the top develops the fervor of the newly converted. He extolls the virtues of "up," boasts to those friends and neighbors he'd been so jealous of that his turn is coming: this dip is his opportunity to get in at better prices. This late phase of the seduction leads, in turn, to a passionate hope: the market will love him . . . tomorrow. In this litany of emotions, hope may be the most risky. Hope is like the ostrich's eyes, seeing until one needs to see.

Sooner or later, what market reality does to hope gives rise to the conviction that you aren't entitled to win. *Fear and anxiety come together with greed and envy to give birth to guilt.* Sometimes the guilt materializes as partner to success; it begins to gnaw even as prices are still rising: you don't deserve this extracurricular thrill. At other times and/or for others, guilt emerges in company with loss: you didn't deserve the profits, so you don't have them anymore. Guilt becomes a burden of one's past, turning the paralysis of the moment into longer-term inertia: whatever might be done to change life and love, or portfolios, is too weighted with risk to do, as if it would be enormously exhausting to have to swing your feet down off the desk where they are safely and comfortably propped. For what? for the future, that's all. The resulting inertia leads to denial: it's too soon to act, more information is needed . . . until it is too late to sell, and one can wait for a new set of circumstances; it isn't even worth bothering to look that stock up in the newspaper. Denial provides the ultimate shelter against risk.

❖❖❖❖ Others believe they are stepping forward into the world with positive goals, but have an imprecise awareness or inadequate perception of how to proceed, based on opinions a mile long and an inch deep. They flounder instead of feel, taking too seriously a broker's casual advice du jour or turning toward low-priced stocks to make that bundle more quickly, asking politely about Telephone but buying Tosco. Their risk-takings begin to sound grandiose instead of practical as they falter and then rise up to try again. They believe that the "right" decision the next time is all that is needed to proceed into success, and therefore fail, sometimes because they are culturally not ready, haven't learned enough, aren't wise enough in the ways of the world, or—and although undoubtedly valid, this has become a psychoanalytical cliché—their perceptions and preparations are subconsciously but powerfully designed to fail. Haven't we all known men or women who yearn to be married, but somehow uncannily pick the wrong person to date—the confirmed bachelor, the married man. Others talk a good game, but have anxieties that become heightened at the very moment they might win. Whether in life or the market, the fear of losing can be overpowering, but so can the fear of success. And yet, as they'll insist afterward, they *tried.*

Still others "win," but like gamblers can't stop. Such players begin to feel as if they are flying, soaring, can't do anything wrong—and lose all perspective. This is a top-of-a-bull-market emotion, taking all sorts of wild, untoward, untenable risks, the low percentage shots of speculation, in the belief of invulnerability; like an adolescent behind the wheel, the exhilaration of power produces peril. Some undergo a natural progression through the course of an increasingly seductive bull market from investing to speculating to gambling; others leap in one bound from paralysis all the way acoss the chasm of risk to a wild bet on a gold mine in Tasmania being hawked by a broker in Denver.

Along comes hope again, an emotion that produces no real-world help. Since risk is viewed as a "peril," hope is the handy-dandy emotion. The paralyzed have no confidence, the adolescent player is all exaggerated confidence. Both extremes believe in hope: "It'll work," "It'll be okay." Hope is arid, supplying a false and temporary and superficial confidence. With its seeming support, we often view risk as something "nice" we'd like to do, admiring it in others while afraid to take it ourselves. Our imaginary mind sees not the knowable danger of that truck bearing down on us, but an Eden across the street, and our agility as nimble as Nijinsky's in dancing safely across.

What happens when we get to Eden? Nothing. Life is life— that is, every risk is a matter of life's course. That's why marital counselors keep saying "Ask for what you need." Ah, such advice to a couple sitting a full couch's length apart from each other. You'd think they could heed the advice—that's what they're there for—but the mere asking is a risk too big to take. There is an emotion that for want of a better word we can only dub "self-imprisoning"—best illustrated by the person who can't ask for what he needs, can't let anyone give him anything, crosses his arms firmly on his chest. *Risk is something such people aren't "free" enough to take.*

It would be folly to argue that any of this means risk is pure, is a positive. Of course, there is risk; it doesn't get erased, or whitewashed. The difference is between seeing risk out there as a hazard, and seeing it *as a choice*. It is no more positive than it is negative. It isn't anything emotional at all. The dictionary is wrong: *risk is a choice.*

❖·❖·❖·❖ Because it is a choice, *and* we're afraid to make that choice, people—you, me, investors—transfer the risk. Here's a selection of choices: (1) do nothing; (2) leap to doing something hitherto not considered; (3) decide to act, but only after additional information becomes available; (4) act, but do so in such a way (using a limited price order, for example) that you don't get action or in such a way (shorting against the box) as to override; (5) ask someone else for advice, so it'll become their fault if it proves to be too risky; (6) act, but then deny the results if wrong; (7) decide that you'll take not this one but the next risk; (8) take the risk, but then botch it as success nears.

Notice how our own behavior, in life as well as in the stock market, interferes with our risk-taking. We need, we crave, the trust and belief from others, but when information is insufficient we need trust and belief in ourselves. We need the discipline to accept whatever is available, and the experience to understand all the ifs, ands, and buts, and yet still take the risk: we need to be able to make the decision. Freud advised tossing a coin so as to realize, while the coin is in the air, which choice you really want to make by sensing whether you are rooting for heads or tails to win.

⬧·⬧·⬧·⬧ Well, tossing a coin might help pull that decision out of you, because risk is the confrontation between choices. But, of all people, Freud is wrong; there's too great an emotional content to how we make those choices about which side to root for. Who's sure we're going to root for the lesser risk, or the more achievable reward?

Although often used interchangeably, there is a distinct difference between intuitive and instinctive reactions. They are actually opposites. Intuition is useful: "Immediate apprehension . . . the power of knowing or the knowledge obtained without recourse to inference or reasoning . . . *insight.*" But *instinctive* is defined as "innate *impulse* or spontaneous *attitude.*" (My emphasis.) The former is knowing without reasoning (perhaps even could be defined as "knowing without knowing"); the latter is merely emotional.

There is, in fact, little spontaneous about intuition. It is, as the dictionary tells us, "immediate," but that's clocking the reaction, not where the reaction comes from. Although it is "nonarticulatable"—no time, no language—it derives over time from experience distilled into concentration. It is illustrated by the actor who is "an overnight success," after having worked at his craft for the previous 20 years. *Intuition is an intense discipline*, not really as emotional as it seems. One takes the risk without being distracted.

Fear, though, is an example of an instinctive emotional distraction. It isn't so much outside stimuli as the way those thoughts or anxieties wander around like pinball machine balls inside our head. The precisionist, the person who demands more and more information before acting, ultimately acts on an emotional *instinctive* basis. The information that has been gathered has become tainted with the passage of time, while its details represent the external stimuli that clutter the mind. The purity, and not just the price advantage, is gone. The ultimate information wanted is the guarantee—the light is on our side, so it's safe to cross. But the instinctive emotion lurks to warn us not to believe it yet.

Intuition, although seemingly spontaneous, apparently emotional, stems from a form of "information" that has become built-in from past experience. Discipline means choosing what to do unencumbered by the fear of making a mistake. Confidence means trusting our intuition that *what we "see" is what we "know."* There's no escaping to the external, to the objective, and no standing on the shaky ground of emotions. So the question becomes, *How do we create within ourselves the heroic condition of confidence wherein risk is not danger but life?*

· 7 ·

The Risk of Money

SHOULD we argue about money? Should we call it coarse? Is "filthy lucre" more than a saying? Should a Wall Streeter earn more in a day than the teacher of his children earns in a year? While the French, straightforward about sex, find money indecent, have Americans transferred sexual passion into financial passion? Have we like Victorians moralized the stock market? Why have Chinese peasants brought up on communism left home, land, and sustenance to pursue more money in the slums of a city? Does money make sense as a force so powerful we risk—or fear to risk—our future? Being comfortable enough, why do we need more? is it younger, prettier? does it feel like a new wife in one's metaphorical wallet? Does money represent? or is money itself the risk?

◆◆◆◆ In the stock market, the moment of actually entering the order is different from any other moment. There is validity to the judgment that "he who hesitates is lost." Every New York City cab driver can recognize the person who, after watching, waiting, hesitating, finally steps out off the curb to cross the street—just as the light is changing. Every tennis player can recognize the hesitation (passing for concentration but actually anxiety) that accompanies standing at the baseline having just missed your first serve. Will you get the ball in? One reason that a seasoned professional double-faults at match point is that, having successfully served several dozen second serves, *this* is the one that leaps into consciousness. *There is the penetrating concern that you are on the verge of doing something "wrong" that will cause you to lose . . .* and when you act, there'll be no calling it back to do again; you'll have committed yourself.

So there you are, standing up at your desk, perhaps pacing as far as the phone in your hand will let you stray. Should you act? You thought the decision had already been made: you like the stock you're about to buy; you've been watching it; it makes sense to you; you've considered the (apparently reasonable) downside risk; it's already starting to go up so you damn well better not procrastinate; and so on. And yet, there's the moment of hesitation: it's your money. The money has been abstract. We suddenly realize it is real. The reality of it becomes blown up out of proportion to the actual amount.

Much the same happens in the moment before you want to enter a sell order: is it only a temporary fainting spell or is the stock in jeopardy? should you take the loss? or will it go back up, perhaps soar, the moment you've sold? Wall Streeters have a perpetual joke that they should sell half of their position, thus tricking the market into thinking they're out, so the stock will finally go up. If it is a holding that has already gone up, should you cash in now? suppose it keeps going up after you sell? That's your profit, your gain, your victory; you'd be selling out your own soul.

What happens is the bubbling up of an enormous concern about money. Money—because it is our own—takes on an out-of-proportion domination: like sex, it distorts our senses. The value of the money—knowing exactly how much the amount is—becomes secondary to the fact that it is ours.

The thought process *leading up to* that moment of, so to speak, stepping off the market's curb, is *abstracted* from the money: is it a good stock? No matter what process you use to consider the buying or selling of that stock, the consideration itself does not involve the personalizing of "your money." It makes sense to buy; it "feels" right; your broker has a forceful personality; and so on. You might be examining the stock itself, on its chart; the company itself via its annual report or a broker's report. You might say to yourself, "I like it; I'd like to buy it lower, but someone else's order would be ahead of me because right now the quote is 33 bid for 1500 shares and I might never buy any if I also bid 33. Oops! someone just bought some at 33¼. There are still 1000 shares offered at 33¼, so if I take the entire offer, it might start the stock on its way. But if someone else takes it ahead of me I'll have to chase the stock up and if that's what happens I'll be not only sorry but furious at myself for hesitating. . . . "

Yet there you are with the phone dangling in your hand. Why the lingering hesitation? Because the decision has abruptly shifted from being abstract—involving study, thought, style—to one in which the abstraction is overwhelmed by the realization that actual money is at stake. *For the first time the money involved becomes real.*

All sorts of protections such as using a stop order so you'll limit your loss if wrong, all sorts of realizations that you are "good" at this game, that you feel excitedly sure you're "right" in buying this stock at this time, are overwhelmed by the intrusion of the thought of real money. For some the hesitation might be paralyzing, and they'll back away as the stock moves up and up without them until they can't stand it anymore and then plunge in promiscuously. For others, the hesitation might last only a second or two. It surfaces in all but the truly professional trader who has survived in the stock market successfully because it is easier for him—upbringing, childhood, considerable experience and discipline—to relax into the abstraction, maintaining it *throughout* the entire transaction without ever considering that it is the rent money he is playing with. Perhaps most important of all, even when that rare breed of professional botches a transaction—from hesitating, from carelessness, from simply being wrong—the ability to keep his judgment distant from (although *not* deny) the notion that it is real money being lost enables him to cut the mathematical loss to a minimum. You may know you haven't double-faulted in three sets, that you always—*almost* always—get your second serve in, so why suddenly does the anxiety well up toward paralysis at match point? In the stock market, entering an order always feels like match point *because the potentially losing act immediately becomes irretrievable.*

◈◈◈◈ There is something—is it inherent?—about money that creates tension. Every broker will tell you that clients get *more* upset when they sell a stock that keeps going up—no matter how much profit they themselves have already taken out of the trade—than if they buy a stock and it immediately thereafter goes down like a textbook example of a lead balloon. And yet, in a sense, that additional gain they've forgone isn't even *their* money. Why aren't they more upset to find themselves in a position that is losing them their own original stake?

The answer seems to be that such a losing position swiftly becomes abstracted out of the realm of real money into a clichéd notion about the stock market: "Well, that's the way the market is, no one can ever tell"; "It'll come back if I hold it long enough"; "The loss is just on paper." "It's just a paper loss" is the way the typical investor transposes the diminishing of his capital into an ostrichlike "Why worry?"

Thus once the action, the deed of entering the order, is past, the anxiety about money shifts back into abstraction: what you now own is a bunch of letters at a varying number, paid for by a check rather than the cash in your pocket. It represents an abstract piece of American business, not a stock, paid for by a bookkeeping entry in your account at the broker's so that it doesn't even feel as if you've paid out anything real at all, the way digging into your pocket for a quarter would feel. This gives rise, eventually, to the absurd abstraction of a paper loss rather than something that has happened to your own money, to the point where, if the loss gets big enough, you don't even read the newspaper stock tables anymore, so that there is "no loss" whatsoever. Even the seller who sits around stewing that the broker let him sell—advised him to sell—a stock that kept going up is furious not because of literal money but because of a wave of envy: someone else has something that he wanted, desired, that was supposed to be and ought to have been, as if by all rights, his.

So the thought process leading up to the decision is abstracted; the thought process after the order is filled is abstracted. We are almost back to the near paralysis of risk-taking that sets in the moment before the order is actually entered. I say "almost" because for the most part the hesitation is overcome, the act finally taken; the investor doesn't stand rigid and never serve that match point second serve.

And yet the paralysis is frequent. Everyone, including the pro, has an embarrassing litany of anecdotes about the ones that got away, the stocks they almost bought but didn't. Maybe they had stepped out to the bathroom; maybe their lover had called to say goodbye forever; maybe they simply didn't want to take on a position just before going on vacation. (Everyone also seems to have an anecdote about the stock sold *because* they were going away on vacation, only to see it turn into a huge profit in their absence. A friend of ours had sold short nearly a million shares of Oracle; it had already gone down from 24 to 15, so he decided to close out the position before going on vacation—ORCL thereupon proceeded to head down to 5 in his absence.) The rhythm of maybe they meant to, but couldn't quite bring themselves to, gives rise to the classic "woulda, coulda, shoulda" war cry. The decision becomes enmeshed in the hesitation: let's wait and watch it for a few more minutes, or a few more days; oh, the hell with it. Sometimes, this peculiarity leads to what might be called switch and bait: after hesitating to the point of paralysis about a trade that has been thoroughly mulled over and makes sense, especially in hindsight, so much so that when it appears the opportunity has been lost because that stock is "up" already, the investor will abruptly switch to a different, less soundly considered and typically much more speculative stock, making an emotional, even hysterical, decision to "do" that one instead.

This may seem as if I am advocating carefully reasoned, solidly based stock market decisions, when, rather, I believe in the intuitive risk-taking. That's because it isn't like that in the market any more than it is in real life. What becomes "reasoned" gets entangled in the need for more information, always more information, because the additional information ought to open the window into the future that will assure that the risk will surely succeed. Indeed, whether one "knows" enough or not, the hesitation at the moment of acting is the short-term concern that only intuition can overcome *positively*. If an honest record could be kept of each such behavioral moment, we'd find that many of the orders that weren't entered would have been much better than the ones actually, and stressfully, done thereafter. In one way or another—price, choice—the moment of hesitation is likely to prove costly.

That introduces the psychiatrist's subject of whether or not there is a subconscious desire to lose. This is hard to picture in sensible terms, just as is trying to grasp why a battered wife sticks around, although for all the jargon—is it guilt at having? is it self-hatred?—there is undoubted validity to such lurking roots. People *do* botch, by behaving differently from how they know they should, or usually have done in the past. More readily believable as a pattern of human behavior is the underlying yearning to do something more risky—the leap to the gamble, the need for some kind of affair (with a sports team, dice, neighbor's spouse). Instead of the smooth transition of the thoughtful (even if intuitive) decision carried out promptly, the hesitation stumbles over all sorts of neuroses.

Is there perhaps something that creates a paralysis when the risk is worth taking, that creates, in turn, the emotional fling when the risk is incomprehensible? a "something" that exposes an underlying desire to be seduced. Are we not like that?

At the racetrack, isn't there a *longing* against the odds to bet on an appealing long shot that "just might do it"? Many older men are teased by the inner knowledge of being a patsy for any youthful body. Indeed, this can be carried to an extreme of the aging married man who feels that boy bodies are safer for his marriage and place in society, but, of course, are actually more speculative than a heterosexual affair. In the market world, such emotional inserts are what happens at a major top when all sorts of experienced portfolio managers and investors, who really do know better, and who already have been expressing theoretical anxieties about a potential top ahead, nevertheless keep buying because at the spur of *each* moment the market looks as exciting as seeing the pot of gold at the end of the rainbow. They buy junk—the classic speculative fling that is one of the ingredients of a top—and might even mutter, "I don't know why I'm buying these cats and dogs," but they do. Back in August 1987, one of the more experienced technical analysts acknowledged that his buy list consisted of names he'd never heard of before and that whenever that had happened in the past it was a sure sign of a top—but he felt compelled to publish the list regardless. The much *less risky* decision—"Let's start selling because this market doesn't feel right anymore"—isn't acted on because of that paralysis cum siren song of the crowd. They don't "know" enough to do something fresh like selling, so they'll try one more OTC name and will sell "later" when the bell goes off—in the crash case, down a terrifying 1000 points later.

◇•◇•◇•◇ It is evident that at the moment of decision there is a distinct tendency to bypass the entering of an order that will prove to be a positive act *in favor of an emotional order*—or no order at all (which in its own way is even more emotional)—thereby assuming exactly that which was feared: a much greater actual risk. The nature of money as real life *infests* the moment of that decision.

· 8 ·

Money: The Opium
of the Investor

THE other night my young son sat down with a box of crayons, not to draw but to practice his counting. He set 6 crayons down in a row, left a space, and then set down another 7. Next, adding them one at a time, he double-checked to make sure there were 6 in one row and 7 in the other. The final step was to count them, starting at 1 and getting to 13. He was then proudly able to announce that 6 + 7 = 13.

Of course, this was his beginning venture into addition; the adult style would differ in that, having counted and then double-checked that there were 6 in the first pile, a grown-up would start counting at 6, 7, rather than going back to the beginning. The reason seems clear: my son didn't trust the 6 yet. We know that such numbers are immutable, but a child still isn't sure that 6 will always be 6, especially when he needs it to be 6. The lesson is clear: *information requires trust.*

No wonder it's so difficult to take a risk. No wonder it turns out, in the stock market, that we are risking more than money. Whether we do vast and detailed research, believe a chief financial officer, or take a broker's advice, our sense of trust is at stake.

Isn't this sense of trust at work in the way we ourselves are so terrified of the baby's risk-taking that we leap across the room, calling, "Be careful," "Don't," "Wait for daddy?" Is it not also

at work, in perverse fashion, at the racetrack where we bet frivolously because we don't believe there's any way to tell which
horse is going to win? Doesn't it manifest itself in the bitter
belief that only insiders, in the stock market or in the paddock,
know who's going to win? Do we play the match point, with its
sense of finality, by hitting the ball "all out" in the manner in
which we practice, or do we become increasingly cautious as the
ball bounces across the net toward us? It isn't just anxiety about
the potential loss involved—it is the surfacing of that lack of
trust about our own strokes, and the increasing conviction that
we might be about to make a mistake, that causes the change in
style from what had successfully brought us to one point away
from victory to a nervous wreck. Our lack of trust in ourselves
stands exposed.

Similarly, when we go to cross the street, and look both ways,
and see that the path is clear to cross—light properly red, no
cars moving—isn't there sometimes a lingering semisubcon-
scious doubt or perceptible squeamishness that we may have
missed something? Perhaps we've made a mistake, perhaps our
eyes are momentarily flawed, or our senses slightly blurred.
Crossing the street becomes increasingly risky the more choices
we have and the more action there is around us; the cars may be
moving toward us, but we see they are far away, and yet we
may not quite trust that judgment of ours. The light may be
about to change, and although we "know" we have time to get
across, we don't quite trust that judgment either. We run across
because of an insecurity we don't even realize we have. Or,
amazingly, we saunter across in speculative confrontation with
the now onrushing traffic just to prove to ourselves that we're
in control of the flow of information . . . and in defiance of our
doubts about ourselves as well.

The old man's darting with his cane out into the street just as
the light is about to change is his angry attempt to confront the
world with his skills. He curses the cars coming at him, waves
the cane like a sword to prove he is still a gladiator. With the
same defiance coupled with lack of trust, the risks of being in

the stock market are often transferred away from ourselves to the external. There's the constant loser's cliché, a verbal throwing up of one's hands, of "How can you ever tell about the stock market?" When one loses, the market seems to have defied logic, sense, analyzability. The information can't be trusted. Gambling on tertiary stocks, like betting on a lucky number or hunch name or the jockey's silks, takes over in a speculative "What the hell?" defiance of a part of ourselves that should have known better. The broker's argument about options that one's risk is predetermined to what one pays in—a 100 percent loss limit—becomes the acceptable way to defy potential/expected stock market loss, just the way my son, in looking at the crayons spread out in a row, doesn't trust his experience, his intuition, his ability. To us it seems readily obvious how many crayons there are; we can "see" the number. But a child has to actually touch them one by one, just to be sure. There is too great a risk of being wrong.

And yet, what is that risk to him? There is no punishment to his being wrong; he is not going to have his hand slapped; his parents aren't going to laugh at him, yet he sometimes will pause to the point of paralysis even when we know he knows the answer. A fear seems to surface in his hesitation that this is more than just a game; his future is at stake, not that he needs to know that $6 + 7 = 13$ but that he knows how to know. Every counting at this age is as if match point to him, until he is sure enough of that stroke to move on, until he has developed enough confidence—about what? that he won't get hurt if he is wrong, that he'll be right if he has to do it again, or that if he does it again, it is resolvable even though he was wrong the first time, or that if he does it again he'll be able to "win" even though he was wrong the first time, or even, that it is fun to play, right or wrong? Is it the eventual triumph, or the absence of fear, is it trusting his parents or himself or the crayons, that helps him play the counting game? A child's trust in his own intuition is the path to reducing his "risk." Confidence does not arrive full-blown; it grows with experience.

But *not* when it comes to money itself: play money lacks the intensity of the risk of losing (or making) actual money. Monopoly money provides no emotional experience in handling the pressure. In an adult game—the stock market—one of the problems in taking a market risk is that we feel as if we can't be trusted in the market, or can't trust the market—either or both—because we'll lose something very real. This anxiety grows in intensity as it passes from a paper loss to one that is all too real. Some people, therefore, exercise total avoidance; others advance with trepidation, turning the process over to a mutual fund manager, or to their broker, having been told, by "experts," that they don't know enough to trust themselves, and thus should abandon the game to the pros. Others sell too soon, and then, thinking they have learned a lesson, hold on too long the next time, and so swing wildly from one extreme to the other. Some do only the blue chip, or the conventional, or consensus thing; still others leap well beyond the available information—light changing, truck coming—and in defiance take the speculative risk instead. And all too many swing wildly from one extreme to another, as they "learn" a lesson from what they have just done: sold too soon, so the next time they hold on too long.

Is that risk in the stock market because we are staking something as evidently important to us, both practically *and* emotionally, as money? Is it a modern form of alchemy we believe in—that money can be turned into more money? What is it about stock market reality that gives rise to the cliché that "it's only a paper loss," so it doesn't count (although profits on paper always count when boasting about or borrowing against). Is money such a big deal because it measures our own worth or because whatever form it takes can be bartered for whatever it is we need to live on? How true is the snide remark that "we are what we buy" (or, what our purchasing power is)? Don't some people pursue money for its own sake, others in the conviction that money is power? still others in the belief that one can never have too much money? If we have enough to live comfortably, why do we pursue more? Are we risking something more than money? If money is ephemeral, why does it matter so much? Hasn't money become increasingly invisible over the centuries, over the years? until, today, money's "shape" is binary impulses. What *is* money worth? and what *is* its value?

Visible money—paper money itself—is current money; currently, U.S. currency is more often used to pay for taxis in Bangkok than purchases in Bloomingdale's. When I was a child, a nickel bought the best ice cream cone in memory. We kept coins in little purses, and then in our trouser pockets. As young marrieds we dumped our pennies in jars, and then, as children came, all our coins. In turn we stuffed dollar bills in our pockets the way we had once treated those coins. After a few years, we began to find wadded-up $5 and $10 bills mixed in. The worth—our feeling about them—had changed, even though the value—their intrinsic desirability—remained.

Now some of us, at least some of the time, don't even carry cash. We rely on our credit cards as money, so it isn't really invisible—no cash—but merely different (plastic instead of paper). But if our transactionable assets are away from us—instead of in jars on the bureau or as paper in our wallets—then our money's value is found in monthly statements and is otherwise invisible . . . well, not quite invisible because we know it is somewhere in the pile of papers on the desk. Such "money" is increasingly ephemeral as it comes and goes untouched, unseen—it loses its context as meaningful, important, solid; as it becomes increasingly abstracted, it becomes easier and easier to unthinkingly use up. So we've had a steady progression from a nickel clutched in a child's fist to a multitude of possible ways to exchange bookkeeping entries for products.

That's one way to look at money—it is whatever we use; at Club Med it is once again beads. Another way to look at money, however, is as our own value: compensation for what we do. Try to explain *that* value of money to a youngster. ("Don't break that toy; it costs money.") Money—the real coins and bills the child sees—is as abstract as anything within a child's realm. This kind of money is mysterious, mystical. A piece of paper with a number on it becomes something essential for our survival. Worth—its emotional content—takes over from its literal value, almost precisely in proportion to our need for its value.

◇◆◇◆◇ Consider exchanging dollar bills for the work of an artist. What you would be doing, literally, in making such a purchase is exchanging the actual currency of the realm, the value of which remains relatively static—a buck is a buck, despite inflation—for something else that is believed to have some kind of worth, but a value that fluctuates depending (entirely?) on the desires of the marketplace. For one thing, you are taking an enormous risk: the known for the unknown. For another, the risk includes the near total inability to be sure the price is right, or reasonable, or, indeed, that anyone at any time subsequently will want to take the artist's work off your hands regardless of price.

Now consider that the trepidation you are experiencing as you are about to make that purchase cannot be ameliorated by the traditional psychic-reward salesman's remark: "I like it, so even if it isn't worth the money I can get pleasure seeing it on my living-room wall." The work of art you are purchasing is an engraving conceived and executed in an artist's garret, but, rather than being of meadows or nudes, is of a dollar bill. What you are doing, in effect, is exchanging one engraving for another in the hope that the engraving you now hold will eventually be worth more than the engraving of currency from your wallet that you gave in exchange.

Similarly, replace that artist's engraving with the engraving, also formally done by an artist, of a stock certificate. Again, as far as the piece of paper is concerned, the literal exchange is of one engraving, green, for another, white and admittedly fancier. And when you sell that stock, the white engraved certificate is then exchanged for a green engraving. In the old days before everything became binary impulses, and you preferred having that handsomely engraved stock certificate in your safe-deposit box, that is how a transaction in the stock market literally could be described.

◆•◆•◆•◆ For these remarks (and historical research), I am indebted to a remarkably perceptive and entertaining essay, first read in *The New Yorker*, and subsequently published in *Shapinsky's Karma, Bogg's Bills, and Other True-Life Tales*, by Lawrence Weschler (North Point Press, San Francisco, 1988). Part of the charm of the story is how Boggs, starving and struggling in the standard artist's tradition, hit upon the notion of drawing a picture of actual currency and trying, then, to exchange his portrait of the dollar, or $5, or $100, bill for a meal, or a six-pack, or a pen to use to create the next drawing. The transaction itself, which involved trying to convince the other party to accept the created bill in lieu of the government's literal amount, became part of the work of art. A few who were offered the trade were willing; most couldn't bring themselves to take the risk, didn't recognize the opportunity, or were afraid to seize it. Nor did it seem to matter that the work of art might increase in value manyfold. Exchanging a fixed amount for something of fluctuating value was often not a familiar concept in itself.

Those on the buy side of the transaction did not understand the risk/reward possibility of the situation and/or were unable to take the chance. Some were fearful of their boss or the manager; others were concerned about being embarrassed, as if they were being offered the Brooklyn Bridge. One waitress so badly needed the real cash that she felt compelled to say no. Having worked hard for her money, scrimped and saved, she preferred the $5 she knew to the work of art she wasn't sure of. A lottery ticket, with its dreamlike chance of winning, seemed more real, less chancy, because it had a literal definition, than a work of art with a vague and floating sense of value. (Similarly, an out-of-the-money call option, with its betting characteristic, can be appealing, even though one can lose every cent, while shares in a NYSE listed company seems like too dreadful an abstracted risk for some to take. The widespread acceptance of options as having less risk can be seen in the multiple repeated commercials for options on Financial News Network (FNN), much of whose audience consists of retired men.)

Of course, as the interest of collectors grew, Boggs's original works of art became worth many times what the original transaction had cost. But those who had forgone the risk never knew what kind of profit they had rejected. *The ability to take a risk, without having enough information, and perhaps even while doubting one's instincts* (the visual quality of the work in front of them), was put to a severe test by Boggs. The person who was willing to accept artist-drawn currency instead of government printed engravings tended to make up his or her mind decisively, compared to the mulling over and hesitation—should I? am I being tricked? can I get away with it?—of those who were unable to act. Those who agreed revealed a sense (or experience) that there was some kind of recognizable value involved, not just a chance-taking. *What they seemed to be trusting was themselves,* an "I'm okay" sense of life itself.

◇◆◇◆◇ Once one has framed the question "What is art worth?" one has accepted that the transaction is a question of value rather than of risk. We are not here talking about an out-of-the-money option or a lottery ticket. In such instances the risk and the bet are interchangeable. But here the risk becomes judging the potential value of what you are exchanging something known for, "feeling" that there is some, albeit uncertain, degree of value involved. What one brings to that judgment—in terms of experience in making such judgments, intuition, hunch, artistic awareness, and so on—is all you get to "know" before you have to decide. *Trust has to supplant anxiety.* One decides whether one's estimate of potential future value—more or less than the $5 or $100 bill at stake—is correct, rather than whether one is going to win a bet. *This changes the nature of the risk to one of judgment rather than threat.*

In Boggs's case, affecting the exchange risk was the reluctance, the inability, to do something different—that is, personal experience. Routine, standard expectations, the nature of the clerk's or bartender's job, all got in the mind's way. Part, too, was that Boggs introduced a notion of exchange—barter—that was "different" from the customary method of that particular place of business and was, therefore, scary. Who could do what they had not done before? better to say no.

The question raised—Would you accept Boggs's bill?—has ramifications beyond why not? "What is art? What is money? What is the one worth and what the other? What is 'worth' worth? How does value itself arise, and live, and gutter out?" Those issues raised by Weschler can be transferred, for our purposes, to the stock market: "Would you make the trade?" becomes an issue of which engraving is preferable at that moment, the green or the white? How does one determine the worth of one or the other? especially in a fluctuating environment, and what substance—if any—does that notion of "worth" actually have? How does the value judgment get made, how does it grow, how does it shrink? Who—which gnomes of Wall Street?—take rising stocks that seemed to be okay back down again? and why?

In pursuit of some answers, Weschler quotes Georg Simmel, author in 1900 of *The Philosophy of Money*. In words that read as if the stock market was invented to give money a playing field, Simmel concluded: "There is no more striking symbol of the completely dynamic character of the world than money. The meaning of money lies in the fact that it will be given away. When money stands still, it is no longer money according to its specific value and significance. The effect that it occasionally exerts in a state of repose arises out of an anticipation of its further motion. Money is nothing but the vehicle for a movement in which everything else that is not in motion is completely extinguished."

Money as a white stock certificate stored in a strongbox becomes translated on the exchange floor to money in motion. Here, too, is the way the nature of the risk changes. One swaps passive behavior for dynamic action—life itself, if you will. It is not money pinned down like a butterfly, but a vehicle whose value and significance is on the go. But, to quote Simmel again, "as a tangible item, money is the most ephemeral thing in the external-practical world; yet its content is the most stable, since it stands at the point of indifference and balance between all other phenomena in the world. . . . " Stock certificate money is even more ephemeral; as "value" it seems to have stability even as it is constantly changing in relation to everything else in its world.

The mindless frenzy of exchange is slowed as the closing prices compel us to heed them. But that briefly forces the age-old monolithic stasis to "budge and shudder." It's a sort of magic. But then: "All art is magic, and so is all money."

◇◆◇◆◇ Weschler goes on to cite Fernand Braudel in *The Structures of Everyday Life*: "Money has never ceased to surprise humanity. It seems mysterious and disturbing . . . and complicated in itself." "It is a difficult cabbala to understand," with the cabbala, remember, replete with numbers signifying meanings in an attempt to make magic literal. Although it may seem that numbers are changeable only as they increase in size, there are magical meanings attached to the perceptions of size.

Norman O. Brown, in *Life against Death* (1955), wrote: "It is essential to the nature of money for the objects into which wealth or value is *condensed* to be practically useless. . . . This theorem is equally true for modern money (gold) and for archaic money (dogs' teeth)." (Increasingly worthless as a store of value, one might add 35 years later, are the computerized records, rather than transfers, of who owns what.) And: "with the transformation of the worthless into the priceless . . . man acquires a soul. . . . " An interesting theorem indeed, for the very objects to which "value" becomes the mysterious and fluctuating estimate are precisely those which are "practically useless"—consider not just art, not just gold, but also the ownership of stocks and bonds. The money itself was useless, as Boggs would testify, while *the transaction contained the value*. (That is, the end result of profit or loss is deadness, compared to the value of the risk itself.)

Brown goes on to note that money consists of the transubstantiation of the worthless into the priceless (of the "filthy" into "lucre"): "The sublimation of base matter into gold is the folly of alchemy and the folly of alchemy's pseudo-secular heir, modern capitalism. The profoundest things in 'Capital' are Marx's shadowy poetic presentments of *the alchemical mystery of money and of the 'mystical, fetishistic' character of commodities*. . . . Commodities are thrown into the alchemical retort of circulation to come out again in the shape of money. Circulation sweats money from every pore." That, too, is testimony to the dynamic movement of money. *The mystical aspect of "value" or "worth" is what keeps money and its engraved equivalents moving.* The nature of risk becomes part of that circulation, so that *the movement of "value" itself becomes the determinant of risk*, obscuring the belief of risk as danger.

And then along comes Freud, whose critique of sublimation foreshadows "the end of this flight of fancy, the end of the alchemical delusion, the discovery of what things really are worth," and "the return of the priceless to the worthless." Money as an alchemical delusion is what we fear from our childhood's first tentative steps of "Watch out," "Don't," and "Be careful." *Money*, like all those delusions, *is untrustworthy*. Freud admits: "I can hardly tell you how many things I (a new Midas) turn into—excrement."

◆•◆•◆ Where did paper money come from? Weschler refers to Horst Kurnitzky: It seems to have its origins in *ancient rituals of sacrifice and expiation*. Thus the earliest vaults were temples, and the creation and control of money was a priestly function. Here, too, at the very outset of the notion of money, is the transfer from the filthy, or the worthless, into the priceless—into substantiation, as human sacrifice was substituted for by pigs. One entity was changed for another, in a manner in which "value" was created. The pig became more valuable because it paid for the prayer; dogs' teeth became worth something, instead of nothing, because the "world" attributed a value to them. That priestly control enhanced the notion that there was something magical about money. An ephemeral object (paper being even more ephemeral than dogs' teeth) moved through our ancestors' lives, our lives, adding or subtracting "value." It has that effect on us even though it "isn't worth the paper it's printed on." As with all magic, we are terrorized by the power this "nothing" has over us. No wonder we view money transactions as fraught with risk!

Commodity money—the physical gold nugget, or sack of potatoes, abstracted into something transactional—developed into an incomprehensible relationship, "complicated in itself (Braudel), in which man no longer recognized himself, his customs, or his ancient values. That which he exchanged for this abstraction called money—his work—itself became a commodity, and himself a thing. Money earned for produce was given to the doctor or lawyer that one had previously never known, so that it seemed as if one never had anything of substance, just a magical abstraction that came and went, and yet constantly had an effect on one's life."

"Money's flexibility and complexity are functions of the flexibility and complexity of the economy it brings into being." Thus, step by step, money has passed from dogs' teeth through barter, the first pieces of paper exchanged as IOUs, government printed scrip, checks, credit cards, and now binary inputs. In the 1960s a takeover frenzy whose magic words were *synergy* and *conglomeration* built temporary empires by swapping temporarily overvalued but real pieces of paper for equally real stock certificates in apparently undervalued companies. But the leveraged-buyout frenzy of the 1980s came into being chiefly because there was no longer any such rooting to such old beliefs of a cash-and-carry economy. The new wheeler-dealers were able to borrow "cash" because it didn't exist in sufficient quantity anymore, but, rather, a new form of paper—"junk" bonds being the simplest description—was created out of virtually nothing more than men's minds. Their ability to "play," their willingness turning into obsession, put them above an increasingly worshipful crowd in a form of the Emperor's New Money.

As has happened throughout history, starting with the

priestly class and on through knights and kings, it became the secular elite who created and thus controlled this monetary function. Their maneuverings brought with it sharp variations in prices, dependent on fanciful offers or the rumors thereof, again with no basis in "real" cash because the paper being offered was so easily created, although as immaturely developed economically as a 19-year-old sexpot. Even as we thought of ourselves as increasingly sophisticated because of such devised products, the economy itself lagged behind the novelty of their magical forms of "new" money. In our secular era, the secular priest—the man who could borrow vast sums of nothingness and magically turn it into "junk" with which he could buy priceless objects—proved the innovator. Henry Kravis and the saga of RJR became the cover story; Ivan Boesky was so sure of its "virtue" that he reinvented insider participation as acolyte to the raider priests; Mr. Campeau was permitted to be a spear carrier. Once such action is accepted by peers, is taken over by the monetary elite, it then gradually spreads through society. *Money becomes increasingly unreal—just terms, line items, numbers stored in computers*—while we who used to clutch nickels firmly in our fists on the way to the candy store find ourselves stuffing $5 and $10 bills in our pockets like supermarket receipts. What we knew of money is left to us as scraps of paper, while "unreal" money is becoming more and more invisible.

John Law's words of the early 1700s, "The business potentialities of the discovery that money—and hence capital in the monetary sense of the term—can be manufactured or created," marked the beginning of this trend toward invisibility. This is a lot better than alchemy. Paper money did seem to create wealth out of nothing. Experience also showed that in times of contraction the value of such notes could disappear as quickly as it appeared. Thus, in a leap past what is now fondly remembered as the marble substance of Mellon and Carnegie, there became the illusion of newly created wealth that did not come crashing until the UAL deal, concocted in the belief that anything was possible with "junk" paper, collapsed in an hour's trading

(October 1989) as the final feverish manifestation of this invisibility of "unreal real money." It turned out that the person assuming the risk actually didn't assume any risk at all—although sometimes overstaying the performance before walking out. If Drexel Burnham et al. gets blown away, that's the nature of the magic wand being waved—what wasn't, now isn't . . . that's all. At that elite level, there is no loss, because there never was anything of substance to begin with.

But eventually, of course, the elitist games filter down to the masses. As Simon Schama, in *The Embarrassment of Riches*, notes, it was the transformation of the tulip from a connoisseur's specimen to a generally accessible commodity that made the mania possible. People weren't so much trading the tulips themselves as paper futures on next season's tulips (just as in our own time futures and options are becoming more readily tradable than stocks themselves). *Money has a distressing counter-propensity: the ability to convert wealth back into nothing.* But it is the late-coming masses, as in 1929 and 1987, who bear that burden, who, thereafter, hold the "junk" bonds.

In the "good old days" of our youth, we accepted as an article of faith that the engravings we submitted (bills) would be exchanged for a different engraving (stock certificate) on demand. Although traders didn't want to be bothered with the transfers, many investors, not trusting the brokerage firm's preference for "street name" accounts, insisted on having the actual certificate in their own vaults, as if that piece of paper in itself possessed real value the way the circulation of paper money became accepted. But increasingly our transactions—not only with bills but credit cards and checks—have become even more ephemeral than paper money. We don't transfer the engraving in our wallets for another's, we don't keep carbons of our credit card transactions anymore, nor, in many accounts, are copies of canceled checks returned to us. Instead a series of numbers—"our" numbers—represents us on a computer, which, as binary sequences of pulses, does all the swapping for us. Money clips are becoming a collectible along with tick-tock watches.

One of the results of this has been the *acceptance* of program trading, which is, after all, not the old-fashioned transaction of our engravings for those engravings, but a momentary portfolio adjustment, with shares plucked out of thin air—albeit brokers go through the motions of making it look as if there is a "real" transaction taking place. In effect, though, program activity is designed to be ethereal, so no one will be disturbed. Paid professorial hacks like "expert" defense witnesses proclaim "nonvolatility," although we have all experienced the up 17 points while we've bent over to pick up the pencil we've dropped; or down 23 points while we're glancing at the sports scores. Look at how quickly the Japanese market turned and how steeply it fell when it switched from rising prices based on speculating in *real* estate to the introduction of program-trading, the making of money out of nothing but transactions. The elite survive, while the shop clerk wishes his life savings were elsewhere.

Those of us who have grown more conservative in our old age long to return to the good old days, but we are no different from the peasants of the seventeenth century who found that the introduction of money made them feel adrift and worthless. In the same way that trade became baffling to them when the old barter system was abandoned, we find the tape baffling when program transactions dominate the activity. We know it's important, but we don't know how to interpret it. Thus the now frequently heard vote of confidence for programs and futures is, as it was then, an elitist confidence that they are onto something that works and therefore is "good." We peasants have got to understand that just as paper money took over from gold, gold having taken over from barter, and checking and credit cards taking over from paper, the market ahead is going to be composed of invisible binary transactions that others play. It's not going to be any fun, but the lords of the manor are going to insist that it is good for us.

· 9 ·

Handicapping Equines
and Equities

To me, a horse is hardly even an animal
with four legs that runs around the track.
I hardly even remember the names. To
me, a horse is this slim piece of paper with
numbers written on it—a line of
development.

You have all these random factors that are
very hard to understand. You comb them
out and weight them properly, and the
end product has an amazing beautiful
simplicity. . . .

—*Leonard Ragozin*
(Jeff Coplon,
The New Yorker,
December 21, 1987)

IT is easy to make a stock market comparison to horse racing—in racing's favor. After all, in a couple of minutes you
know whether you've won or lost. Racing has a win-or-lose
clarity to it. There's no way to rationalize defeat into the possibility of regaining your investment, as there is for stock market
enthusiasts who often insist that "it's just a paper loss," thus

hiding from the ongoing risk rather than reducing it, holding onto the "ticket" in the lingering stressful hope they'll be able to cash in when they "get even" again. The race itself tells all, at payoff odds usually much greater than any the stock market ever produces—that is, if you've bet on the right horse, and especially if, like boastful advisory services, you annualize your rate of return for those two minutes.

Because it is called betting, does that mean racing is to be scoffed at as gambling? Is Wall Street so pure at heart that investing has no element of the gamble to it? Can taking a risk be separated from a moral judgment? Or is risk just a more dignified word for gambling? so that brokers wear suits and ties while racetrack touts are identified by sport jackets apparently made from horse blankets.

No one, it must be added quickly, is talking about the sheer gambling at Las Vegas or Atlantic City. Such betting on cards or dice is rooted in luck, the luck of the roll or the draw. Even the evident skill of a poker player, the need for discipline and control over one's emotions, is tempered by, and dependent on, the initial hazard of the unanalyzable, unhandicappable way the cards fall in random, or accidental, fashion. There is gambling for stakes—something, usually money, although often ego, too, has to be at risk—which are games of chance and those games that can be handicapped, however imperfectly, so as to reduce the risk of losing that stake.

Horse racing, for all its lack of dignity—no matter what the well-bred owners themselves want us to think about the sport of kings—qualifies for the risk-reducing category because it can be analyzed. The risk can be reduced by study and deduction, the scrutiny of the numbers and patterns of past performance, the bluechipness of the breed, and, of course, intuition. And *that*'s no different from what can be said about reducing stock market risk.

When it comes to handicapping horses, we scoff at old ladies who make their bet based on the color of the jockey's silks; we laugh at the odd-lotters who gamble on the horse's name; we deride as amateurs those who bet lucky numbers, or who follow some guy with manure on his boots to see what number he's betting on, just as media tipsters from Winchell to Dorfman abandon news to tell us what the biggies or the analysts or other tipsters are doing. There are those who blindly bet the jockey without any "real" analysis, those who like to bet the favorite or prefer playing a long shot, and those who buy a tipster's sheet as they get to the track, just as there are portfolio managers who will react to a brokerage firm's recommendation du jour.

A "professional" handicapper—by definition, one who believes his analysis can reduce risk and increase the odds of picking a winner—tries to concentrate on available meaningful data. There are those who believe in the horse's lineage, as if it were blue chip stock analysis on the "who can blame me if I'm wrong about IBM" approach. The racing data are used like balance sheets, cash flow numbers, and earnings expectations to determine if the classiness or lack of same of the sire and dam has been passed on. When there is relatively little to go on, this becomes meaningful—for example, how well might the horse run in the mud when it has never run in the mud before? "The horse's grandmother was a superb mudder," the blue chip analyst will say. Others scrutinize available fundamental information in the racing form's tables, concerned primarily with how well the horse has been doing, as if races were earnings reports. They concentrate on the data for each horse in comparison to the data for other horses in the race, so as to determine which is the more likely "value," although sometimes they come up with two or three answers. That's suitable to the stock market, but not so helpful when there is to be only one winner.

In this manner, handicappers of a fundamental bent try to pick winners. The more one knows, the less one can be blamed for the ensuing loss. It is all done—don't scoff—to use information to reduce risk. Does it not do so? favorites win more than one-third of the time, which is not a bad batting average. Should they not find more longer-shot winners if they are so smart? no, because to find the favorite is the object of such analysis. What is believed is what is recommended. They can't be criticized for the profit problem—that the favorite doesn't pay off at big enough odds to make winning one-third of the time sufficient because most investors (bettors) will buy (bet on) what is believable and therefore must inevitably affect their own odds (just as the more stock buyers there are, the more the price is already up by the time believability becomes well known). Besides, those few handicappers who make a living at this can further refine their style by confining their betting to races in which only one potential winner stands out. *This is relative analysis:* which horse among several is likely to be better than the other horses in that particular race.

But there is a different, more objective—more technical, if you will—style of handicapping. This approach concerns itself only with literal physical factors: the jockey's weight, the wind speed and direction, how fast the horse has actually run a race (that is, momentum), what kind of shape the horse is in (its base), and even the resilience of the track's surface on the day of the race (how the "market" is behaving at that time). What this objective analyst tries to do is to pull together all the seemingly random factors so as to discern "the physical animal underlying all the variables," just as the stock market technician analyzes only that which is actually going on in the marketplace itself via volume, breadth, new highs and lows, plus the action of the individual stock/animal itself.

This technician/handicapper then proceeds in a belief that is surprisingly unknown—nay, unthought of during this era of relative performance—among stock market handicappers. That is: *to compare a horse with its rivals in the race is not as important as to compare the horse to itself.* What does its own chart look like?

That means making a "chart" of how the horse has been doing in its own previous races—not relative to other horses so much as against itself. Relative performance choices may win a race or two when the race is over in two minutes (or two or three weeks in the options market race), but it doesn't work as well in an ongoing, never-ending stock market race. Such a horse's chart would show—shades of Edwards & Magee—"patterns that repeat themselves beyond statistical coincidence," just as head and shoulders or triangle patterns show up in stock charts. What is the horse's condition at the time of the race?— at the time, that is, you are about to place a risky bet. Ragozin states: "By analyzing condition, one can see how horses are affected by layoffs or overuse, how certain lines on the graph signal imminent improvement, and others sure decline."

The analyst/handicapper must consider "the complicated ebbs and flows, the two-sidedness of every development. *When a horse runs a good race, it's both good and bad.*" The analytical question becomes: "Which is predominant? *Did that race hurt him, or would it be a springboard for further good efforts?*"

When a stock begins to top out—particularly a pet stock that has done well—there are all sorts of denial questions: Why can't this be just a consolidation? Why can't it be a pause, as it proved to be three or six months earlier? How can one tell "for sure" it is a tired racehorse when it has been doing so well? Who is that guy buying when the chart suggests he should be selling? Keep in mind that the market has a two-way race going on, for such denial also works at bottoms; after a stock has fallen in half, its developing bottom is derided coast to coast; no one, especially those who have ridden the stock down, is the least bit interested in hearing that it has become buyable again. Something changes, doesn't it? not only in the animal/stock, but in the bettor's attitude.

At the track, one can consider clockings of predawn trials and workouts; the observer can consider whether anything more can be expected of that physical animal, or if it has "peaked." In the stock market, tape readers look for volume and price-change clues: is the offer being taken, are blocks being sold to the bid, does the stock close well, is there any follow-through on the next day's opening, and so forth. Chartists or racing-form devotees search for patterns developing in the summary statistics. In both races, tops are characterized by going too far, to an excess, to a degree beyond which it can do no better.

But apart from the minutiae of ticks on the tape and the daily penciled squiggles on a chart, such clues are more apparent in hindsight. At the track you may buy a ticket on the horse's next race, perhaps too overconfidently expecting another win because that previous race was thrilling, or powerful, or a runaway, although by then the horse has become the favorite, even as his winning momentum has peaked. Similarly, in the market we may overconfidently (greedily) hold on—while others buy, as someone has to, right at the peak, because of all the enthusiasm, because no bells go off at the final new high. Big-shot bettors go to the window to plunk down thousands on the favorite to show, and sometimes lose the whole bundle as the overwhelming favorite finishes fourth, but the stock market player still has a chance to salvage most of his bet by learning from the surprising/disappointing action that damage has been done: the equity's decline goes to a lower low, an attempt to rally falters under the high on much less volume, and so on. The question becomes: how much damage? The horse race is over and the bettor knows for sure, but in the ongoing stock market damage becomes harder for us to evaluate, in terms of both price and time.

In the stock market, just as Ragozin noted about the racetrack, "this is a very live problem, and not a dead statistical problem, or a lot of people would have solved it." The ebb and flow, the fluctuations, of the market create both the tools for analysis and the problem itself. Is this particular rally over, or does the end of the rally presage the end of the entire move? Is the pullback buyable—"the springboard for further good efforts"—or is it the beginning of a bear trend?

Ragozin found one consistent pattern: that after a "best effort" by the horse, the next race would be a "relatively poor performance." This should come as no surprise to stock marketeers. What is identifiable as "strong" becomes clearest *after* prolonged and apparently continuing success; an exhaustion of buyers leads to a similar "relatively poor performance." In humans, aging sets in just when we feel we are at our peak, which is why high-priced athletes fail to earn their contracts. In the stock market it begins as profit-taking. *There is a letdown after the glamour of winning*, whereas the glamour of the quest, the being-fully-alive striving for the win—and thoroughbreds must feel this as well as humans, which is how they earn the honorific of "thoroughbred"—intensifies the drive toward that win. The risk of life becomes making life ever more vibrant—or retiring. World Series and Super Bowl winners rarely repeat—the glamour has been enough—while Picasso, Casals, Roy Neuberger, Martha Graham, and others like them must feel they have to keep going *toward* that peak. And when we can't get back up to that peak level, man, beast, or stock, then, in hindsight, we know the peak has passed.

Of course, it is easier to measure "peak" performance in a horse because the race has that definitive end, and a reasonably definitive limit of skill in relation to the clock—whereas stock buyers can keep coming in past reason. It doesn't make picking that top eighth any easier, but it does provide a means of reducing risk by avoiding, or selling into, a feverish burst of strength if it might prove to be (has the ingredients of) the final peaking, and, often enough, a "reversal" pattern itself makes the end as clear as if it were a race. Like aging in life, aging of the move has its waves. At one point—the most important point in the trend, actually, because it may be the end of that trend—*strength does not follow strength.* It is then that we can be thankful the stock market has no finish line to measure the end of the race because as we begin to see failures unfold—belief is required—there's time to get out of the way.

◆◇◆◇◆◇ Look where we have come to! Market analysts—technicians, portfolio managers, and individual investors—have become consumed with relative performance. They are like once-a-year visitors to the track who bet on every race for the fun of it—often on one horse to win, another to show, or (you've seen them) even against themselves by betting on two different horses to win because they can't decide. Similarly, strategists play their self-defeating game of diversification by allocating group ideas to the S & P weightings, shifting, always shifting, relative evaluations by infinitesimal amounts, so that if they are on the right track it scarcely matters, and if they are on the wrong track even a mild underweighting always costs them performance. "Am I going to beat the Standard & Proor's?" is but one obvious example of relative thinking. Someone will seek out cats and dogs in a December effort to catch up; another will resort to down and out stocks in a defensive effort to own only stocks that oughtn't to go down any more. Still others temper the challenge by betting on the favorites, most comfortable with what is doing well at the time because they understand the reasons why others are plunking down all that money.

"What's the market going to do?" is the question every day, because "the market" is the quintessence of relative behavior turned into an average. Which stocks are going to do better, or best? Is there any new leadership? and what about the old leadership? Which stocks will go down relatively less? Which is the best stock in a group? Will the small stocks do relatively better than the big babies? How one does in comparison to an average, other money managers, or a next-door neighbor is all relative, a relativity that has nothing practical to do with analytical decisions.

When one's viewpoint is geared toward relative performance, handicapping includes not only the attempt to pick which horse ought to win that particular race, but also to buy place or show tickets, because that spreads the risk and thus may be good enough, relatively. But then the literal performance of each stock becomes less important. A money manager buries poor performance within his entire portfolio rather than having to confront the fact that something's "absolutely" wrong. The risk is masked by relative performance. Individual stocks become analyzed in terms of how they are doing relative to what the market is doing rather than on their own terms. Peak performance becomes comforting—helping one to win the race of the moment—rather than a potential warning. The first decline in a new downtrend is not only ignored but is frequently bought into because the relative trend performance makes it seem like a good idea.

Technicians, introducing their indicators—which are, after all, relative pronouncements (is this oversold enough? when did we have as much bearishness as now? will there be one more rally first?)—tend to bypass how each stock itself is performing in relation to itself, even though, if you ask them at a cocktail party, they'll seem brilliant in telling you that many stocks top out ahead of a market top. They begin waltzing to their theme song of "One More Rally, One More Rally" because failures—tops—are not absolute but relative. When everything is relative everything becomes blurred; decisions are postponed, or deemed unnecessary; a cry of "Let's wait until tomorrow, let's watch one more tick" takes over, the way bettors, tearing up useless tickets, vow to make it all back on the last race.

Unlike the racetrack, where there is no overall "market" or "Dow average" for the day's performance, we have such readings, but each in its own way is relative: the unweighted approach distorts in favor of little stocks; the S & P is procapitalization; the Dow is the breeding index, including genetic failures like Navistar. Others try to measure how many stocks are above or below their moving average lines as a summary approach. The closest a market indicator comes to telling us about "the market" for individual stocks is not breadth, which measures relativity rather than absoluteness, but the highs and lows. Here is an objective statistic that at least tells us the positions of individual stocks coming round the eighth pole. Each new high tells us whether each "horse" is making any money for its backers, and, in total, whether the market rally itself has increasing or dwindling profitability, as a measure of its increasing or dwindling potency. The statistics, though, don't tell us which new high is going to be the final one. Attempts to calculate which of those "new high" stocks eventually closed lower on the day, although useful for traders to identify such exposed incipient weakness, are not consistent enough to make a separate indicator of, nor does it matter mathematically if calculated after deleting new listings, splits, or preferreds. We've never found "common stocks only" sufficiently different as an indicator—although such a list is easier to glance through for individual names. Such rationalizations turn the absolute "raw" statistic into a relative one. (All of this, of course, is identical philosophically when describing or observing or living through the number of new lows.) This indicator's statistical summary report on impending market trend changes is the only indicator that hasn't missed an important turn because it is the only indicator reporting the absolute action of individual stocks.

How is the stock doing compared to itself? *that's* what matters. What a chart is theoretically supposed to do—measure the degree of buying and selling—it really does. Although peak performance, and the question of when a good performance leads to more up, or to exhaustion, is more decisive in equines because the inputs are fewer, and self-contained within the physical animal, it is vital for us to keep wondering about as we attempt to handicap equities. A stock can be—is—buffeted by a stream of new, and frequently shifting, inputs that come from many different, and often unknown to you and me, external factors. The action is affected by, and hence our problem is made more difficult by, the very nature of the continuous auction market process.

The problem splits into two general sectors: the stock that does, and the stock that disappoints. The latter, constantly running back in the pack down the track, shouldn't be bet on; it may someday come in as a long shot, but that's too risky a bet. The stock that does—keeps rising, consolidating, coming on again—is more readily analyzed. Chart measures such as a confirmed rising trend line, or even the longer-term moving average line, or the number of Elliottian waves like our aging selves, define the climb and will warn of trouble. A gradual shift in the weight of supply versus demand will appear; even though the rise—the race, so to speak—is still upward, momentum will begin to wane. "Peak" performance—that final new high—will be made on *less* volume. Eventually, but often hardest to believe, *that best effort will be followed by a relatively poor performance*: a lower low, a subsequently failing rally attempt, an even lower low. The advantage of the stock market over the racetrack is most clear at this moment—when the race is over, you have to face reality; if you've lost, you tear up the ticket and drop it on the cement, whereas in the stock market you learn a lot after the race is over, including the fact that it *is* over, but you still can keep perhaps 90 percent of the peak price . . . if that reality can be accepted. Except that portfolio managers just like odd-lotters respond to the appearance of a problem by (a) hoping it'll go away; (b) deciding to sell when it gets back up to its high; (c) when and if it does so, getting greedy and therefore ceasing to worry about it anymore; and (d) if it doesn't, blanking out because "it's too late to do anything about it" anyhow.

That's easier to do when you are playing a relativity game than when your concern is concentrated on how the individual stock is performing against itself. In the latter case, when you see a top you sell, when you see a bottom you can begin to buy. But relativity will blur those tops and bottoms. Relativity masks choice.

No one says this is perfect. The fascinating thing about it is that even in using such charts to handicap horses, the equine analyst can still lose money. Neither the horse nor the stock races in an absolute unchangeable vacuum. Producing "a piece of paper with numbers written on it—a line of development" that can be turned into a chart—should aid and abet the ability to be disciplined about placing one's bets. But gradually one's ego becomes seduced by success. Ragozin comments: "Instead of doing what I had done to build the stable, which was to go into situations I understood completely, I was looking for a brilliancy prize. I was trying to lose, and, since I wasn't completely crazy, I had to work out a rationale for losing money. . . . "

Something similar takes place in the stock market: a feeling of power bred by success leads to an ever-increasing desire to be perfect; players try to make it work *all* the time and in the rankest speculations so as to win "the brilliancy prize." This accounts for the incessant, and costly, efforts of investors to guess at the bottom or top eighth for a stock. I've done this myself: feeling cocky because the market has been behaving the way I said it was going to, I've announced one extra, unnecessary sentence, such as "Yesterday was the high for Apple." And then (stubbornness being a component of that quest for brilliance), when the market has proved me wrong, I try again.

What Ragozin expresses in that marvelous phrase helps to explain how even successful and experienced stock market players become undone near important tops. Often, speculation in cats and dogs becomes the betting game to show how "brilliant" one can be, precisely when that "leadership" in tertiary stocks comes along to help identify such tops. Their "brilliancy" serves to lull the players—how can they become bearish (and sell stocks in their managed accounts, even though they "know" the market is deteriorating) when the $3 stocks they own in their own accounts have gone to $7?

Having let ego take over, what happens, every time, is that excuses abound. Owners and bettors prefer to hear excuses—the horse got dirt in his eye, or got wedged in at the rail. They don't want to hear that the horse simply wasn't fast enough. Nor do buyers want to admit that the stock they bought simply wasn't good enough—its "condition," when analyzed, reveals that, even though the stock "ought to do well"—got a nice name, has a blue chip past, has earnings and a number (price) that says it is undervalued (the odds)—so if it doesn't do well, it must be the crazy market, the relativity, not the stock itself. The actual action of the stock itself is denied. What had been a promising chart starts to look shaky, but it can be harder to admit that the stock you heralded has begun to deteriorate than to believe in it in the first place. "Something's wrong," you mutter, "I'll give it two or three more days," and then, when it's down, you have to say, "I'll sell it on the next rally." The chart that forces analysts to be objective is too concrete for them to handle. No wonder people are hostile toward technical analysis. In its purest form, it forces you to look at the stock's behavior, just as the bettor at the track can yell and cheer all he wants to, but if the horse doesn't get up fast enough, all the belief and yelling, all the crowd together tearing up tickets, isn't going to do any good.

What the stock market racer has to do is the equivalent of putting blinders on. Although, of course, decisions should include consideration of what the few important market indicators are "saying"—the "condition of the track" kinds of indicators—there is a vitality to doing objective rather than relative analysis of each stock. It is the only path to selling ahead of market tops and buying ahead of market bottoms. And that's the path to reducing risk.

· 1 0 ·

The Risks of Language

WE can't pin down the stock market the way we can pin down butterflies—even though we'd like to. Adults run through fields with nets, and children are told that a box full of pinned-down butterflies is a collection as desirable as stamps or baseball cards, as if by tracking down the vast number of individual species one can become "sure" of their essence. A butterfly pinned is more understandable, and the pinnee feels more comfortable knowing that it isn't flitting around freely and irresponsibly. The pin represents the rational man. Isn't the guy who pins down butterflies the same guy who condemns Freud?

Being rational is what distinguishes us from other animals. It comes as a surprise to children to learn that a cat or a dog or a horse has a better sense of sight, or smell, or hearing, than a human being does. Humans are the best at everything, or so goes the grammar-school party line, and what makes us better than those dumb animals, who are better than we are at some senses, is that we are rational. Of course, we often don't really act rationally, but the capacity is there.

Americans—let's call us the Stock Market Public—had a postwar surprise: an alien culture turned out to be able to think. The Germans, okay, but how come the Japanese? The notion that the Japanese were terrific at copying deceived us into not worrying about Asian economic creativity. Volkswagen's Beetle, for example, was received rather cheerfully as "cute," while the subsequent Toyota/Datsun invasion was marked by a considerable denial of what was happening because it was not just foreign but alien; eventually, we became angry about it because it was being accomplished by people who were not us. This prejudice has as much to do with language as with color or race. Those who use a different kind of writing are "peculiar," are not like "us." It is not just Asians; consider the status of those who use the Cyrillic script; keep in mind the Jews.

Another language in a different script or style—be it written differently, read differently, or understood differently—almost automatically becomes less believable. There's a lack of trust, and sometimes, as such prejudices will have it, a fervent denial that goes along with the hostility. How can that other, different, language be as "right"? Such problematic languages include that of animals, of babies, of the feel/touch senses, of modern music or drip paintings—and of the stock market, too. Being rational, we like what is obvious; *our* language prefers soup-can paintings, soap-opera emotions, dictionary definitions. We trust what we can understand.

It is more than being convinced that those alien hieroglyphics are so hard to learn, are so complex and time-consuming, that they cannot be as useful. The more specific our own language, the prouder we are. At least, chauvinists mutter, we still have the lead in scientific research even though we can't produce a decent car or VCR. As a result, rational use of language is believed, whereas nonscientific communication—even what can actually be felt with our own skin, like a hug—bears with it the seeds of doubt, doubt that sprouts into distrust until it is defined by literal language. "I love you" becomes scientifically specific, redeeming the doubt.

◇◆◇◆◇ Consider this stock market oddity. If one takes all the various market statistics and feeds them into a computer—volume, price, money flow, and the like for each stock, for each tick, for each day, for ten-day or ten-week or ten-month moving averages—an answer spews out. It is "scientific." It is the computer speaking a very precise, very exact language. We believe that language because we believe the computer is the ultimate rational Western mind.

But the computer's digestive speed can do even more. Having turned stock market inputs into computer language, one must also devise a means of turning the sum total into something called "advice"—not opinions, which are to be sneered at, but *action*. The computer's means of communicating advice also has to be in absolutely precise language. A fuzzy answer of maybe, or might, or probably, or possibly, won't do. Thus a variety of software systems produce "action" signals. Such "readings" are typically crossings of pairs of lines, or oscillators, or crossings of a zero line, or at predetermined parameter extremes, using averages of historical measurements so as to be precise. Like "Simon Says," such advice—"The computer says do this, do that . . . "—is automatically obeyed, because the computer is so scientifically well behaved.

Even so, it is insufficient. Some money managers, handling billion-dollar portfolios, have two or three different machines in their offices, and constantly hit a few keys to put something up on the screen that each software program can "teach" them about what's going on. That a variety of different software programs, all speaking a computer language, are available, with none of them containing a surefire way to beat the market, and each of them differing in details, has little to do with the willingness of investors to believe that the computer, because it is so "objective," has the answers in it somewhere.

There is an assumption that the computer language is but an extension of our own rational mind—faster, less errant, but basically the same genes, like a smarter cousin. The conviction that science will carry the day, that it will solve our quest for an absolute answer—after all, the computer may be wrong because of our weaknesses, but can't be wrong on its own—makes computer language "user friendly." The excuse is always: "Garbage in, garbage out," without considering the computer's garbage grinder structure.

Someone came by the office the other day to try to sell a

particularly sophisticated computer software program—at $1,900 per month. Up on the screen went what the salesman thought was the most useful, or eye-catching, or maybe even terrific, part of his demonstration. "It compares," he launched his pitch enthusiastically, "the this with the that, and down here you can see the relative strength whatzis compared to both of them" and so on. There may have been half a dozen windows on the screen for various comparisons all at once. Seeing me standing there with my arms crossed on my chest, he hesitated, and then finally blurted out: "Isn't that terrific?"

"Now what do I do?"

"What do you mean?"

"I mean, having looked at all those nice pictures, how does it, where does it, tell me something useful?" Then I felt I'd better elaborate. "Do I buy the relative strength? Or do I decide to buy the weakness instead, on the theory it'll catch up? What do I do? maybe you've got a button to push that'll give a signal."

"Oh, sure," he said, warming up again from that bewilderment. He threw another set of windows and zigzags up on the screen, and demonstrated that one roller coaster had just started scooting across its zero line. "There's the action signal for you."

"But I don't want that signal," I said. "How many inputs did it take to get it across that line? I want the message that told some guy to buy back down here as the roller coaster was coming to the low of its ride and arcing upward. He's probably rubbing his hands with glee to sell to your guy who is going to buy because of your signal."

And so on. Such data are marvelous information—except that it is presented in the rational language humans crave. Where are the "artistic" data that speak of impending turns, of imminent life, of what might be—rather than of what has already been? Both the computer and our charts gather information in an everchanging environment; the inputs have to be of things that have already happened. But the computer can only be precise. It is good scientific study stuff, including, although we don't know which is which, placebos. The market scientist can use the machine to go back in history rapidly and easily to determine, say, that 67 percent of the Fridays after Thanksgiving are "up," for an average rise of whatever percent. But so what? surely you wouldn't want to buy, sell, or even hold, based on such precision, when you could base it on overboughtness, or fading momentum, or an individual stock chart that has just broken out across its neckline. When the computer does give a buy or sell signal, how reassuring it is; how believable. It is a language our culture approves of. But it isn't really the market speaking.

Take *the very same data*, and jot them down on the back of an envelope. Calculate, as the extent of this "scientific" approach, a 10-day moving average because that math can be done in one's head (while the "clever" computer experiments with 9-day, 11-day, and 17-day moving averages to see which one is more "precise"). And keep the data in a kid's schoolbook. Use a pencil, albeit mechanically sharpened, to stick a line or two on charts showing nothing more than the day's trading. "Feel" what the market, or that stock, wants to do. And then talk about those factors in the gypsy tea-leaf language of an old-fashioned technician, or the Greenwich Village language of an old-fashioned artist, and what's the result? disbelief, prejudice, scoffing. It isn't anywhere near scientific enough! Who could go to a client and say, "I bought that stock because of a few squiggles."

The technician, the chartist, is not trying to say anything very much different from the computer: buy this, sell that, and do it now, or wait. But if he is any good—*that's* the problem—what he is trying to do is anticipate what is going to happen. Now, of course, he has to use the same already-in-hand data that the computer uses to do his forecasting, but what he can "do"— and the computer cannot—is *imagine* what is likely to happen next, and three weeks hence, and maybe even three months thereafter, *using the language of the market*. And that's different from relying on the language of the computer, as in, "The computer says . . . " The risk is in his mind—no wonder it can be so hard to believe! *The computer is preferred because it has no apparent risk to it;* its exactness suits our scientific era. It is a rationalist's euphemism.

◆•◆•◆•◆ While we insist on precisely definable language and denigrate other kinds of language—written, sensory, or the stock market's—we abuse our own alleged clarity. When you pin down word definitions as if they are butterflies, even to the extent of making up one's own words so they will be specifically and narrowly rooted, you may think you are avoiding the risk of error, but what you are avoiding is the reality of a world full of ambiguities. (Certain clever word coiners believe in kings to try to solve the same problem.) Attempts to discuss and describe the stock market are as permeated by fear of rejection as were all those men who, caught up in the criticisms of the women's movement, took "feeling" classes, met to learn to touch each other, and were told at every group therapy class that they had to learn to express themselves better. Why else is there such reluctance to say "I hate you" about a stock or the market? Is it because the stock, or the market, won't like us back ever again? In the stock market, only the outright optimist, with a grin on his face, cheerfully takes the risk of saying everything is marvelous in this best of all possible worlds. Maybe that's the way to avoid anxiety, even though not the way to avoid actual risk, as *Candide* made clear.

That grin, of course, is a distortion of "language"—we know that life, especially in the stock market, isn't that simple. The outright optimist of today is not going to be as blatantly cheerful at a market bottom; indeed, he may suffer the pangs of a lapsed believer instead. The grin won't return until after a long run up, precisely when risk has once again increased.

Nor does the grinnee take into account that while the appearance of the market averages may make him cheerful, individual stocks are busily shifting from out- to underperforming, and the deterioration inevitable with aging sets in even if as yet scarcely noticed. Like those who want newspapers to print only the good news, the eternal stock market optimist distorts with his grin out of a similar fear that the day's messages will be too painful to bear. A story about the homeless or an earthquake produces feelings of helplessness, yet one can at least send a check of one's own hard-earned money. What's painful about stock market news is that the feeling of helplessness requires more direct involvement, to overcome the discouragement, especially since you're not as "sure" as seeing photos of the earthquake in the newspaper: you can always hope prices will rise again "tomorrow." The grinnee hides his anxiety in the same fatalistic way someone, when interviewed at the airport after a terrorist explosion, invariably says, "It could happen anywhere; if it's going to happen, it's going to happen; I'm getting on the next plane without any worries." *The grin is a body-language euphemism.*

Others mask their fears with verbal euphemisms. A respected analyst writes: "We expect auto stocks to underperform during the coming year, but [sic] for those who desire exposure in the auto group. . . ." No advice, said with feeling, of "Stay the hell away." Consider what that word *exposure* masks—risk, vulnerability, danger—implying as it does some nakedness out in the howling winds. Instead of saying "We'll let you know when GM is okay to buy again," brokerage firm advice consists of sequences: "Buy," "Okay to buy," "Hold," "Neutral," and "Switch" (usually carefully qualified by having more optimistic evaluations appended for the longer term). There's no "Sell the damn thing" category because, this being an imperfect "science," the adviser might be spanked for being wrong. And when a company is involved in the comment, the corporate officers insist that the analyst not say anything negative—or they don't disclose to the analyst anything negative to begin with—which can only be because they risk their jobs or ego if their incompetence is evaluated.

These euphemisms help make the market appear not as risky as it really is. The "passed away" phrases have the same effect of hiding from the reality of "he died." By the time we become accustomed to the euphemisms, it becomes acceptable business practice to see no sell recommendations *and therefore to sense no risk*—unless, of course, the stock or market is starting to make a bottom, when commentators take heart to announce, grin gone, that it is awful, and going to get worse. Attempts to reduce risk by use of euphemisms and insistence on computerized precision only serve to mask reality. Such linguistic blindness increases actual risk.

· 11 ·

The Ambiguities of
Market Language

WHATEVER happened to the "language of feel"? Well, yes, we've bought books on body language and listened to our spouses complain about how men don't show feelings enough. For many it has had to be couched in scientific terms—"62 percent of all married men," and so on—or written down in a book to give it validity, but we've accepted the fact that there is a separate, nonrational part of humans called "feel," and that, with conscientiousness and consciousness, we can learn to express that language of feelings. But it is learned behavior; we still insist we're rational animals, even though we don't think particularly rationally, or communicate particularly precisely. Damned if we'll purr just because our belly is being rubbed! especially since we *know* it is going to cost us, somehow, later.

But, ah, now here comes the curve: what about the language of the stock market? We expect the stock market to be like us: rational, consistent, agreeable, cooperative, understandable, with capitalistic genes. We treat the market as if it is a white, upper-middle-class male. We analyze it on the assumption that it has familiar characteristics like a familial TV series: the market as Mr. Brady, sound, stable, its blunderings acceptable. And then get furious when it behaves more like a stereotyped woman; the throes of market losses produce such cries as "I'll never understand the market." "It's always changing its mind." "I'll never get married to a stock again."

The reason this is important is that there are questions that come up—in life, in art, and in the stock market—that exist in areas apart from the boundaries of language. Can one trust what is being communicated, without its being conveyed in word form? Maybe that's what's wrong with hugs and kisses? they don't get believed. What a risk, if unaccompanied by words like "I love you," and "I do," illustrated by a computer graphics chart comparing 1987's with 1989's hugs. I don't think that's going too far, but you might, because maybe you've grown up to believe that the hug means love. Clearly, though, many "investors" in marriage do not trust the language of feel, of guts, of the several senses, because there is a risk contained in that intuitive concentrated form. It's sort of like that Western Man saying: "I know you're a nice guy, but cut the cards."

And all the more so, when we are dealing with the stock market. Who can trust something so remote from words as a bunch of numbers that jump around so erratically? Nor can a chart itself be defined with precision. Often, it is the head and shoulders pattern so obvious that everyone can see it in the *Wall Street Journal* that is the one that fails.

◈◈◈◈ "The market did it, not me" becomes as handy an excuse for losses as "The devil made me do it." The Fed tightened so prices fell, "but how was I to know they were concerned?" The stock had been going up for six days in a row, but "how was I supposed to know it was about to fall when I finally bought it?" There is always an external excuse—the straw that breaks the market's, or the stock's, back (such as the previously discussed Iraqi invasion of Kuwait)—to account for losing behavior. As if seduced by a smiling siren dancing naked across the ticker tape, this ignores internal behavioral responses, thereby transferring fault somewhere else.

Some things actually are not—ice on the road that causes the other driver to lose control even though you've fastened your seat belt and are proceeding carefully. But the events involving risk, as driving does, that ignore internal messages—"I had too much to drink" being an obvious example—have excuses built in so often that one has to wonder about an inner desire to have them turn into losses.

In the stock market, *what we are ignoring in those "internal messages" is the market's language.* The way it speaks to us is not via grand and noble comments by economists or politicians or strategists but by its own tick-by-tick action. This is not a very big dictionary. It consists of buyers and sellers: *not what they say but what they do, and how they do it.* (It is pseudoscientific in that external stimuli, like shocking a laboratory rat, produce reactions we learn from. The floor trader's aphorism is "It's not the news, but how the market reacts to the news, that matters.") From these imprecise "words" and often contradictory "phrases," we abstract various sentences called statistics: overall volume, volume up and volume down, number of issues advancing or declining, number of new highs and lows, a price range for the day or week or month, how much of the selling was short selling, what those differing dialects of odd-lotters and option players and specialists are muttering, and so on. Obviously, the advent of derivative products, the tails that wag the dog, have increased the style of information to our detriment—like *The Cat in the Hat*, the fewer words, the easier to read—although it is essentially the same language of buyers and sellers and what they are doing.

But there is a low-grade fever annoyance at the contradictions and confusions of the market's behavior. Evidence on both sides makes it seem like a losing proposition to try to fathom what the market is saying. (No politician who hopes to get elected can afford to express his ability to understand rationally and feel emotionally both sides of an issue.) That science will carry the day leads to the misconstrued notion in the stock market that fundamentals can provide an answer, that "value" will win out, if only the analyst could plug the right middle-class numbers in. These relate to the company whose dollar language is that of society's rather than to the stock. There is a belief in corporate-precise numbers as an investment language—balance sheet lines, cash flow or earnings items, net asset value, and so on—as if it is classroom English. (Note that these are all *forecast* numbers derived from past and present numbers, and thus no different in nature from the way a technician uses known numbers to forecast. It is only that the former are presented not as forecasts but as virtually immutable "values.")

When losses continue, investors leap to the hope that if the input language can be made computer-precise enough their risk will be reduced, if not eliminated. By resorting to an accountant-style fantasyland of spreadsheets, in which changing one teensy variable provides an instant revelation of what that change would mean, analysts think they can come up with a reliable answer. Similarly, hordes of dentists and doctors—as well as brokers and analysts—boot up their computers every night to input numbers. They are in search of a language-answer that can be clearly understood, is absolute in its message, and at the same time can be definitively translated into what ought to be a no-risk course of action that, even if right, can only be because the market's future opens up like a cornucopia of possibilities. This "scientimorphism" denies the market's own language, even while plugging the day's hieroglyphics into the machine, because it has preset requirements of an absolute nature whereas the market refuses to talk in such a straight line.

If we believe that the market speaks its own language, it is dangerous to apply our own intellectual form of analyzing.

◈◈◈◈ Before delving further into the market's own language, and the kind of language we need to use as a translation of that hieroglyphic talk, it is important to consider the words we do use about the market that add to the risk. *We apply value-oriented judgmental language.*

Right and *wrong* don't have any market precision because the market isn't precise; they represent human judgments about human failings and successes. *Good* and *bad* are moral words imposed on the marketplace; there is a language-faith that up is the direction of good, while down is inevitably bad. Such judgmental words are papal in the way they are used to try to dispense with the ambiguities and contradictions of the stock market world. Similarly, *responsible* is a word that matters so much in our own daily dealings that we'd like to apply it to the stock market so we'll feel better about being invested in something "responsible" rather than racetrack-disreputable.

Consider, for example, the sports phrase "Go for it." Almost by definition, "Go for it" is not a conservative, sensible, or responsible piece of advice (which is perhaps why it has become a beer commercial's jingle). The sidelines observer views with a mixture of awe and terror the player who does "go for it," believing that for a normal, more careful, can't-afford-to-lose person like himself, the "risk" is too great. Taking that sort of risk is considered irresponsible because it is beyond the bounds of rational (meaning safe) behavior. Although, like stealing home in the last of the ninth, it supplies anecdotes about heroic behavior, it is too risky as a way to live one's daily life. We are not talking about speculative play, the low-percentage shots that weekend athletes leap to with macho exuberance, hoping to hit one spectacular winner for old time's sake, even though they lose the game, set, and match; "going for it" means actually taking the risk laid out in front of you—doing what is doable because your self is comfortable enough to "dare" to do it. You can see how, translated into the stock market, this insistence on the responsible act instead defines risk-taking as irresponsible. By midday on October 20, in the face of apparently huge risk, the "go for it" specialists and other professionals were on the buy side while many brokers, in the interests of being responsible for their clients' money, were selling them out at the low. It infuriates and frustrates the nice investor when the seemingly dangerous risk-taking turns out to be the "brilliant," and safer, course of action.

"How can anyone understand a market like that?" becomes the cry. What seems speculative wins over what is deemed conservative. Note how misleading those words are. *Speculative* takes on the aura of Evel Knievel riding his motorcycle across the Grand Canyon. The word becomes synonymous with gambling, when what you and I are really trying to define is nothing more, or less, than a potentially positive risk-taking. Similarly, *conservative* has become associated with widows and orphans;

non–risk-taking; safe. But many are the widows who were subject to losses while the bond market, proclaimed much safer than stocks, went down and down and down for years. By market-language definition, *conservative* means that which conserves one's capital, although at times that might mean investing in a $7 stock that goes to $10 rather than in American Telephone that goes from $30 to $28. Nor does that mean hanging onto the investment in Telephone because other stocks are going to go from the equivalent of $30 to $25, although there are those who believe it is irresponsible to sell Telephone, irresponsible to take the risk of selling a "conservative" stock even though it makes market sense, the risk, as you can see, being the decision itself.

Stock Market Man doesn't like or approve of such risk-taking. We have our doubts and suspicions because it isn't clear, isn't nice, isn't our language. *The risk of making the "wrong" decision becomes more important than the event risk.* We want to apply moral words to what happens: right versus wrong; up is good and down is bad; positive and negative as market timing signals; success and failure equating profit and loss; even bull and bear personality traits. A case can be made that this viewpoint is that of a white, sports-oriented male. The market is viewed as a kind of indoor game, with its winners and losers. Today's TV announcer tells us that "the market had a good day; the Dow was a winner for the fifth day in a row." Bulls are winners, bears are losers, as if this is a tag-team wrestling match. Bulls are potent, macho; bears are surly predators.

How are we going to understand the risk of buying if reporters call the market "good"? How can a 60-second TV spot accurately reveal a deteriorating but rallying day? although the "good" Dow was up, the market's language may be showing us there were more declines than advances, fewer new highs than the day before, and so on. Suppose the announcer in his acted-out enthusiasm tells the country that "the Dow continued its winning performance, rising for the fifth straight day," while the market is telling us that each day has shown increasing deterioration, like an old man trying to climb the steps of the

Old North Church to hang a warning lantern or two. Then, when the market gets smacked, the same announcer says, "The bears came out of hibernation today, but experts [sic] could find no reason why the market plunged."

Similarly, how are we going to understand the risk of not buying if the day's action is described as "bad"? if commentators invoke the image of a growling bear rearing up on hind legs waving claws out to get us. Maybe investors should be selling into a "good" day, but how are they to know from such morally loaded words? Or perhaps one should be taking the risk of buying when—and because—everyone else is frightened of the bear. How does the armchair stock market fan react when he watches an analyst being interviewed on TV who believes stocks should be sold even though the announcer has said "Today was a good day on Wall Street"? It's a lot like being told one's favorite team, although it has a winning record, isn't going to make it to the Super Bowl. Is the analyst crazy? or is he merely antisocial? "Good," "up," "bullish" markets being desired from the administration in Washington on down—any anti-American bear should be squelched. What we think of as our rational language has in its "secret" emotional context a style of trying to prejudice us. *By prejudicing our view of market behavior, morally loaded language increases the chance that we won't understand the risks.*

Of course, we have to use words with meanings, so the task is to try to take the moral and emotional content out of those definitions and keep them literal. The objective is to be as objective as possible. Up is not good and down is not bad—up is up and down is down. Knowing *that* leaves room to think about what to do. As another set of loaded words, consider failure and success. In a manner of speaking, there is no such thing as success in the marketplace—profits, yes, but *success is really just another word for continuation.* "The stock succeeded in making another new high" tells us only that it is still going up; there is no objective information as to whether it should be bought or sold. On the other hand, *failure* is a word that tells us something all the time, *if* it is translating a market message, and *if* it is interpreted literally. Where was the "failure"? what does it mean? The usefulness of this market-language word is that *failure always tells us that something has changed.* There are failures of the bullish case, failures of the bearish case. For example, when the DJIA succeeds in making a new high, but the number of individual stocks making new highs is less than before— that's a failure, consisting of hitherto successful stocks that had been making new highs but subsequently fail to do so even as the market continues to rally, thus warning that the all-time high may be history.

Typically, however, because of our prejudices, the word *failure* is not used near market lows. How can we speak of "failure" about a potential buying opportunity and hope to convince someone to act? Yet that prejudice can interfere with seeing an important bottom develop. It just happens to be a failure of the *bear* case. For example, during the first half of 1982, the DJIA made three or four successively lower lows, which conventionally would have been dubbed failures; yet on *each* occasion there were successively *fewer* new individual stock lows, as a message in market language of a failure to keep the bear trend going for an increasing number of stocks. *If all you know is that the stock has successfully held, you have to worry if it'll hold tomorrow; the phrase that "it has failed to continue its downtrend" announces that something has changed.*

Because down is bad and up is good, and in the same way that the English-speaking world has never overcome "sinister" for left-handed, the entire jumble of judgments gets mixed up emotionally. *Unless the same market language is used, unless bull and bear are equal kinds of animals, each with their failures, how will we understand?* Emotional connotations of our own distort our ability to perceive what is actually happening in the marketplace. When we ask "What kind of information do we want so as to reduce risk?" the answer should not be couched in nonobjective words.

We are talking about two different "beings"—ourselves and the stock market. Have you ever noticed how frequently the stock market is described in anthropomorphic terms? Jokesters might dub it the "mother-in-law" syndrome. We describe the market as perverse, bewildering, out to get us, never making life easy for us, refusing to help, always embarrassing our egos. It seems to criticize us constantly by handing us losses as if to teach us a lesson. We apply to the market many adjectives from our language that have angry or negative connotations: "That goddamn market did it to me again." Indeed, a Wall Street cliché goes: "The market will do whatever it takes for the most number of people to lose the most money." Inevitably, that happens because/when the most number of humans have succumbed to its blandishments. As it happens, that is another definition of a top: everyone having already acted, no buyer is left to take the price up another eighth. "I love that stock," they say, and then, sadder but wiser, "Don't get married to a stock." But the market, of course, doesn't care about such human concerns—it has no sexual desire even though it seems to satisfy perversities of ours.

How can we understand the market's behavior unless we accept the market's concept of itself and not impose our own on such a different "being"? The market as we know it certainly speaks a standard language for all to see, to read about. Its behavior is exposed to the analyst, to the buyer or seller; it can be charted, and the charts "read," like archaeologists deciphering hieroglyphics. What else is supply and demand but two specific words from our language applied to the way the market responds to, and "speaks" about, the probing behavior of buyers and sellers? The market certainly has a consistency to it, even if that consistency is what we deem perverse. It tries to make sure that it is never easy to understand, even when it appears to be just churning. The market often seems to proceed like a suspicious and cranky elderly person who doesn't trust anyone, not even someone who might be trying to help.

◇◆◇◆◇ At least some of this comes from insecurity, and that insecurity, in the same way it produces dictators, produces an attempt to coerce the market into behaving in a rigorously sensible fashion. Isn't that what we are trying to do with applied science? compel the forces of the natural structure to behave the way we want them to. In its own trivial way, and with less success, that's the explanation for why investors never seem able to compel the market to do what they want it to do.

Thus cycle after cycle has a rhythm to it, beginning with distrust, wary acceptance, puppy love, and ultimately a blindly passionate conviction that everything is going to be marvelous forever. Investors begin to believe that each particular stock they are individually in love with will continue to go up eternally. It may be a honkytonk affair with Blockbuster or Home Shopping Network, or it may be the homey hug of Wal-Mart earnings going higher every quarter or the seeming reliability of Phillip Morris's earnings. In times of stress, one gives up the stock-mistress and returns to what's dependable: stocks with earnings, dividends, cash flow. And when love is in bloom, previously suspicious fundamental analysts, finding that their cautious earnings projections are being exceeded, go to the romantic extreme of projecting stupendous earnings five years out into the future. We are trying to impose what seems entirely sensible to us, because it can be expressed in our own language. But then the market takes over: since everyone has already bought because of that "good" forecast, when the news actually is announced, there is no one left to buy and profit-takers ease the stock down instead. Everyone is furious, while the stock begins an affair with sellers. It didn't do what it was supposed to, which was to be faithful to those married to it. And yet in the market's own language of revealing that people had already acted in advance as the information became widespread, the warning was "readable."

In our quest to understand the market, to gain the information that we think we need so as to reduce the risk of buying and then owning stocks, we want it to "talk" to us in our own terms. We want the market to have our characteristics, or rather, the characteristics Mr. Kant wanted his neighbors to have. No stereotyped mothers-in-law need apply. But that kind of orderly bureaucratic thinking, that expectation of consistency of behavior, of being "nice," is what *we* want; it is not the market's culture.

We so believe in our own scientific rational approach that we will not accept that the stock market has its own language. We use our language not objectively but in emotional, judgmental, moralistic ways to describe the market. We permit this to determine and define the nature of stock market risk for us: "good" causes buying at a high; "bad" leads to selling at a low. If we do not watch our own language, if we do not believe the market has its own language, we are going to increase the risk of our participation. It's as simple as that.

· 1 2 ·

The Technician's Language

> What gets lost in translation is, proverbially,
> poetry: the penumbra of associations around
> words, their resonance. . . . Translation
> alters meanings, dislocates emotional
> registers. Feelings are estranged from the
> words that are used to embody them. . . .
>
> (New York Times, *November 5, 1989,*
> *review by Peter Conrad of* Lost in
> Translation *by Eva Hoffman*)

WHAT applies to the language of literature is as true for the stock market's language. How are we going to translate it successfully? Poetry be damned, many people would say. Those very resonances cannot be trusted. They want what is known to be precisely defined. More, their rationalist minds want to know the unknowable, so as to reduce risk.

Poetry can be dangerous. In itself, it is a translation of feelings. Is the writer sure he is getting it all out, truth included? Is the reader sure he understands what the writer is trying to say? The eduational system demands a conveyance that removes this apparent risk from the poetry, hence the manner in which it is taught in school or "revealed" by the cottage industry of critics.

Yet the opposite is really happening. Kids get *Message to Garcia* on their path to disliking poetry, disbelieving in it as useful, when "my father moved through dooms of love" would provide the resonances they'd understand. If we do not demand that it be precise, "feeling" language does its best to actually reduce risk. Whatever it is, the more that is "felt," the more can be believed. If you really open up enough to believe that those arms embracing you are truly saying "I love you" without requiring additional definition, the more other bits of poetry and feeling you can believe. The more confident you become, the more confidently you can proceed. *Does that not reduce risk?*

The child who is expected to come home with all A's doesn't dare try to do something until she's sure it's right. But the child who is told "We love you anyhow" can step forward into the world with the freedom to go after whatever she's good at. Thus on the one hand we have scientific language and on the other poetry. In between stands the translation. As if it were poetry, as if it were a painting, as if it were a hug, the stock market's language needs to be both conveyed and understood. The precisionists, however, talk like professors: they concentrate on the translation instead of trying to convey the feeling.

❖❖❖❖ On the day I first sat down to write this chapter, a *New York Times* columnist stated that when AT&T was broken up, analysts analyzed that PacTel and Nynex would be the poorest performers of the group of regional companies being spun off, with what must have seemed at that time good reasons. Yet over the ensuing five years, PAC proved to be the star performer of the group, up 228 percent, while NYN was in third place, up 197 percent. What kind of information did those analysts have that was "right" at the time? What information did they miss that made them so wrong? And how did "the market," as revealed in its trading activity, "know" before they did that PacTel was the one to buy? Hard as it may be for humans to admit (especially with a portfolio full of losses), in the market what you see—if you can see it—is what you get. *Fundamental analysts are disloyal to their own ability to ana-*

lyze intellectually if they acknowledge that the market speaks its own language, so of course they can believe no such thing.

It perhaps seems easier to study art through the eyes of the critic, and in the case of the stock market, the critic's role is that of the fundamental analyst, for it is he or she who is criticizing the behavior of the company, the performance of the economy, the precision of the balance sheet. People, not understanding how art is valued, have trouble accepting the risk of owning a work of art ("I wouldn't have that piece of scribbling in my house if they paid me") because they don't understand the language. Those who speak the stock market tongue are similarly derided; "Shoot the messenger" is a cry heard throughout the land when the market's message contradicts what society prefers to hear, especially if one talks about money (market price) in terms of "feel," of sensitivity, of touch, instead of specifically defining corporate results. "What do you mean by 'tired'?" they ask.

When we do use words to convey the market's language of ticks, trades, sentiment, and short selling, consider the problem. The technician talks "market talk" almost like an astrologist: "when the advance/decline line's 10-day moving average crosses the 30-day" sounds like Uranus's and Saturn's positions in the heavens. How else can it be said? the language the analyst is trying to "read" consists of individual transactions, ticks as plentiful as grains of sand. There is a need for summary statistics. One explains in our language, for example, a bottoming the market's language is whispering about, using a sentence such as: "When the Dow Jones Industrial Average makes a new low, yet the number of individual stock new lows is fewer than it was at the previous Dow low . . . " It's not precise; no one knows whether this is all the subsurface strengthening there will be, or but the first of several messages developing. Similarly, to call stocks "tired" is a valid adjective to convey the way they are acting, but it is considered unsatisfactory because it has no measuring mathematics attached. Such language—technical jargon or sensory adjectives—is a way to "translate" what the market is telling us is happening, without precision, without timing,

Chart 4*

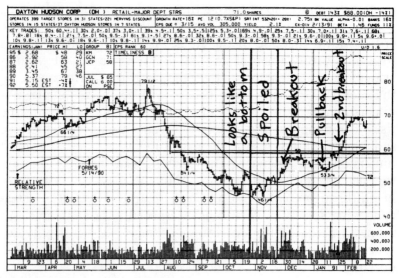

*Courtesy of Mansfield Chart Service

without dictionary definition handholding, *but it is practical enough to rely on for taking action.*

Consider this sequence of daily chart action in Dayton Hudson: (1) First it looks like an appealing bottom, but then (2) when the stock drops to a lower low, you can feel totally wrong, until (3) a rebound makes that lower low look like the "head" of an even bigger base, thus reviving your faith, so that (4) it turns out you were *very* right the first time, but merely lacked patience.

I make a joke of saying that I don't know what's happening or what is likely to happen next until I put my pencil to the piece of chart paper and sketch in the day's price and volume action. It sounds silly because there is obviously no artistic leeway to change where I draw that line; nevertheless, there is a kinship with the artist creating a drawing in that we both use the objectivity of our pencilings to take the next step into the future. Our needs for sensitivity are similar. As you can see,

Chart 5*

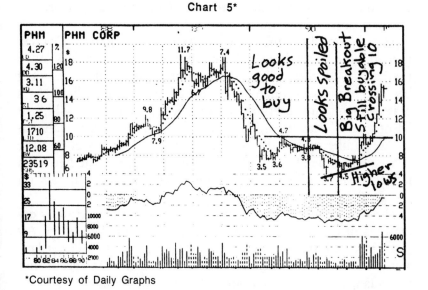

*Courtesy of Daily Graphs

now we are talking about a third language: first the scientific; then the market's; now the artist's.

◇•◇•◇•◇ The photographic image as art is preferred by those who want to be sure of what they are looking at. Realism gets hung behind living-room couches. Distrust of the artist's language is most vivid in the art world itself where there is a tradition of initially rejecting anything new, different, unfamiliar, but the people who "play" the stock market are part of that distrustful world. Unless there's a potential investment gain to it, which they have learned to accept, Wall Streeters are not good customers for art. And this generation's mass investor— the public—is not interested in art either.

This distrust carries over to the technician's squiggles. Realism of information is preferred to feelings conveyed, when defining what is being said or, in the stock market's case, recommended. No one can deny an "Okay to buy" rating, except that it has no nuance to it: what does "Okay" mean? and when? We get euphemisms. "Switch" means "sell." "Underperformer" equates with "passed away."

Translation of the market's language is little better. "Overextended" and "Overbought" are attempts to bring precision to the analysis without making anything at all precise. "Can't it become more overbought?" "Can't it stay overbought?" (As a matter of historic usefulness, "overbought" or "oversold," or "sentiment," "extremes," and the like, have predictive value as to impending market turns, but *none* as to the extent of the subsequent move.) Well, then, investors mutter, "the hell with it." If it can't be predicted precisely, why believe? why act on the prediction?

Those translations, being imprecise, are rejected. More is demanded of the outsider/technician speaking an alien lingo. Although we are trying to use it to inspire more, the market language creates lack of confidence because it is hard to accept that it is a language of ambiguities, requiring no judgments. Technicians, who are full of doubt as a matter of course, because they know how surely the market has no absolute answer, are therefore alien to today's Stock Market Man culture.

◈◈◈◈ Furthermore, *investors have a superstitious notion that to have no reason to believe a forecast is the same as having a reason to assert that the forecast is false.* Thus investors blithely go into a top 100 percent long but stay away from bottoms because there's no scientific "reason" to change one's position. *Denial in the market is superstition.* Or, by extension, having anxiety that a proposition may not be "true"— note the emotional language that word conjures up—or that something that appears to be happening is not to be trusted— therefore becomes the same as denying that possibility, so the risk is not taken. Instead that hesitation creates the demand for more information before action. Important bottoms, for example, are invariably dismissed as "just a technical rally" because the daily news is still entirely negative (and expected to be worse the next morning) and there is nothing else to go on to believe a real turn is taking place.

In this manner, the market's language, as expressed through the technician's "art," is what is not believed. This is akin to the mass of opinion that would gag at the sight of cubist or minimalist paintings, or deride someone who "spends money on that junk." It is simply hard for many people to act on the perceptions of an artist whose vision is different from what has become generally accepted, and in the market's case the art is the technical, the fundamentals are the rational. Because charts and indicators *cannot* be the path to *certain* knowledge, they are asserted as false.

You may not know this is a top. What you do know is that right now there is nothing of consequence to buy. You may perceive that the averages are still going up while certain statistics (easily obtained in the newspapers)—breadth, new highs—have begun not to. Or that in an undefinable (that is, nonstatistical) sense, investor sentiment from comments on TV or in the papers has become comfortable *at the same time* those failures have begun to surface. Not only is there no precise timing to the potential trouble, but it may even be short-lived, it may be speaking of a simple correction before the move is resumed in better fashion. It may be August–September of 1987.

Or it may be that the market is trading poorly already, deep into a downtrend. But you find a stock that looks buyable, and then another, and another. Are they temporarily improved, or valuable signs of reversal? If it were easy, you remind yourself, we'd all be rich.

What has to be understood is that the market, and what we know about its hidden life as conveyed by its language, is not precise, not perfect. The same, of course, can be said about our real, our daily, life. The absolutes are what we never know. The stock market can teach us that it is only when we accept the ambiguities that we can use language to clarify and thus reduce risk. Yes, this; yes, that. On the one hand, maybe, perhaps, possibly, probably. The coin toss; the odds. Those are the ambiguities you are about to question. *What you may not know precisely turns out to be practical.*

· 1 3 ·

What the Market Says

NO T long ago, a *New York Times* article, entitled "Forecasters' Art in 1929 and Now," noted how the economists of that earlier day were unable to foresee not only the crash but also the ensuing depression. Some researchers, using modern techniques, recently went back to that era and demonstrated that even today's fancy computer-driven approaches would have failed as miserably. Their conclusion was that there was no way to anticipate such disasters. "The scary truth," the author of the article wrote, "is that the limits of macroeconomic models reflect inherent limits to economic knowledge."

Imagine! an entire essay about a serious limitation on the ability to anticipate economic trouble, and not a sentence, not a word, not a phrase, about the economic forecasting tool that works—the stock market. The "market" is smarter than you, I, and economists' computers. To be sure, in 1929 the "market" didn't know the Fed was going to make a mess of things, or that "depression" would become the dominant economic force. But many months before that crash an increasing number of individual stocks had ceased to advance, creating a vast nonconfirmation of that final Dow fling. Without knowing why, the market did "speak" of selling in advance of trouble. Nor did it know—who knew?—in February 1980, *before* a six-week 20 percent collapse, that the Hunts were trying to corner the silver market. But some of us were already short "too soon," simply from the tops in many (particularly oil) stocks that had begun to appear that January on the charts. Nor did the market know, before the October 1987 crash, how fast and how far prices were going to fall. But the market somehow "knew" in the summer of 1987 that trouble was brewing, widespread enough for me to sit down and write a special report for *Insights*, the market letter I was then publishing, entitled "The Philosophy of Tops" (July 30, 1987), which cited the array of classic top conditions that already had appeared and thus was able to warn that, although precise timing was elusive, it was time to sell.

Isn't that all a forecasting tool needs to do? is supposed to do? The stock market has anticipated, via its own language, every severe equity price decline in my lifetime. (By definition, a severe price decline is one in advance of which you would have been pleased to have sold.) Not knowing "why" keeps investors from selling, when it is the "what" that counts. "Why" is answered later—too late. Indeed, in this century every severe price decline in the market with two exceptions has had an economic reason for it that did not become obvious until near the end of the decline itself. And in both of those exceptions—the conviction that there would be a post–World War II depression and the fear, in 1962, of a recession that never materialized—the downtrends began because of anxiety that there would be economic trouble ahead. Isn't it astounding that the problems that *didn't* materialize were the ones the experts anticipated? And in *every* instance (including those two), ample market language stated, sufficiently in advance, when the message was changing back to "okay to buy."

In the preceding chapters, you will have noticed a considerable reliance on the number of new highs or new lows as an example of a useful market-"language" statistic. The reason for this is simple: it works. No other indicator—whether readily available, as this one is every day, or not—has such a consistent success record.

A diminishing number of new lows as the Dow Jones Industrial Average chalks up a lower low is a divergence telling us

Chart 6
10 DAY MOVING AVERAGE OF HIGH/LOW NET DIFFERENTIAL
1987

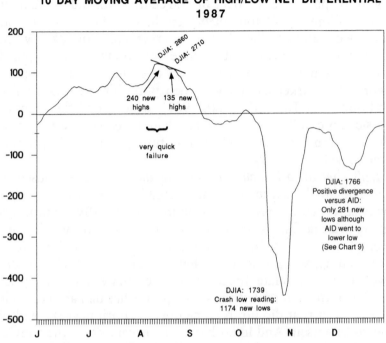

about an impending market bottom. Similarly, a diminishing number of new highs as the blue chip average itself keeps chugging higher warns of a forthcoming top. This has been helpful at *every* important trend change. But that doesn't mean it will ever ring a bell at any one specific "guaranteed" moment in the image of the circus strong man. One such divergence may not be enough, except for day traders; the greater the magnitude of the trend change, the more a sequence of such statistics unfolds. Thus if you believe the first divergence, you may be out too soon (or, if it is a bottoming divergence, buying while there is still a further fall in the averages). If you wait for another, you may have ignored the only signal. Going into the major bottom of mid-August 1982, there was a succession of four instances of fewer individual stock new lows versus lower DJIA lows. Going into 1987's major top, there was a similarly successive sequence of fewer new highs each time the Dow itself kept spurting higher.

Which means, of course, that what the market giveth, it nevertheless still doesn't make easy. You know, but you don't quite know. You get the warning of a change in trend, and then the damn market keeps going further. The way this indicator "spoke" the past time isn't necessarily the way it is "speaking" this time, so you aren't ever really sure enough. You rely on this indicator to alert you and just when emotions are at their most powerful—the terror toward the end of a bear market, or when a bull market's enthusiasm overflows—it has a message but it is an incomplete message. When you want to know something specifically useful at that very moment, it is small consolation to know that the message is becoming more and more important. The temptation then is to try to squeeze one more trade even though you know it's late, even as the indicator is telling you the odds are changing. Like King Canute trying to stop the tide, it may be your chance to defy the market's scientifically imprecise language.

◆·◆·◆·◆ Divergences are a variation on the old saying "Do as I say, not as I do." The market's thesis is "Do what I'm doing, not what the averages say I'm doing." In principle, what happens is that the market is acting like a jury. It collectively/consistently comes out of the jury room with a decision—even if the plaintiff or the defendant doesn't approve, or the law forces the decision past what seems obvious to an outsider—that has its own very practical message. While you might not want your fate in the hands of any one juror, would never buy a used car from that juror, juries work with incredible collective wisdom.

In the market, individual stocks peel out of the trend for various, sometimes apparently irrational (or not yet known) reasons. It doesn't matter why; indeed, most often we don't know, and probably, even if we searched assiduously, couldn't find out why. We are dealing with a collective statistic. Some one day, others another day. As the market approaches a top, individual stocks get sold for profit-taking reasons, for switching purposes, because their own trends are late and tired, or even, sensibly, because holders have perceived that something has changed in their underlying fundamentals. Maybe one institution sells and another notices that the stock has stalled, and so on until a domino effect develops. Maybe the stock has simply gotten "pricey." Institutions in particular make such decisions to sell individual stocks along the way. Of course, at the same time, it is customary to switch more and more into secondary and tertiary stocks because that has become where the action is, which is why an investor selling near the top still usually winds up owning too many shares at a market top.

Buying more even while thinking you are smart by selling something else is the psychology of a top. Switching is tempting, especially since a top of consequence takes a prolonged period of time to form. Despite the narrowing, it doesn't look so "bad" because some stocks are still going up, because the averages are still okay. But bottoms unfold in a differing, more market-oriented and market-simultaneous manner: there's the plunging, panic low, subsequent tests, and erosion to lower lows.

At bottoms, someone has to be early, and those purchasers are as apt to be wrong—after all, the price keeps going down—as foresighted. Buyers nibble at what they perceive as "bargains," but they are usually so only in relation to previously inflated peak prices. Stocks with *currently* desirable fundamentals begin to appear on "value" screens simply because the price has tumbled, but it has nothing to do with anticipating the future: such computerized screens fail to take into account the behavior of the market to always go to an extreme, and are unable to relate to the change in future leadership that the big top and bear market are foretelling. A bear market changes economic realities for the next cycle; but "bargains" are perceived only for past winners.

But someone "knows," someone is foresighted. It just doesn't happen to be you or I, nor need it be, so long as we can witness what those someones are doing. The "right" stocks made their lows in September 1981 during the first whack of that new bear market, and were the very stocks that stubbornly but successfully made higher lows *each time* the DJIA didn't, thereby accounting mathematically for the steadily improving "fewer new lows" statistic. Such bottoms are made not by guessers but by those who understand. The crowd is bargain hunting in what was; the knowing are buying what will be. And because the former were so popular and successful, those stocks get some play during bear market rallies; it is on sell-offs, therefore, that we learn where the new leadership is likely to be.

Relative strength works. The characteristic of bottoms forming in market-oriented chunks makes it easy to identify which stocks to sell on those bounces, what to buy on declines. In 1981–1982, the defensive sector (foods, tobaccos, and the like) showed initial relative strength, but it was presumed to be only because such stocks made safety sense as the economy slid into a recession. But they blossomed into "defensive growth" as the new bull market chugged along, and ultimately came to be called "growth" stocks, as if they were going to sell an ever-increasing amount of cereals, soaps, and cigarettes. That these formerly mundane companies proved to be the big winners of the ensuing seven-year bull market goes to show that someone(s) made an intelligent decision early on.

At that time, what was knowable was (a) those stocks were not bargains related to previously high prices (like the previously terrific oil stocks) but were bargains because they had gone nowhere (basing) for seven lean years; (b) they did not make new lows during the bear market, thus showing relative strength; which, in turn, (c) was confirmed by the participation of almost all stocks in these groups, thus telling us these were not random selections; and (d) required *believing* in what the market was telling us about those stocks. You didn't know their moves were going to last seven fat years; you didn't have to be an economist to understand the root virtue for such companies was the benefit they were going to get from the Fed's easing of long rates (although a hindsight explanation made that clear). All you had to know was that the market was telling you, in no uncertain terms, which stocks were showing sufficient relative strength to be buyable.

Relative weakness is the language of the market as tops form; relative strength works when identifying what to buy. Such patterns develop divergences that we can "read" in our indicators. The "jury" verdict is that, regardless of why, at important turning points the market language changes. Instead of agreeing with the trend of the averages, as it had, the statistics begin to speak differently. Each individual stock seems to see through the surface appearance of the average, and to perceive something changing. The Dow Jones Industrial Average—best used for this litmus-test purpose—keeps going on its own momentum and mathematics; individual stocks don't. So we get the "fewer" number (of new lows at bottoms, of new highs at tops) in contrast to the DJIA's continuation.

Aha! did you think it was that simple? If so, the market throws you a curve, a spitter, and a slider all at once. Remember that *any* divergence counts: at those late 1987 lows, it was breadth (the advance/decline line) that kept going down, while the blue chip average held—a pattern that repeated itself frequently throughout the rest of the decade and on into the 1990s. Yet in prior years, it had been the Dow Jones Industrial Average that often made the new low for the move while breadth held. And, at the 1982 low, both breadth and the Dow were falling together, causing most technicians to stay bearish even though the statistically fewer new lows were telling us that stocks themselves were holding, and actually wanted to go up, not down. Same message, different packages.

So market language is not easy to interpret. But the number of new highs (at tops), of new lows (at bottoms), is the most useful market message of all because *it is the statistic most directly related to the action of individual stocks themselves. If the number of new highs is diminishing, then the odds of your owning a stock that has/will make a new high is also diminishing.* Similarly, if the number of new lows is diminishing, it provides statistical comfort for buying one of those stocks that seems to be holding; the odds of being punished have materially diminished. And, of course, the more individual stocks are defying the apparent trend, the more the underlying trend is changing. You might equate it to the repressive behavior of a dictatorship making it look as if everything is under total control—so that daily life seems to be getting worse and worse—when individuals are becoming more and more emboldened to change that trend.

◇•◇•◇•◇ The consistent ingredients of a bear market that leads to an important bottom are the following:

1. The initial breakdown and collapsing phase that because of its vehemence seems to be a sufficient decline in itself.
2. Because of widespread conviction that the worst is now past, some successful testing of that low is followed by bear market bounces that keep investors hopeful, and even convinced, that the market is okay again.
3. A surrender, and fresh slide that, as they come to "know" why prices have been falling, can go on and on like Chinese water torture.
4. The give-up phase during which the pain increases because the "known" reasons seem to be getting worse and worse, and feel as if they will be even worse tomorrow. (See E, Chart 7.)
5. Signs that almost everyone who had owned has now sold begin to materialize when more bad news fails to carry prices any lower, followed by a bounce that is dismissed as "merely technical," and thus is deceptive enough to keep the crowd too fearful to believe.

The consistent ingredients of an important top that leads to a serious bear market are the following:

1. A prolonged distribution of individual stocks so that breadth statistics and the number of new highs gradually begin to "fail"—registering readings that are less than statistics seen at previous DJIA highs.
2. In contrast, the averages, especially the blue chip Dow, continue upward. The "news" is cheerful, often even glowing.

Chart 7
EXAMPLE OF A MAJOR BOTTOM FORMING

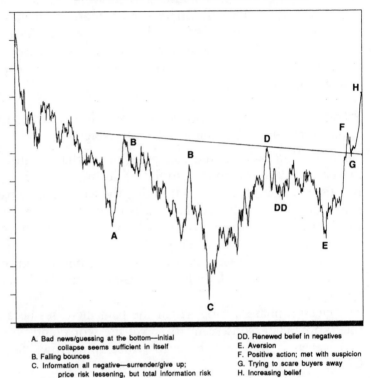

A. Bad news/guessing at the bottom—initial
    collapse seems sufficient in itself
B. Falling bounces
C. Information all negative—surrender/give up;
    price risk lessening, but total information risk
D. Denial of positives

DD. Renewed belief in negatives
E. Aversion
F. Positive action; met with suspicion
G. Trying to scare buyers away
H. Increasing belief

    The apparent narrowing is masked by the excitement of large gains concentrated in a few conspicuous stocks.

3. Declines that ensue still look like "normal" corrections that bulls have bought into any number of times along the way up, but this time rebounds have lessened volume and vitality, to go along with the increasingly negative statistics. Some stocks are already starting down seriously, as switching into what is still "okay"—typically, both the bottom of the barrel and the blue chips—intensifies.

4. Eventually there is a sufficient break in the averages to cause the longer-term moving average lines to finally roll over and head downward.

5. In turn, this means that individual stocks have left resistance overhead, so that rebounds will run into trouble at those resistance levels that happen, with remarkable consistency, to coincide with the by-now-downturning moving average lines. Having given a stock every chance, that last-gasp belief rally is the best opportunity to sell before the bear market starts in earnest. You now see the proven downtrend, and know where the stone wall is.

Tops, as you can see, are made stock by stock, over a prolonged period of time; bottoms, in contrast, are made with stocks pretty much in unison. To be sure, you would prefer something more precise. It would be nice to have an indicator signal that says, quite clearly, and often enough correctly, "Now." Let's take all these statistics and shove them into the computer. Why shouldn't that work, if the statistics themselves do work? When it comes to the number of new highs or new lows, the indicator either fails or confirms. The reported numbers can't be tinkered with.

Can the semiscientific approach hold your hand? Obviously, the computer can print out the statistics and show you how the numbers have changed; it can produce a chart that illustrates the change. We keep a substantial number of such charts on our computer, ranging from the London and Tokyo market statistics to currency charts to the market internal numbers that work, just to see their pictures. That's all useful stuff; one picture is worth . . . and so on. But there is little added value to having the computer do all sorts of other calculations; beware, in particular, of comparisions that apparently tell you what is happening—the DJIA versus Value Line, for example—but are incapable of telling you what to do next. Only individual stock action—long before a "spread" becomes clear—can tell you if a trend is changing *and* can continue to tell you if it can continue.

The problem is not in using the computer; we do. A chartist who looks at pictures ought to. But you see, we don't know *how many* divergences it is going to take to change the trend—

to move the ocean liner around, as the cliché would have it. Nor, to be sure, do we know whether or not to make allowances for a trivial failure—two or three might be a statistical freak, an accident, to be offset a day or two later. Or whether we should use, for comparison, the Dow's closing price or intraday price, or one time the former, the next time getting an otherwise unclear message from the latter. Or whether the move that ensues is going to be the last rally—as was the signal on April 30, 1990—or tipping the market's hand for seven fat years, as in August 1982. And if it takes three or four successive divergences, as it did heading into that particular major bottom, look at the hysteria along the way. You think you've got the signal pegged—it wasn't hard to turn bullish near the end of June that year—and then along comes another wave of selling that not only looks scary but puts the advance/decline line, which had been trying to hold, into gear with the Dow on the downside . . . *except* that one shaky indicator stubbornly saying "fewer new lows."

"Hey you guys," it says, "don't be so scared."

◆◆◆◆ Note that *what works is what the market tells us about the action of individual stocks.* If you'd bought, in 1982, at any one of those intermediate divergences along the way, you'd be in trouble as the market continued down, wouldn't you? well, no, *not* if you happened to buy any of those stocks that was responsible, by holding, for making the market speak of "fewer new lows." And why would you do that? well, if you were going to buy at all, would you be guessing at some darling stock's *potential* bottom or would you decide to buy, practically rather than romantically, a stock that was *already* showing relative strength by refusing to go down any more?

And *how* would you know that? by *feeling* them as you posted your own charts, or by going through every page of a chart book regularly until they began to stick out. Because you wouldn't know which ones they were merely by asking the computer. If you tried to put these lower lows into a computer, how would you have gotten the signal? Each "number" the market spoke of was a different number, only the first of which, the peak number of new lows in September 1981, might have registered at a machine-designated extreme. But the extreme was not the signal, *only the lessening,* and only the lessening several times thereafter *while* the Dow Jones Industrial Average was making its own lower lows (and while the economic news spoke of recession), not on any other day. So the computer couldn't speak as well as this indicator *before* the market bottom, nor could it specify which stocks you ought to be buying. The only way you could "hear" this was to pay attention to the market, and even then, although the market's language was able to put you on the right track, you still had a dozen or more decisions to make. That's why, *no matter what you know, you still have to take a risk.*

· 14 ·

What the Market Says II

I T would be nice, of course, to get additional useful messages from the market's language. An apparently easy sequence of actually timing a major bottom was available from the market's language in the fall of 1974, which produced not only a diminishing number of new lows, but a similar failure on the part of breadth (the advance/decline line) to refuse to continue on down with the Dow Jones Industrial Average, plus, at the end, a Dow Theory positive divergence when the Transportation Average refused to confirm the final new low in the Industrials. Throughout the 1970s, such signals "worked."

Unfortunately, there has been a change since then, as humans have tinkered with the market environment and replaced helpful indicators with the equivalent of acid rain. It was hard enough before, but now technicians have fewer and fewer valid tools. The derivative products—futures and options, plus the program trading that makes use of them—have so grossly distorted indicators that used to work that they are of no real value anymore. Among these are some that I had advocated a decade ago in *When to Sell*, such as member, specialist, and odd-lot short selling.

Specialists offset positions with options, so that while they still do have to go against the flow of orders, selling short when no one else is willing to sell at all, their statistical activity no longer consistently provides its previous message of what the professionals on the floor have been doing. The parameters have changed—shrunk, to be exact. Identifying heavy professional shorting has changed the most because of option use. We haven't seen readings on the short side (as a percentage of total shorting) over 50 in a long time, so the upper 40s is now the warning range. (See Chart 8.) Because specialists are required to buy shares to maintain an orderly market, they accumulate substantial long positions as the market slides, shares that they have to sell on upticks before they can do any shorting. Accordingly, they do less and less short selling as the market declines. The indicator is worth tracking because occasionally an extreme low reading arrives—at the end of April 1990, their percentage dipped under 30, thereby perfectly catching a 300-point rally (albeit the final one), and there was a return to this extremity of low short selling (31 percent) as the market bottomed in October and November 1990.

Members trading from "upstairs" tend to buy individual stocks, as a matter of habit, I suppose, but also because of "information" and "opinion" and, for some old-timers, pure tape reading. But on the short side, they overwhelmingly use the OEX and XMI options, and the stock index futures, when they think the market is going down. It is a simpler, one-decision choice for them; they just have to be right about market direction. As a result, their calculable shorting no longer completely reflects their professional judgments.

Nevertheless, it helps to keep track of the percentage—it is, after all, one simple division problem (total short sales divided into member short sales) once a week—so as to be aware when a significant change does take place—as in November 1990 when these professionals both on and off the floor greatly *decreased* their short selling. But it is not so much a leading indicator anymore as it can be a valuable *confirmer* of a bottom forming. The same, however, cannot be said about the odd-lot statistics. Odd-lotters also can use put and call options much more easily and for the same kind of small sums as they formerly used for less than 100-share orders. At the same time, programs using 99-shares have destroyed the odd-lot short-selling statistic seemingly beyond repair. Because odd-lot short

Chart 8
SPECIALISTS SHORT INTEREST
January 1990—January 1991

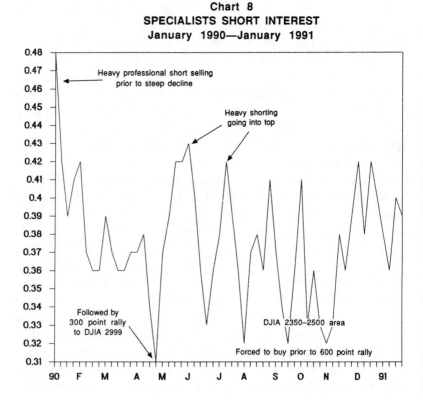

selling was one of the best bottom signalers—small investors would finally become convinced the market was going to continue to collapse, precisely as the panic selling was ending—we miss this indicator greatly, so let these words be "in memoriam."

These are not the only distortions over the past decade. Dividend capture activity affects all manner of volume-related indicators, while the frequency of program trading at or near the closing bell can distort any reading tracked on the basis of closing statistics, so that upside and downside volume, TICK and TRIN, and the like have no consistently reliable validity anymore. Their tendency to become generalized has been reinforced to the point of imprecision.

Other indicators I wrote about a dozen years ago seem to me, on more mature (or bored) reflection, to be trivial. What does it matter if a minor-league indicator is speaking, if the major indicators are not; and if the key indicators have a message, what difference do the secondary ones make? I'm referring to such items as the big block statistics, secondaries, and the like, which *Barron's*, and even the *Times*, now calculate for everyone. This popularizing acceptance is a contrarian's clue that they are not to be relied on anymore: what everyone knows is too known.

Another example of an indicator that has changed because the climate changed is the Mutual Fund Cash Ratio. During the summer of 1987, for example, bulls kept insisting that there was still plenty of sidelines money around to be invested, but that was just an expression of the "Greater Fool" theory that even if you buy foolishly someone else will come along later to buy from you at an even higher price. Two things have happened to change this indicator: (1) The proliferation of telephone switch funds, and thus the ability and willingness of holders to get in and out of mutual funds by dialing, as a trend-following means of "timing" the market; their flow of funds has changed the way mutual fund managers manage their portfolios and how much cash they need to keep on hand for potential redemptions. Often, it's not buying power anymore so much as a cash reserve. And (2) there are times when much of that alleged buying power becomes stale; rather than burning a hole in his pocket, the money manager has held the cash for so long, and it has been so helpful to him, that he learns to live with it (and the high no-risk yield it brings him). In recent years the virtue in trying to identify the amount of sidelines cash has not been its potential buying power, but through *understanding* that a rising percentage of cash means no further selling needs to be done. The market can have an upward tilt due to that absence of selling pressure, rather than a real rise fueled by actual buying. Cash (Treasury bill) positions are positive when their yield helps performance, and can become a market factor if, near the end of a "grading" quarter, the manager does not want to show too much (or too little) cash—depending on his competitive relationship with other comparable money managers. (Calendar-year comparisons count with clients and their consultants.) "We can all go down together," is the slogan, "but I can't let them go up without me." An indicator based on such factors is no longer accurately reflecting how they feel about the market itself.

The lesson is that indicators exist in a real, everchanging world. They are not so definable that you can put them in a computer, with parameters that ring bells, because a human being still has to interpret their subtleties. *But a few indicators do still work, the most important of which can be described as the divergence pair.*

The reason divergences—nonconfirmations—work is that they are telling us about what is literally going on in the marketplace at a time when things are changing under the surface. *They are statistical summations of what the individual stocks are actually doing.* The virtues of the high/low statistics were discussed in chapter 13. They have the added appeal of not being anywhere near as closely followed or understood as breadth—the advance/decline line. Even nontechnicians talk about breadth, and yet it has developed many disconcerting style changes in recent years. The most glaring deception, as previously noted, was in July 1982, when the advance/decline line remained in gear with the declining DJIA during what proved to be a final wave of selling. And after the 1987 crash, an entire sequence of nonconfirmations came "backwards." That is, instead of what had been the customary style of seeing the Dow Jones Industrial Average keep sinking while other market indicators were holding, the other way around became the norm. Since the crash, each meaningful positive divergence has been signaled when the DJIA held, as did the number of new lows, while the advance/decline line went to a lower low. (See October and December 1987 examples, Chart 9.) Hence the rule that *any divergence is a valid divergence.*

On the subject of the advance/decline line, an intriguing historical fact is that breadth peaks have frequently materialized in March: March 1961; March 1971; reconfirmed in March 1972;

Chart 9
CUMULATIVE ADVANCE/DECLINE LINE
June 1987—December 1987

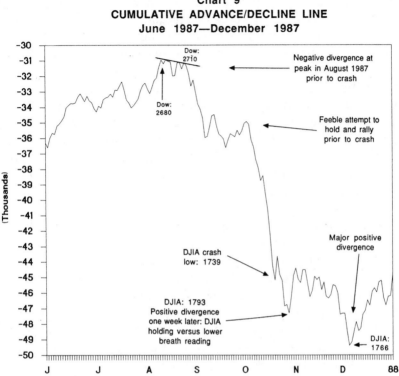

and, more recently, March in both 1987 and 1988 (although it was September 1 in 1989). Are the cycle folks onto something, after all? March advance/decline problems appear just about as frequently as October collapses. The question of seasonality or cyclicity is an intriguing one in the search for indicators that will tell us something "reliable" about the market.

This does not extend to the Super Bowl indicator, and other such foolishness. (Before the emergence of pro football, a similar indicator was based on the Rose Bowl game results.) The problem with all seeming calendar consistencies is that you can *never* tell if or when a particular year is going to break the pattern until *after* the time is past, in the dependable manner in which you can see, say, that a head and shoulders pattern, as the classic repetitive chart example, is failing at the precise time that

the failure is taking place. Others use more statistically oriented, number-of-days kinds of market cycles with what they
claim is some reliability—although they add, apologetically,
"plus or minus" two or three days, or even weeks—but those
"cycle" notions have always seemed to me more a matter of the
normal ebb and flow of a market that fluctuates by nature, in
the same way that certain aspects of life fluctuate with the sea-
sons (an increase in suicides during the holiday season, for example, or spring fever itself), but are in no way consistent
enough to plan a ski trip around in the fall. If the 30-day and
four-year cycles are bottoming within the same week, but the
16-day and 52-week are out of sync, such work is getting into
guesswork.

Divergent market language, of course, becomes clearer when
it is accompanied by similar divergent "talk" about the number
of new highs or lows. Consider, for example, the sequence immediately prior to the 1987 crash when a very rapid failure
provided a marvelous warning. That August, the Dow seemed
to be roaring upward almost unstoppably; at 2680, there were
240 new highs. However, only ten trading days later, at what
was to prove to be the Dow's precrash peak of 2722, there were
only 135 new highs. Warning enough, we'd say.

Lest you think this is always and only New York Stock Exchange–oriented, consider the sequence over-the-counter in
1990. (See Chart 10.) Using the NASDAQ Composite as the
litmus test, the sequence was as follows: May 22, 208 new
highs (Composite at 453); June 4, 185 new highs (Composite
465); and finally, less than two weeks later, with the Composite
Average at 467, only 168 new highs. As the averages continued
rising you could "hear" the market telling you, "It's worse, it's
worse, not better." It becomes a bewildering test of love: if the
"market" shows it loves me by going up, why aren't I making
any money? Of course, this deteriorating love affair was accompanied, like a private eye reporting on an errant spouse, of other
divergences, nonconfirmations, and overly bullish sentiment
readings.

The same kind of behavior can be seen at major bottoms. The

Chart 10
NASDAQ COMPOSITE
High-Low-Close

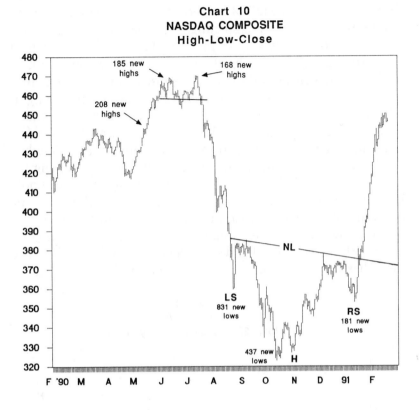

truly remarkable thing is how divergences make it clear that the crowd, still heading in the about-to-be-wrong direction, is refusing to believe that a trend change is under way, so that both sentiment extremes and internal readings confirm each other in ample time to act. On August 23, 1990, stock prices dove to a panic closing low of 2483, causing 707 new lows. It is not unreasonable, noting that substantial number, to surmise that any subsequent lower Dow low will *not* be confirmed by even more new individual stock lows—thus you can rather more confidently than just about anyone else actually look forward to such a Dow sell-off, so as to increase your perception of a bottom forming. In October, amid increasing Middle East fears, the Dow went to a lower low, closing at 2407. (Hindsight shows this as the "head" of a major bottom developing, but no one knows that as it is happening.) But there were "only" 375 new lows—obviously a lot of individual sufferings, but of great cheer to the technician observing the nonconfirmation. Obviously, this has little to do with the subsequent explosion three months later—it doesn't measure ultimate extent, or timing itself; but it does tell you, and in simple, believable form, that a bottom is beginning to form. The fascinating aspect is how few noticed, let alone believed, so that when, on January 15, when the Dow was trying to sell off once again, thereby creating the "right shoulder," there were only 69 new lows. Stop! Look! Listen! do not require mechanical signals—even when they are our fondest divergences. Compared to 375, compared to 707, 69 new lows is message enough in itself. Seeing that, in company with the huge head and shoulders bottom that had formed (see Chart 11), how could anyone have been "surprised" at the

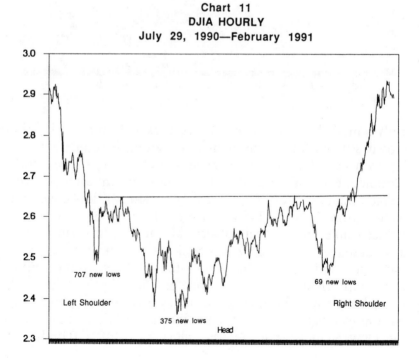

Chart 11
DJIA HOURLY
July 29, 1990—February 1991

rally that followed? but the explosive 600-point upward thrust not only surprised but bewildered everyone else.

◇◆◇◆◇ The advance and decline statistics (or, as the British call them, rises and falls) as well as the highs and lows are readily available in the daily newspapers, and thus are no secret. To tabulate the raw data, to calculate their differentials, need take no more than two minutes a day. I may be a bit old-fashioned, or locked into habit, but here's what I do for a couple of minutes every day.

In a simple standard "Collegiate Notebook" bought in any stationery store or supermarket, each morning I record the DJIA's high, low, and closing price, its price change from the previous day, NYSE highs and lows, the advances and declines and the day's volume. On the notebook's facing page, I then record the net differential between advances and declines and calculate the 10-day moving average of that differential, quickly done by noting the difference between the eleventh day back— the statistical day that is being dropped—and the latest day, and adding or subtracting that answer to the 10-day total, which, by moving the decimal point, becomes the 10-day moving average. (To avoid careless math, from time to time I add up the ten days of advances and the ten days of declines just to make sure I'm using the correct number. If you are so inclined, using the computer as a notebook to record these statistics directly is one way the machine can help with the math while also being capable of producing indicator charts of your own.)

This particular 10-day moving average of the net differential between advances and declines serves several functions: first and foremost, it functions as the overbought/oversold oscillator and is the only appropriate source for using those overused words. By measuring momentum extremes, it can, as much as anything we know, *predict* market turns with genuine timing skill. You can see, directly in front of you, the numbers ten and nine and eight days previous—that is, the statistics that are going to be dropped—and thus you can calculate when this oscillator is likely to reach an extreme reading. Trivial reversals don't matter; the market is not set up for much of anything more than choppy moves when the numbers ahead to be dropped are +200, −312, followed by −60, +203, +127, −318, and so on through a variety of switchings back and forth. Ah, but when you have, for example, a rising market and can see, ahead of you, four more minus numbers to be dropped before the plus numbers of the rally come around, you can then reason that further rallying, producing additional plus numbers to take the place of those minus readings, will *no more than* four days hence reach a maximum overbought reading. Such "forecasting" (you are actually only "reading" the market's language) works almost all the time when heading into an extreme. Directly from your notebook, therefore, you can time the market.

Additional virtues of this particular indicator—identifying waning moves; identifying the start of a powerful market rise; and serving as the dynamic half of the mechanical signalling device of a 10-day/30-day crossing—are discussed below. For its several sensitive purposes, the 10-day moving average of the a/d is extremely reliable, but the 30-day isn't as useful, and all sorts of attempts to jiggle with 9-day or 13-day alternatives not only don't work any more consistently, but lack the virtue of the decimal system's easy calculation.

The same daily differential is then subtracted (or added) to the cumulative advance/decline line. The cumulative line has an historic negative bias so even if you start at 0—and you can start keeping this indicator at any point in time by using any arbitrary number—you'll quickly be in the minus column, which means watching your addings and subtractings; it may be better to start at +50,000. It doesn't matter what the number is because in terms of warnings of a change in trend all you are looking for are *comparisons* with previous peaks and bottoms in the DJIA. The best divergences come virtually simultaneously with the Dow; the longer apart in time, the more generalized the *timing* significance. The best comparisons for timing purposes are contained within the same market swing. Note on Chart 12 that there are two comparisons: a short-term (what is happening *now* between the blue chips and the rest of the mar-

ket), which may require several increasingly glaring nonconfirmations before the major trend is turned, and serious warnings of longer-term failures (the current reading compared to
past swings).

I then also calculate a 10-day moving average of the net differential between the highs and lows. In recent years, *the raw
data have proven to be the significant comparison*—this day's
number compared to that day's; this day's DJIA compared to
that day's. This degree of divergence works best for intermediate length (a few months) swings. A longer-term comparison, in
search of divergences, can also be helpful—not so much during
periods when market life is a series of swings, as in 1988–1989,
but when there is a more prolonged trend, as in 1973–1974 or
1985–1987. Often, a reversal of the 10-day average can be *coincident* with longer-term trend changes. When the change in
trend "bites," this indicator will show a significant divergence.
Thus it serves as a useful *confirmer* of the raw data's timing.

On the next page of my notebook I then record the high, low,
and closing statistics for the S&P 500, the NYSE Composite, the
Dow Transports and Utilities, the ASE average, and the
NASDAQ Composite. (You also could do this on a second line
of the same page.) This effort is the easiest path to spotting such
important divergences as the Transports compared to the Industrials (Dow Theory stuff), or if the Utilities have begun their
traditional performance of "leading" the market, or if the S&P
500 is out- or underperforming the 30 Dow components. I also
jot down the raw highs and lows and advances and declines data
for the American and OTC marketplaces; from these simple
statistics one can see at a glance whether action is shifting to
secondary and tertiary stocks, or if they are failing to keep up.
For example, you may note that the NASDAQ new lows are
diminishing while you've already recorded that they are still
expanding over on the Big Board (a sign that smaller stocks may
have begun to perform better).

Lastly, I calculate a simple ratio of the readily available CBOE
and OEX put and call numbers. Others keep a seemingly infinite variety of option indicators, but they have never appeared

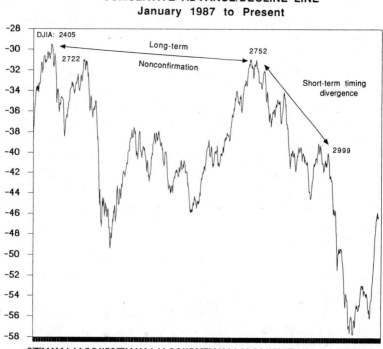

Chart 12
CUMULATIVE ADVANCE/DECLINE LINE
January 1987 to Present

consistent enough to be useful, or else they are defining the narrowest of universes. As the now-obsolete odd-lot short-sales statistic used to provide, the CBOE number tells of emotional changes—when it reaches an extreme of optimism (a low put/call ratio), it is invariably followed by a market correction. An extremely pessimistic reading sometimes persists a few days into a market decline (just as odd-lot shorting did in the old days), but has consistently preceded a tradable rebound.

Unfortunately, these numbers are beginning to lose their effectiveness—too many watchers, too short-term in nature, too frequently used for hedging purposes rather than for the speculations we want to measure, and too glibly used by professional players, especially near expiration, to perform complicated or sophisticated (or both) tricks, as part of program trading as well as on their own. (The "married put"—which is an attempt to establish large short positions while sidestepping the "uptick" requirement—and the "sport short" are but two recently popular option descriptions that have surpassed the by now standard "butterflies," calendar spreads, and the like.) Despite these increasing reservations, keep track of the option numbers through messageless days so that a *change* to an extreme degree on one side or the other leaps out at you: when the bettors are placing their money because of an emotional extreme, they are *not* going to be rewarded. Thus the option ratios can serve best as a check on getting too excited late in a rally (the put/call ratio coming down into the .40 range) or too interested in shorting very late in a decline (when there are actually more puts being bought than calls). *Don't join option trading crowds; be contrary.*

◆◆◆◆◆ Let's pause here for a fuller discussion of additional useful messages derived from the 10-day advance/decline statistics. One of the "leading" technical services that supplies charts on an array of indicators ran the statistics through their machine (makes one think of a meat grinder, doesn't it?) and announced that there was absolutely no predictive value to the 10-day advance/decline oscillator. To the computer, it never "said" anything because the assumption was that a signal would be given when the reading crossed the zero line. But that was a human's rational expectation; the market was saying something earlier, more anticipatory, and more important, although not as precise. By serving as an oscillator, the 10-day moving average of the advance-decline differential reveals extremes. What's an extreme? you get the same answer as the classic response to the question of the cost of a yacht—if you have to ask, it's not an extreme yet. (With the exception of the 1987 crash reading, which went off the bottom of the page, minus 6000 is, roughly, the extreme "oversold" bottom [and often of "overbought" top readings] of the 10-day's scale. For example, it was reached in the first emotional panic selling in August 1990 that stemmed from the Middle East crisis.)

Past its extreme, our pet 10-day advance/decline oscillator

Chart 13
ADVANCE/DECLINE LINE
10 and 30 Day Moving Averages

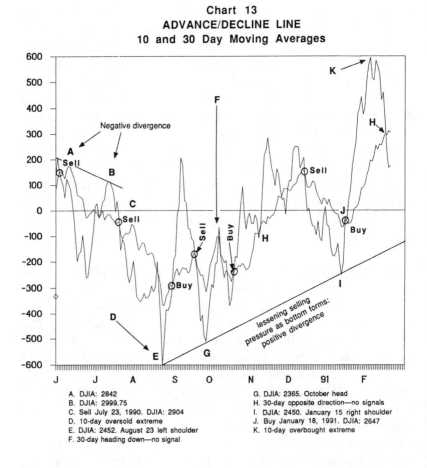

A. DJIA: 2842
B. DJIA: 2999.75
C. Sell July 23, 1990. DJIA: 2904
D. 10-day oversold extreme
E. DJIA: 2452. August 23 left shoulder
F. 30-day heading down—no signal

G. DJIA: 2365. October head
H. 30-day opposite direction—no signals
I. DJIA: 2450. January 15 right shoulder
J. Buy January 18, 1991. DJIA: 2647
K. 10-day overbought extreme

then begins to report on diminishing momentum. In a rally, for example, the oscillator will go to a *lesser* extreme even though the DJIA is continuing higher. In standard (if anything in the market can be so identified) uptrends, the oscillator tends to show three, occasionally four, successively lower peaks as its momentum wanes. *It is the diminishing that is the message.* The 10-day moving average can then anticipate that the market has gotten "overbought" *enough*—as overbought as a waning market is capable of achieving—because we can see which numbers are about to be dropped and when the maximum reading can be reached. Ditto for waning momentum on the downside, serving as a divergence indicator in itself: Dow still falling, accompanied by successively *lessening* oversold readings.

At the other extreme from waning is the significance of a particularly explosive swing from an oversold extreme to an extreme overbought reading. This can happen only when a plunging market has left behind an entire sequence of minus numbers, so that a powerful reversal replaces those negatives with big positive readings, leading to the traversal from the bottom of the chart to a peak overbought reading. You've got, for example, "−820, −754, −786" recorded as the market collapsed, so that those big numbers are set up to be replaced, as the market reverses, by "+990, +820, +780." In only the first three days of such a rally, therefore, a total of −2360 is being dropped with +2490 replacing them, causing the indicator to shoot up the chart like a bullish fever. A few more such days of minus readings being dropped and plus numbers added, and the reading has gone from the bottom of the page to the top. *This big overbought represents such potency that it is invariably the start of a major move.*

Oh yes, the market has quickly gotten overbought and needs a pullback. But while traders who had been short, and investors who are still out, scoffingly announce it is only a "technical" rally, you want to buy into the pullback because the market's strength will return. And don't expect much of a pullback, either; remaining shorts need to cover, all of those wallflower cash-rich investors need to join the party. *Every worthwhile market turn upward blossoms from a plummeting of the 10-day moving average to a deeply oversold reading, followed by an explosive reversal.*

But there's no comparable message from an overbought extreme collapsing directly into an oversold extreme because that's not the way the market declines: overbought extremes come at the *start* of moves; oversold extremes come as culminations. In serious straits, a bear market can stay oversold for a prolonged period while even the best of bull markets never stays extremely overbought because there are always profit-taking fluctuations.

Such action will, of course, also produce decisive trading buy or sell signals as the 10-day crosses up through the 30-day. Accordingly, since the inputs are already available, you should track one more useful indicator: a 30-day moving average of the advances and declines. While this will give you a more intermediate-term measure of overbought/oversold readings, that is only of peripheral importance. It is much more useful plotted together with the 10-day oscillator. This joint venture produces a mechanical signal when the 10-day line crosses the 30-day, and is the only such mechanical "signal" we've found that works *often enough and early enough* to pay attention to. The best such signals come after the 10-day has reached its own oversold or overbought extreme reading, so that when it crosses it does so with potency and not mere kissing and hugging of the 30-day. Even so, to help diminish (although not entirely avoid) the chance of a whipsaw, an added rule is that *both lines must be moving in the same direction when crossing.*

◈◈◈◈ Note how complex the market can be when a simple indicator requires clauses and parenthetical additions to explain its various market points. No wonder investors embrace the computer. That machine, for all my complaining, is a useful machine, particularly in making *your* work easier. As chartists, we are, after all, accustomed to looking at graphic representations, but just as with stock charts, *we* have to do the thinking. Once experience has been gained in understanding the market language of these indicators, the computer can do all of the math much more accurately and efficiently than human beings. Thus it can serve as a notebook into which you enter and store the statistics and then can put them up on the screen to see, graphically, what the comparisons are. You can also—again, after you become experienced at how these indicators work— play "what if" games that can be quite helpful. In effect, *the computer can become your notebook, but it can't become your mind.*

Others *keep* weekly statistics, as well. I used to. But after a decade more of experience, I'm convinced the daily data comparisons are the significant statistics because they measure *directly* how the individual stocks are doing in the face of the Dow's move. An advance/decline calculation is a summary of the day's action; thus the weekly statistic is an abstraction of an abstraction, a summary of a summary. (And besides, it frees you from having *Barron's* around the house on a lovely spring weekend.) The often-cited weekly breadth line has no predictive value that I've ever seen, but is, instead, a deception invariably used, as the market begins to falter (and while serious negative divergences begin to appear in the daily figures), to defend the uptrend as still pure in heart and mind and spirit. It never warns of tops, because it typically makes its own peak coincident with the averages. It is the last refuge of perennial bulls, always surfacing to defend an uptrend that other indicators have told us has already begun to deteriorate. It belongs in that category elsewhere defined as "you can make statistics mean anything you want them to mean."

◇◆◇◆◇ Other ways the market speaks to us—also readily available either in the daily newspaper or, in some instances of refinement, *Barron's* or via your broker's desktop machine—are the following: (1) TICK; (2) QCHA; (3) overall volume, as well as upside and downside volume; (4) and TRIN. (There are others, but I've become jaded.)

The problem with TRIN is that as an overbought/oversold measure it seems to add little if anything to the 10-day advance/decline oscillator. Sometimes it holds its ground for weeks at a time without doing what an oscillator should do. And as believing technicians discovered during the oil crisis that surfaced in August 1990, one strong sector while the rest of the market is weak can wreak havoc with the statistic itself. In sum, TRIN adds little to what you can see for yourself by glancing at upside and downside volume and comparing it to breadth figures. Was there more "this" or more "that" is what's important—not a number itself. Computer software programs provide many indicators like TRIN that make you feel you know something even though that information doesn't carry you anyplace significantly further.

Overall volume is important, but in differing ways, often more like pin-the-tail-on-the-donkey; you know there's a proper place for the pin but you're moving around blindly. Instead of being a sign of a fresh rush to buy as it used to be, in recent years *extreme activity has consistently come at the end of a short-term rise.* Volume generally should ease on corrections if the dip is to be taken buyably, but then you run into the problem of a market that just keeps going down on low volume. So let's refine that statement: low volume on a correction within a bull trend is a good sign for individual stocks even more so than for the market. The saying of "never short a dull market" is rooted in reality. But keep in mind that a dull market is different from low volume. Once the underlying trend has changed from bull to bear, going down on low volume is no longer positive but, rather, is typical of the *middle* of the decline—that is, as people are beginning to suspect something is seriously wrong. The big volume comes out when, believing their pain is going to go on forever, they panic near the low. The introduction of program trading and other esoterica has changed many of the old volume guidelines. A rally on noticeably lower volume is a reliable message in helping to define bad rallies. While continuing low volume for the overall market typically defines the middle of a bear market, it is also the case that *after a prolonged decline* in an individual stock, low—disappearing—volume is the way extended major bottoms are formed. A big increase in volume is vital in identifying a genuine breakout (or breakdown); failure to follow through after a poor volume breakout or breakdown is a consistent frustration. Always sell a "good news" up opening that features delayed openings and gaps everywhere. Even if you are excited too, the delays should alert you to be on the other side.

I do have a fondness for QCHA, which is available only on Quotron machines. (A reprise of each day's closing number can also be found every weekend in *Barron's* back pages.) QCHA represents the market's *unweighted* average when calculated cumulatively. (Since it is provided as a percentage statistic, it is easy to create your own market average simply by multiplying the previous day's reading by the current gain or loss and adding if the day was up, or subtracting when QCHA is negative.) What it does on a moment-to-moment basis is to give you *instantly* a measure of the general market compared to the blue chip average. QCHA is provided as a percentage figure—the percentage change of all NYSE stocks. Thus by comparing it with the DJIA's percentage change at the same time—an easy calculation in your head because there's no need to be mathematically perfect—you can tell immediately if the market's move is narrow and blue chip based, or if stocks generally are matching up well. For example, a 48-point rise in the Dow, with the average at 2400, amounts to 2 percent. If that day's QCHA is +150 (1.5 percent) that's not a bad comparison, rather typical, in fact. But if it is only +50 (1/2 of 1 percent) that's a stinko rise, much too narrowly concentrated in a few blue chips. As another example: when the Dow is up but QCHA is in negative territory, it is a message of a very weak market. Less frequently, but revealingly, there are days when QCHA is on the plus side, while the DJIA has closed down for the day—on November 28, 1990, for example, QCHA read +38 while the DJIA was down 8.66; a message that the market was in good shape, despite the Dow's dip; a week later the market was up over 100 points. Such divergences can be signs of heavy sell (or buy) program interference, but there are times when a persistent outperformance by QCHA, such as occurred on the war rally that began on January 16, 1991, when strength far beyond that of the blue chip index revealed powerful leadership coming from the secondary and smaller stocks. QCHA is a figure that helps keep your mind honest.

In much the same way, you can use TICK to measure moment-to-moment *quality*. TICK tabulates the net differential between the number of stocks trading up from their last different price (a "+" or "0+" tick) and the number of stocks trading down from their last different price (a "−" or "0−" tick).

Beware of DJIA rises or falls if TICK is going nowhere—plus or minus 100, or less. One wants to see strong confirmation from TICK for the way the market is currently moving because it establishes the degree of actual participation, and therefore helps evaluate the quality, extent, and importance of the move (up or down) that's under way. Unfortunately, however, big TICK numbers that surface abruptly nowadays are almost always program-engendered; thus one has to be quite wary of rapid shifts in readings. What you want to "believe" are *understandable* relationships between TICK, QCHA, and the DJIA—not necessarily placid relationships, but ones with an understandable market message. These are all very short term by nature, so that rather than producing signals they are most useful in helping you "feel" what the market is saying. Peculiarities, contradictions, differences, are messages that all is not as the Dow makes it seem. Your market mind should be like a fictional detective's, always asking about why something is not as it should have been.

◆◆◆◆ While we've lost many measures of the market that had been helpful, there are still enough to heed—enough, for example, to notice all the things that were already going on in the precrash summer of 1987 that were typical of important tops: the breadth and volume divergences; the early peaking in the Utility Average and bonds; the diminishing number of new highs; the grand rush to sell closed-end IPOs and mutual funds to taxi drivers and shoeshine men; and so on. A frequently heard precrash remark was that "one of these days the market is going down 100 points," and then someone would half-jokingly say, "Maybe even 200 points," and everyone would laugh agreeably.

Thus the only thing that wasn't anticipated—or anticipatable—was that the Dow would crash 500 points in a day instead of a mere 100 or 200, or, actually, since the overall percentage decline was approximately the same as in other previous bear markets such as 1969–1970, that it did the entire distance from breakdown to panic low in a few days rather than going down for months and months and only then culminating in a selling climax, just the way such climaxes are supposed to look but of monumental proportions. The wonder was how many people actually did see problems developing, yet kept buying and holding. A frequently heard comment was—"*after* the market hits Bob Prechter's 3600 target, *then* we're going to have a bear market." Investors knew, and yet they didn't know. The biggest deception of the impending top was that, thanks to turning Prechter from a guru into a god, everyone knew in advance what the "ultimate" target was, so they didn't have to worry until the Dow got there. Although Prechter had issued an interim "sell" on October 5, clients told me, "we can see the problems you're talking about, but we've still got another 1000 points to go before we have to sell." The bane of technicians, and the problem with investors, is to *always wait for one more rally before selling.* Market letters always advise: "Sell on the next rally." The technicians' theme song—you could waltz to it—is "One more rally." It's a way to avoid the risk of doing something.

◇•◇•◇•◇ Why does this happen? There is, of course, the greed that inhibits selling at a top, expressed as an anxiety about being deprived of something that isn't even theirs. There is the simple reluctance to act—the apparently exhausting effort to take one's feet down off the top of the desk. It's hard work to actually do! There is the fear of being wrong, and the fear of doing something different from the crowd. There is the desire to avoid being antisocial. There is the "fact" that doing means going against what seemingly has been happening. Many portfolio managers have hot low-priced stocks in their own portfolios, exactly the speculative stocks that are one of the warnings of how late in the bull market it has become. But they've been going up—so how can the money manager turn bearish when he is making money? There is the desire to wait for more information, to have it "proven" before acting. Many investors set guidelines—if it gets worse, if it gets better, as various forms of mental "stop" orders, so that one does not have to act now . . .

sort of the way, in a bad marriage, there is a belief that "tomorrow it'll be better."

Most of all there is the reluctance: there's a risk in opening your mouth *before* something happens; better to wait, to be sure. Many portfolio managers now have machines that can be programmed to ring bells when stock targets or alerts are reached. How many bells have to ring before they'll act? Why, when they've made such determinations in quieter more objective times, do they then call me to ask: "The bell's gone off; what do I do now?" And then, of course, because they've missed what now looks, in hindsight, like an obvious turn, they start singing that same old "One more rally" tune.

Something similar, of course, happens at bottoms, when the market is so punishing that anyone and everyone, it seems, wants to have nothing more to do with it. The portfolio manager who eagerly bought "bargains" on the way down now sits with serious losses. How can he believe anymore? There it is— holding! but who would dare buy? Bounces are dismissed as "just a technical rally." And then, when the rally is so vigorous as to become acceptable, "Buy the next dip" becomes the bottoming theme.

What market language does—is designed to do—is provide corrective messages to what your own head is doing to you. It is in the perverse world of the stock market that we perceive with clarity how life/market choices require taking some degree of risk. Risk is reduced not by waiting and waiting to learn more, because the more you know the more the "price" (your choices) will have already changed, but by taking a leap to the belief that what you know is enough to know. You have to use the indicators as messengers, not as bell ringers.

· 15 ·

Trying, Not Winning,
Is Freeing

CHILDREN, animals, and the stock market refuse to be coerced into behavior patterns. Animals can be trained, to be sure, but one always knows they know it's our patterns, not theirs, that we are trying to force them into. They'll do it, until they don't want to, as any cat owner can testify. Children, as they first learn to speak, will say "No" as a first reaction even when they want to say yes. Offer them two pieces of chocolate and they might even say, "No, one," just to remain free of our benign coercion.

The stock market is the same way; we try to force it to be and do what we can understand, but all it will provide is superficial and temporary acquiescence, just enough to lure us in, or ease us out, before the "real" move begins in the other direction. Like a pit bull, it has a habit of appearing under control, only to, almost carelessly, do something dangerous. What's worked before, especially in the recent past, becomes an acceptable pattern of behavior—except that the market will then do something similar, but different enough to deceive us. What we try to know, what is familiar to us, what previously has been useful, can help until we run smack into the problem of trying to coerce the market into a familiar behavior pattern, and the market, in its own language, says "No." Like a stubborn toddler, it wants to do what it wants to do, even though it was an angel five minutes before.

The biggest single problem I have, in giving market advice, is changing my mind. I can overcome being stubborn—the nature of technical work is to force me to look at objective behavior. The hard part is conveying to my audience that the market itself has changed. U.S. Air looks absolutely awful—"Sell it," I proclaim, and when it goes down, in a day, from 14 to 12½, I crow. But then it bounces better than it was expected to; doesn't make a new low on the next sell-off; rallies again to a higher level, so I start to mutter to myself—"This damn stock is getting better, not worse"—and finally go back to the client and admit, when the stock is at 15, "I think it's buyable now." He understands that the market has a continuous life of its own, and that I was right to say "sell"—it did go down scarily—and right again to say "buy"—it did continue on up to 22—but that rapid change of opinion, however perceptive, doesn't do his portfolio management any good. As the advice-giver, I have the luxury of changing my mind with successively new information, but the money manager can't use that excuse in talking to *his* client.

Accordingly, as every investor eventually learns, the more you know, the more you feel you need to know. Often, the more you know, the less good it does you, because it begins to inhibit. But how can you take a risk, if you don't know enough? It's easy to berate and deride other approaches—fundamentalist, economist, monetarist—for failing us like weathermen. Their basic flaws, obviously, are in believing that markets can be coerced into their own upper-middle-class views of proper behavior. But then, of course, our mothers thought that about us, and look at how difficult, and often defiant, we've grown up to be. Even technicians will admit that *the market's own message isn't clear, isn't consistent, isn't perfect*—at least not as perfect as the computerists believe the computer can be coerced into being.

So there's a flaw. And one way to understand that flaw is to see the process as our attempt to force the market (substitute daily life, if you will) to do what we want it to do *and* what we expect it to do . . . so we can win. Is the message contradictory?

Is it unbelievable? Is it different? *The flaw is our absolutist belief in winning.* The subtext of Vince Lombardi's remark that "winning is the only thing" is belief. Like dictators, in order to win we need to coerce. And oh boy, how we want to win. Winning is the be-all, so exaggeratedly sometimes that it seems even modest winning is not enough. You can be criticized (or blame yourself) for finishing second even in a marathon with 300 entries. Whether it is gambling, speculation, sports, or business itself, the American myth prizes best the extreme. That the man who loses his shirt is considered virile, that the sergeant who throws himself on a hand grenade is heroic, is what gives extreme success its pedestal. But *heroism* as the ultimate winning *is an either/or that the stock market isn't.*

Our interest in reducing risk, in sports and raising children as well as in the market, leads us toward understanding that *the goal is not to win, but to keep striving.* The advent of Vince Lombardi's era has discredited Grantland Rice's pre–World War II remark, but in reality, it *is* "how you play the game." To believe in the extremism of winning is never to see change, to acknowledge growth, to understand what's happening along the way. Because the stock market, like daily life, isn't either/or, *how* you play the game—the trying—is the path to coming out ahead.

In a different world, the cellist Yo-Yo Ma has said: "Perfection is not very communicative. However, when you subordinate your technique to the musical message you get really involved. Then you can take risks. It doesn't matter if you fail. What does matter is that you tried."

"Oh sure," you reply angrily, "what makes the stock market a different world is that it *does* matter if you fail *because* you lose money if you fail." You can tinkle all the notes in the world in search of the musical message, and it may wind up being worth it, but if the message/performance turns out to be disappointing to the audience, so be it; you need only retreat, hunched over, to your instrument. As Peter Arno depicted so brilliantly: "Back to the drawing board."

That's not the case with investments. It does little good to argue that on occasion "losing" is not failing—when taking that first loss before the position falls apart can be the grandest trading success of your career. A memorable anecdote illustrating this is the experience of an experienced trader friend who was short 10,000 shares of R. J. Reynolds at 55. When he decided, or felt, or realized, that the position wasn't doing him any good, that the stock didn't seem to want to go down, he covered the entire position at 55¼ for a small *loss*, only to come in the next morning to be greeted by the news of the initial LBO offer up 40 points. His trade, therefore, saved nearly $400,000 overnight, instead of the $2,500 loss actually taken . . . and that's quite a profit.

Since the loss already existed, there was no reason to want to know more; the problem had been stated clearly enough—the position had been undertaken to gain a small but prompt profit, yet there was no profit. Thus rather than a need to know more, the need was to recognize, and to believe, that what one did know identified the trade as wrong, but *not* "you schmuck, you did it wrong," for that transfers the risk to the ego. The brain knows, certainly the gut does; it is up to the ego to be nonembarrassed about taking the loss.

Although loss in the stock market is absolute, the market has the advantage, compared to life, that opportunities keep coming along to make another choice and then another, just as men enjoy golf because they get 18 sequences in a row to keep trying to get it right, and tennis players profit by the requirement of having to win games by two points, sets by two games. You can make mistakes—or the wind, course, or opponent can force them—yet still win; those sports are as remarkable as the stock market.

But games are visibly ongoing. *In the stock market only the upside seems that way.* A losing position becomes stagnant or hostile; both induce the notion that a decision does *not* have to be made. The risk becomes not do I dare step off the curb, but of believing that being on the sidewalk is safe and sufficient. The risk of not buying can be ameliorated by considering all those future buying opportunities. The risk in not selling is often not even realizing you should confront the mistake; it is all too easy to say "Tomorrow the position will improve," or even, when the position is actively hostile, "I can't sell now; I'll wait for the next rally." These are ego-protection decisions that seem scarcely to be decisions at all. As soon as one equates a stock market loss with money, then all those aspects of money that have to do with embarrassment and/or the need to be perfect come into play. ("It's mine and he can't have it," says a selfish part of the ego, which is also involved in the problem of being unable to take the risk of making a decision to sell.)

Stage fright—the fear of initiating a position—is intensified when one can foresee the worry about being "wrong." Conversely, accepting it as part of stock market/life is a key ingredient to becoming more comfortable about taking a risk after all. "I'm a big boy; I know how to take a loss," is a cliché of those asking for advice, and yet somehow they *don't* take the loss well after all. The expression itself expresses their subconscious anxiety: "Once I put my money in, the advice is going to be wrong." Others, of course, as we've noted elsewhere, wait *past* the moment of advice (and opportunity) to see if the stock, or the market, will really move before acting.

Even so, one can initiate a speculation. (Speculating is believing there is less risk than there really is; gambling is enjoying the risk.) How much more difficult to close out a "wrong" position. When the loss is already there, it is as if one has stepped out off the curb only to see the truck already bearing down: panicked at the "mistake," some people start this way and then that (although if they'd just keep going they could save themselves); others freeze in the middle of the road.

Once a risk-position is initiated, we must not let the exposure increase the sense of risk. Stage fright has turned into the equivalent of being out there *on* the stage, exposed. Threatening or actual loss is a different risk from potential loss. "Should I marry this girl?" is an easier question than "How can I get out of this marriage?" One wants out intact, whole, and without admitting to the slightest fault . . . right? There's no way, *no need*, to know more; the problem is *acting* on what is becoming only too obvious. Anyone with market or divorce experience can picture the innate tension built into that kind of situation—should I, or will life be better tomorrow?—which can be relieved only by acting. Often a difficult situation can overwhelm one's mind, one's decision-making ability about all other (established or potential) positions. The tension affects adversely. Accordingly, closing out at a loss not only reduces the monetary risk (it can't get any worse), it eases the ego risk (you can put the embarrassment into the past), and avoids the risk of interfering with other decisions. (Similarly, of course, when there is a profit, we don't want the anxiety that it'll be taken away to cause us to sell such a positive position too soon.) The experience of being exposed out there on the stage alone, and *surviving*, and not only surviving but subsequently profiting, is the path to lessened stage fright before the curtain rises. Thus when the risk of loss gets to be *routinely* acceptable as part of the nature of the stock market/life, it improves the ability to be decisive when initiating the risk.

A professional way to make loss routine is often forced on them by the rules. Many accounts—for example, members' trading for the firm account, specialist positions, trading in stock index futures—are required to be "marked to the market." When I was sitting upstairs trading for a member firm, the day would begin with a computerized run of the previous day's activity, with each position held priced to the closing price. The loss or gain of the previous day was *already* "taken." The portfolio was "marked" to the current "market" price. The result was a *fresh* position. If the stock proceeded to go down, it showed a loss, even if the prior activity had been a nice gain. Similarly, since a loss would already have been taken, if the stock then went up, it became a gain. This made trading activity routine. The loss was accepted, and instead of clinging to hope, or calling it just a "paper loss," you could then start the day by saying "The hell with it, I was wrong," and kicking it out "even." Or if it bounced ³⁄₈, well, then, you could sell it for that "gain," rather than anxiously trying to make your money back.

◇◆◇◆◇ So let's return to Yo-Yo Ma's comment (on p. 179) and break down its contents:

(1) "Perfection" doesn't do any real good. It's romantic, the quest, in stock market terms, for the eternal "up." Like the heroic, that quest for perfection has an element of stupidity to it.

(2) "Subordinating technique"—that is, don't act like a big-shot smart guy who knows so much, gets too stubborn, nor like a teenager who doesn't believe in the virtues of routine practice. Furthermore, you can have a "perfect" technique/execution/style, but technique is not the be-all and end-all. Subordinating technique means not worrying about being "wrong," not letting that "one" way of doing things affect sensitivity to other messages. *One's technique must be used solely as a routine and consistent behavioral pattern.* Thus technique is developed to provide an underlying reliability to perform with skill and expanse, but it comes underneath (3) the market's message itself. It is only then that one can really get involved.

Oops, I stuck *market* in place of Ma's word *musical.* What is the (3) "musical message"? Is it exactly what the composer wrote? technique can handle that perfectly without producing anything of increasing value to the audience. Do we really know the notes literally? that's coercion again. Can't we be flexible? aren't there complex and perhaps even contradictory musical messages? served by the technique, one gets the "message" from the music, in musical-language terms, just as one gets the market's message in market-language terms. The market is telling us, just as the composer's notes are, but *we* must play—*it still requires interpretation.*

(4) The phrase " . . . get involved" means it is the *combination* of technique (whatever style that happens to be, but having practiced it long enough for it to be relied on) with the market's language (notes being music's language) that gives you *the strength* to (5) "take risks."

(6) Because there'll be another, and another, opportunity, "it doesn't matter if you fail," unless you really do need to be perfect. If that's the case, the stock market, as a humbling experience, is not the place to be.

The appeal of heroism is that it represents an impulse to unreasonable perfection, and thus *seems* like an ideal when, rather, it is potentially destructive—"my country right or wrong"—extremism. What "doesn't" matter about failing is not the noble response that "you learn something from your mistakes"—although that certainly ought to be true—nor is it the embarrassment of failing, like bringing a report card home. "It doesn't matter if you fail" is an *inherent* component of taking the risk. You can't take the risk unless you are *comfortable* about failing. Well, comfortable has connotations—let's say, *neutral* about failing. It really doesn't matter (except for the buck or two).

(7) That's why it *does* matter "that you tried." Heroism leaves no room for trying. As Vicki Hearne points out in *Adam's Task*, it is an artifice, a complicated stance of courage, recklessness, simple stupidity, and insensibility before danger that triumphs over the powerful natural impulses of fear and the urge to survive. It is the absolutist approach to choices that dominates our vision even though we know that *life and the stock market are tests that never end.* The false ideal of heroism has no place in places where there is a continuous challenge of testing and retesting (horse racing, cello playing, stock forecasting) of one's ability *and* ego. *The goal is not to win but to keep striving.* The goal of the striving is to channel risk away from the avoidance of loss or the self-denying leap to complete loss to the achievement of a reward. The stock market, having different requirements from heroism, actually cries out instead for making *positive* use of "the urge to survive" so as to be able to try again.

◆◆◆◆ Imagine Yo-Yo Ma up there on the stage, with all the seats full in the auditorium in front of him. He has the tension of being about to take a risk. Is he worried about a squeaky tone, or that a reviewer will find his musical interpretation bizarre? Or does he already *know*, from his experience, that *not* taking the risk would be the failure, so that his tension arises not from the presence of the audience or concerns for his own skills, or the difficulties of the music, but from the anxiety inside himself that he won't be free enough to let go, will be too cautious; afraid of making a mistake, he might then blame himself for missing the opportunity. Thus the concert itself accounts for only a small portion of the risk that lies ahead: *that* moment's risk—"right or wrong"—and no more. The bigger question—his profit or loss, so to speak—*has to do with his own freedom*, being free without using that freedom to voluntarily fall on a grenade.

Obviously, therefore, the problem of "Do you know enough so as to be perfect?" is not the question. Can you be brilliant? sure, once in a while. Can you sell at the top eighth? sure, once in a lifetime. But one must rid oneself of those vainglorious expectations because they are freedom inhibiting. *"Do you know enough so as to be able to act?"* evolves around what the cellist would call technique and we must call experience.

What technique does, by providing a level of skill for the needs of the moment in the concert hall or while the tape is ticking, is take away the risk of disaster, of falling flat on one's face, of being in over one's head. All those clichés become irrelevant with experience. It means *you can go out there and play the game*. Fortunately for us, the stock market is a game that most people can with experience play as well as the pros, by reading, sensing, hearing the market. But it can't be played with reduced risk until one has the technique/experience.

The "all-feeling" of youthful poets, whose brilliance down through history has nothing to do with life experience, won't work in more rationally based work such as the stock market, or even cello playing. Currency market trading, or the "all-technique" of child musical prodigies, may be eye-catching, but it is not so virtuous, being the heroism of youth to plunge ahead recklessly; it is sustainable only as it doesn't tire. We want something more enduring and less risky than that.

Experience, in the stock market, is a matter of *accepting* what there is to know, and not demanding what is not yet, or not ever, knowable. And that knowing breaks down into personalized subcategories of knowing what works within one's own technique. *There is nothing absolutist to experience.* There are all those different life languages to base technique on.

Some will go in the direction of truly longer-term investing, riding out selling squalls and even steeper corrections for an ultimately bigger "hit." Others, especially those coming from years of experience as specialists or floor traders, would find that they aren't very good at holding positions through such market fluctuations, but have a technique that serves to identify those brief moves and the experience to sense when enough, for the moment, is enough. Those may be the two extremes, but there are infinite variations in between, and it is perhaps the compromise, trying to time and trade the market's intermediate swings—when the indicators "speak" most reliably of changes in trend—which is most adoptable.

In this manner, experience grows into consistency. Its presence helps to define the risk one is about to take. Can the toddler, coming down the stairs, do it well every time? even adults slip sometimes, lose their footing perhaps out of carelessness, or lack of concentration, or haste, or some unforeseen and unexpected roller skate underfoot. Experience, which the toddler does not have, helps to right oneself in time. Market experience, when confronted with that precarious moment of being about to take the risk, helps us proceed.

Ah, but there we are now in the middle. We were able to buy the most outlandish stock because, let's say, experience told us it made sense. If wrong—the stock doesn't do what it was expected to to—we know how to react (easy to say, hard to do): sell, start over.

But if "right"? now there's another risk—of selling too soon. Nervousness creeps in. Isn't up from 3 to 5 enough? 6 is a double, isn't *that* enough? how much higher can such a speculation rise? Who knows? but if it is virtually unknowable, wouldn't we only increase the risk of being wrong by presuming to know? All this inner argument, as you can see, is being done in our own anxiety-language, *not* the market's. Why are we so risk-worried that we can't wait for the market to tell us when to sell?

It can't be greed, can it? for we aren't so greedy as to believe that the stock is going back to 50 again. It is apparently fear— fear that the gain we now possess at 5 will be taken away from us. And that, as the couch-analysts would say, is because we feel we don't deserve that profit. Or, in this instance, that perhaps we've earned the gain in hand—*if* we behave properly by taking it—but who the hell are we to think we deserve more!

So there are several layers of technique to build on. The first is to develop the experience, and confidence in that experience, which eventually turns risk-taking into routine. The second is to make the "knowable" choice: how much *do* we know, so as to identify, in time and place as well as choice of vehicle, which risk, what risk, can be taken. (Sell? Hold? Buy more?! holy smoke, never dared think of that choice!) Third, not to flinch as one steps forward into the risk, but *to let the risk-taking become freeing.*

In order to proceed fully toward the richness, there has to be a transformation. Forget, for once, the money. Just as the cellist plays the notes brilliantly via technique, one can be good enough in the market to select a stock that goes from 3 to 5. But in addition to playing the notes well, the musician can strive for something beyond that mere brilliance; the stock market player, too, can take that risky leap past mere profit into the freedom of an *entire move's* real reward, be that at 5, back at 3, or up to 50.

Risk-inhibition is the anxiety of muttering to oneself, "I'd better sell at 5; it's enough; it might vanish on me if I don't behave myself." Risk-inhibition, for the cellist, is saying "I'd better stick to the notes, because I can be good enough that way to get a decent enough review to be rebooked for next season." But *freedom turns the initiating risk into the ability to exploit the moment/position fully.* You just keep banging at the ball whether it is the first point or match point; whether it is in

Central Park or Flushing Meadow. Freedom turns risk into a positive. Freedom is the path past risk to reward.

Let's put this in the form of an analogy: (1) Prerisk is being in bed and wondering how you'll perform. (2) Risk means accepting the requirement that you have to be in bed, and proceeding to do by experience. (3) Freedom means being in bed with the glory of it all.

The leap into freedom is the *exchanging of risk for reward.* This can be done only by shifting from tension to ease, and that can be done only when *one perceives the reward and not the risk.* That you won't win all the time has nothing to do with it—that's life, that's the stock market. *The trying itself is freeing.* And being free has its own reward.

· 16 ·

How To . . .

THE path to freedom is technique. Fortunately, the stock market does not require being one of the best traders in the world to experience that sense of letting go, of just doing it, without the impediment of anxiety, without apparent thought. *Any* stock market player can do well consistently once he or she has accumulated the technique that comes with market experience. Which is not to say there won't be losses. *Understanding* what is going on day after day is what this indoor sport means by technique. I'm reminded of an old NYSE floor trader who once told me: "I don't need your charts; when I make two or three losing trades in a row I know the trend has changed."

◇◆◇◆◇ Although human nature's gambling instinct would argue otherwise, the entire purpose of buying and selling stocks is not for excitement of the risk but for the reward. The *rational* goal is to try to expand the reward while reducing the risk. Those twin demons of greed and anxiety, however, produce an ongoing, continuously fresh sense of risk. Accordingly, from our point of view there is one basic premise contained within all of Wall Street's clichés: *once the risk has been lessened by beginning to reap a reward, don't exchange that proven position for a fresh risk.*

Why? Let's start by repeating: "The market fluctuates." Confronted with that truism of built-in befuddlement, many try to achieve rewards with lessened risk by being conservative rather than speculative. Balance, diversification, hedging, investing in so-called defensive issues, and the like are all techniques designed to sneak away from confronting risk while being "in" the market. But the risk is still there—especially in terms of timing and selection (even Treasury bills fluctuate wildly these days). You can be as wrong as can be when making those choices, even if the choices are allegedly designed to "reduce" risk. The ultimate example, of course, is falling for those commercials huckstering options by promising "predetermined" risk as if that makes it safe—when the "limited" risk is 100 percent of your bet.

A simple starting point might be to confront the risk directly: this is a nonperfect game. "Should I act?" But of course you have to; like life itself, this is a continuous auction market, confronting you with a variety of choices; the ball is coming across the net toward you. Accordingly, your (admittedly ideal) goal is to select, as often as possible, the "potentially up" vehicle at the "almost imminent" moment. (Or, similarly, to sell short, if that is the direction it appears the vehicle is going.) That's *initiating* the position by understanding, and accepting, the "normal" sense of risk—acting on what we know at the time.

Having gone through all that trouble, we come to the next scary consideration: when should we sell if the stock, even after giving it some leeway, doesn't do what we expected it to? In a nonperfect world, and never knowing everything, why should we argue with what the action itself is telling us? Thus failure itself is the proof; needing to know "why" is unnecessary. The failure may be temporary, the "why" may be someone else's anxiety, so the question really becomes: when is some leeway enough leeway? Obviously, that is different for a Treasury bond than for a stock than for a currency option, so the answer becomes rooted in one's own technique of investing/trading. For some, the first failure, no matter how subtle, is enough—the story of the stock and the pea, so to speak; for others, an entire top would be required to form over a long enough period to become big enough on the weekly chart. Leeway requires watching some of one's cherished capital diminish, giving the position a "glass is half full" interpretation until it truly does something more than worrisome but actually wrong. In doing so, we must understand that there is as much risk in giving up a good position as in losing money.

Too many people mutter, when the risk becomes too great to bear, "no one ever got hurt taking a profit." But one does, one does, if that anxiety takes one out of a still-positive longer-term position that one never, despite internal promises, gets back into. So if we are charting the psychological trip through risk, a major premise must be that *having bought a stock that is going up, selling it prematurely*—that is, because of our anxiety rather than the market's—*increases the risk because it requires us to start all over again finding a stock similar to the one we already had.* Because this is a nonperfect game, sooner or later we're going to pick one that doesn't work.

You can see that this stems from a lack of freedom, a return to the prison of risk, because, in reality, once we own a rising stock, our risk of being in the market has *decreased.* That decreased risk not only is because we now have a successful stock but continues even while the stock experiences, as it should, fluctuations back down. Failures—the market's message that something is no longer as positive as it had been—must begin to occur on the upside . . . that is, at a better price. In the market's perverse way, precisely when a rebound is alleviating anxiety, the position may be failing. Risk then reappears, requiring the freedom of openmindedness, and the technique of understanding such failures within the context of an apparent rise, so as to make a decision.

This phase of budding failure has various requirements depending on the style of one's trading or investing. Shorter-term players may simply react to something/anything wrong. (Ex-specialists and floor traders will be out intuitively before anything wrong becomes manifest, but that's too moment-to-moment to define objectively and is, after all, a direct part of what the market's language would be telling the rest of us.) Such trading accepts the in-and-out nature of the risk, and develops a style of being willing to buy anything back, even if they just sold it at a lower price five minutes before.

This can perhaps best be illustrated in the options market. *One buys* a handful of calls in stock X *for two reasons and two reasons only*: belief that X is an "up" stock and belief that the "upness" is imminent. *Were it not imminent, there would be no point whatsoever in buying* the call, even if X were going to triple, because the call premium that you anted up would diminish during the time the stock languished, no matter how positive that languishing were to be viewed. Thus if one does buy that call, and nothing happens for, let's say, one and a half to two days (or overnight in "hot tip" cases), the "call" was wrong; the tenets of its purchase have been proven "wrong" in the marketplace. And because of the option's absolutist nature of diminishing time values, it becomes necessary to admit the "mistake" and to close out the position. On the other hand, if the imminence is proven "right," then one has a limited time placed on the position. Once the *immediate* move is over, and even if the stock itself remains unchanged at its higher price, preparatory to going even higher, that diminishing time value requires cashing in—because you already *have* the profit that you bought for—without regard for ultimate glory. (Besides, the emotional trading that accompanies a stock's initial burst invariably takes the option to an excessive premium that is not matched subsequently, even though the stock itself goes higher.)

Time value aspects make being "right" or "wrong" vividly clear; options traders never need to know more. And yet almost everyone willingly rides a failed option down to its worthlessness at expiration time. The psychological reason for this absence of acting is that the position has invariably been initiated with an anxiety-ridden statement along the lines of "I'm risking only a few hundred dollars." Holding on seems like greed for a lottery-ticket-type hit, but stems from the fact that *one is already mentally disposed to lose the entire amount.*

Nor is this self-destructive pattern exclusively that of small traders with their few-hundred-dollar bets. Many longer-term institutional portfolio managers have "learned" to use options for hedging purposes. However, they lose the value of their hedge by not closing out the position after it helps. They buy, say, 500 OEX puts because they believe the market is going down; it does; they're thrilled at how they've protected their portfolio. But then they let the options expire worthless in the belief the hedge has served its purpose. Somehow, a fear of changing positions becomes overriding, as if the same person who had been discerning enough about the market to put such a hedge on is not capable of also foreseeing when it has become time enough to take the hedge off, reaping the profit rather than just experiencing the temporary alleviation of anxiety. Having done the "right" thing turns into a waste.

I would not argue with the player who can do such short-term trading successfully. Its success lies in understanding imminence when initiating a position *and* when closing it out. But at the other extreme, the longer-term investor, whose technique is understanding patience, must be willing to ride out such swings. There is a *continuing* market-normal risk that the gain might be taken away, but there are market-language messages for evaluating such a risk. The market really doesn't "suffer gladly" those who would turn a legitimate concern about such fluctuations—for, after all, they must be evaluated—into a neurosis. The fact is that you now own a stock that has *proven* it can go up, and that's the best anyone can do in *reducing* risk.

For a longer-term investor, the measure then is not the necessarily acceptable fluctuation risk along the way; during that phase the risk becomes selling too soon. Holding is for the reward; selling is the risk. The ego fear, the embarrassment fear, the money fear—all the stage-fright fears that preceded initiating the position—are now center stage. Risk seems to surround you even though, since the stock has risen, it is now not even your own money. Hence the expression "No one can get hurt taking a profit." *That's* the fraudulent Don Juan. One finds oneself as if in a dream in someone else's house stealing his money. What a risk of getting caught, of being so vulnerable to exposure. Obviously, the path to safety—to no risk, no pressure—is to flee by selling. But the stock, the market, hasn't told you to withdraw yet. Your eye is still on the risk, not the freedom.

Later, though, a transformation takes place: the risk becomes *blindness to the increasing vulnerability.* One must wait patiently until the stock does something wrong enough, serious enough to warrant—finally—*considering* the sale. Actually, that should be something*s*, because an important move deserves several market failures like a series of small shocks before one can say that the stock is done. Along the way, the stock should have short-term dips/pullbacks, as well as deeper corrections and/or intermediate term consolidations. Having survived these anxiety-ridden swings, you should be increasingly prepared for a more toppy pattern of behavior that would—finally—tell you that the risk of remaining in is becoming greater than the risk of being out.

Isn't it fascinating, therefore, that the farther the rise—in price and time—the more relaxed our previously terrified hero has become? His role center stage has become comfortable. Boasting to neighbors, toting up his gains, hearing the applause from portfolio managers down the hall, make him feel there is more to come. Now he can't be gotten off the stage; he wouldn't even think of leaving that grand success behind. Thus fear of selling prematurely is transferred into the fresh risk of euphoria. *Where is the freedom now?* not in what has become a yuppie-ish form of "I'm too go(o)d to be touched by the realities of daily life."

Keep in mind that all this is a simplified passage through the manner in which "stocks fluctuate." At the bottom, an investor may be too scared to buy at all. But then, having actually reduced risk by virtue of having bought the "right" stock, the investor remains uncomfortable: should a quick profit be grabbed? suppose the scary climate returns? Subsequently, a further rise helps convince the investor-turned-trader that it was wrong to sell; having sold prematurely, and vowing not to sell so soon the next time, the investor-redux buys back in via something else either more speculative or already up a lot (or both). Comfortableness begins to replace fear, so that there is a shift from reward back into risk, only now it is the risk of not selling. Our "investor" becomes something worse than being a longer-term holder—as prices slide, he or she becomes a locked-in, involuntary investor.

The shift is in the investor's head, not in the market's climate. During the "wall of worry" period, vulnerability does not develop without the market "talking" about it beforehand. Patience works. No stock ever goes up and up, never says a "word" that it is in trouble, and then turns around and goes straight down without stopping. *The mistake at tops*, therefore, *is not listening*.

◇◆◇◆◇ Unfortunately for the hoped-for ease in doing all this, one must also take the overall market situation into consideration. Most stocks adhere to the market's own moves; a stock that goes up along with the market's strength will tend to get overextended as the market does, and then stage its own correction as the market does. Even those stocks more independent have a cousinly relationship to the overall market's behavior. *But there are two significant exceptions to this general commonality.*

Stocks that have been the leaders of the previous bull move look like bargains during the early phases of the developing bear market. They hang up near their highs because of their reliability and their past leadership, and bounce quickly when a bear market rally comes along, but then will sell off steeply during the final "give-up" leg as that bear comes to an end. Indeed, they customarily continue on down another 10 to 15 percent while other stocks—and the "market"—are already holding and even turning upward. What's more: "last down, least up"; these erstwhile leaders will underperform in the next bull rise, and cease going up months before the market hits its next top. Meanwhile, because a worthwhile bear market cleans out the prior excesses, the change in leadership that classically develops produces newly emerging names that bottom first, starting up well ahead of the literal end of the bear market, and maintaining their uptrends past the statistical end of the next bull.

For example, 1980–1981 saw an end to energy stock leadership. Oil shares had a stroke during the "Bunker Hunt silver" collapse in March 1980. They roared back to a final peak in November, and then, in January, April, and June 1981 experienced failing runs as the averages topped out. During the bear market transition of 1981–1982, the consumer groups emerged, while the oils became the laggards. These emerging leadership stocks never went down after the bear started—making their lows in September 1981—but were dismissed because of their long-held "defensive" reputation. But they survived the market's 20 percent sell-off in 1984, and led the way back up—thereby earning the categorization of "defensive growth"—and came back yet again after the 1987 crash, thus leading throughout the entire seven fat years of the cycle, so much so that they became identified as "growth" stocks. They proceeded to perform relatively well during the first phase of the 1990 bear slide, because portfolio managers sold other stocks while holding these darlings. Finally, however, they gradually began to top out, and underperform, as the market prepared for a change in leadership.

You can translate this into something the market is telling us in its own language. *There comes a point in a trend when investors believe there is virtually no risk at all to buying and owning stocks.* How can this be? (There's also, of course, a point late in a bear trend when investors don't want to own a single share.)

This might be called *The Blue Angel* syndrome. The blind passion, for momentary rewards, takes over. One can see nothing wrong with one's own behavior, so consumed by it has he become. And at this aging point in the bull market, such blindness is due to the passion for possessing. This might remind some of George Steinbrenner of the Yankees, whose possessiveness blinded him to the incompetence of his own behavior, and the fury of the citizenry. And remember Donald Trump's own "passion for possessing," which led him to believe he was at the top when in stock market terms he had already topped out. Just as *Sports Illustrated* covers signal a peaking athletic career, appearing on the covers of *Business Week, Time,* and/or *Newsweek* is a "market" indicator with a remarkable contrarian record. Steinbrenner might have been warned by the boos, Trump by the applause, that irreversible changes were under way.

This seemingly riskless time in the market can come only *after* a sufficiently long rise, during which every little dip, every correction, is repeatedly followed by a further rise until investors begin to believe that such a "safe" pattern is guaranteed to continue. Prior highs are exceeded; the market, like Mr. Trump, starts appearing on the front page of newspapers; television reporters have an excited tone to their voices; down days are expressed as "normal pauses to digest"; individual stocks are up megapoints; and so on. It is precisely at that stage of an uptrend when investors begin to believe they've *got to* own stocks. Indeed, strategists start saying that stocks are better than bonds, certainly better than cash or money market accounts; analysts begin to plug in higher and higher earnings estimates; and technicians raise their targets with every new high in the averages. And the investor who had been unable to listen to the market's language near the lows now joins in heartily; his attitude change is one of the market's most important messages.

But because this "risklessness" comes after a prolonged rise, it is not only a matter of *who* is left to buy, but *what* is left to buy? Almost all stocks except the truly speculative have already been exploited. They are no longer "cheap." Two things happen at this juncture. First, the story changes. Overpriced has to be revalued to "still cheap," even if that means projecting earnings five years hence as if there will be no intervening business cycle during that entire time. Or even if it means, as in Japan's parabolic rise, that Tokyo's stocks were "different." What carried the rise is no longer the key story; a new, and more enormous story is needed, and is created. The market, which has been climbing that proverbial wall of worry, is now going to continue on up forever because it has become the dawn of a new era. Good news abounds, and if it doesn't, everyone will convert seemingly negative news into good. If the Fed tightens, that becomes rationalized as "good," because it will prevent the economy from getting out of hand. After Home Shopping Network soared because it had been undervalued at issuance, the story changed to the notion that the entire nature of shopping was going to change. After the cellular stocks soared, the story changed that the entire nature of telephoning was going to change. The climate becomes Dr. Panglossian. The result is that even those stocks that have already risen to a parabolic extent find fresh buyers.

The other thing that happens is that because so many market leaders are already up, there is a natural t(r)endency to start looking for what's left. A handful of recognizable names have lagged the entire rise and thus seem cheap. Forgetting that the absence of a genuine (that is, knowledgeable) buying interest is a warning that something may be seriously wrong, the unsophisticated seize on such stocks as a chance to get on board without taking the perceived risk of a stock that is already up. A 1989 example was IBM: what a nice stock to buy still down near its postcrash lows, even as it drifted lower. Investors talk turned IBM from its previous role of a good old-growth stock into a "yield" stock paying over 4 percent for the first time, so as to be able to justify putting a lot of idle buying power to work at once. But when it began to look as if the growth was in trouble, they forgot about the yield and dumped.

At the same time, in that search for what's left that is still "cheap," investors switch to lesser names: the tertiary stocks, the low priced, and eventually, the "cats and dogs." Hot tips abound. This phase represents a willingness to ignore risk.

This sentiment, accordingly, represents a form of market language, telling us that the end of the rise is near. A cycle begins with stocks climbing "a wall of worry," and ends when there is no worry anymore. Even after the rise tops out, investors continue to believe that they should buy the dips. A correction during the bull move tends to be sharp enough, and deep enough, to maintain the "wall of worry," to re-create fear that the rise is over. But when it reaches the point when advisers insist that investors should not worry about sell-offs but, rather,

Chart 14
EXAMPLE OF A SIMPLE SENTIMENT CYCLE

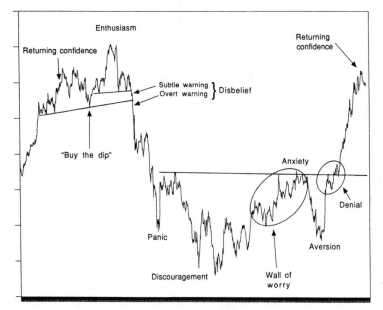

use them for buying, the nature of the correction has changed to becoming the first decline in a new bear market. Unwillingness to believe in that change marks the first phase down: "It's just another buying opportunity." The second, realistic, phase down is the passage from bullish to bearish sentiment as the reasons why stocks are falling become manifest. Selling begins to make sense. It culminates with the third phase: investors, in disgust, decide they don't want to have anything to do with the stock market ever again. They dump right near the eventual low in the conviction that the bad news is never going to stop, that there is going to be worse news tomorrow. They decide, in effect, that there is no longer any risk to selling.

In this manner, we can construct a sentiment cycle.

· 17 ·

Diversification

AS the market proceeds through its sentiment cycle, the very notions that are advocated as protection against undue risk—caution, conservativism, carefulness—actually increase risk.

One of the wonders of modern portfolio management is how consistently professionals hired to manage money actually underperform the averages. (An almost offhand comment in the *Wall Street Journal* noted that investment clubs matched or beat the S&P 500 two-thirds of the time—they're less unwieldy, for one thing—while those paid to do so were successful only 25 percent of the time.) In order to offset this, a huge sum of money has been invested in "index" funds that are designed to mirror the averages precisely. Whatever the S & P 500 (the average customarily used) does, that fund will do, up or down; it can't do better, or worse . . . except for the management fee. But *reducing responsibility is not the same as reducing risk.* Such abandonment is a means of increasing risk. Simply put, the indexer has acquired precisely what he wishes to avoid: the entire risk of being in the stock market at all, because he never cashes in enough of the profit when prices are up, presuming they might go higher. And presuming there will be no crash, he bears the pain when it is down, having used the "index" as a monetary parking garage, subject to having the vehicle banged around and given terrifying rides in the elevator while he isn't watching.

Other portfolio managers, anxious to keep their jobs, will become closet "indexers." They take, say, 90 percent of their funds and surreptitiously mirror the index in the way they structure their managed portfolios, and then try to use the remaining 10 percent to enhance their performance. This avenue leads them to think that since 90 percent is going to perform in line with the market—that is, a controllable performance— then they can be more aggressive with the remaining 10 percent. They take more chances, buy more promiscuously, trade more frequently, keep trying, trying, trying, to come out an eighth ahead.

Others, caring only about relative performance because they are being measured not against the averages but in competition with a similar batch of managers—the "value" league, the "growth" players—will try to play a totally defensive game. They become "specialists" in stocks that have already been battered on the theory that if the stock is already down it won't go down any more—or, that is, won't go down as much as the market will any more. The averages may go down 16 percent, but if such holdings go down only 14 percent—do you believe this logic?—they will have "outperformed"! But while they may be pleased at losing less, the doctor or shopkeeper whose funds these are is out 14 percent of his retirement money.

Why be in the market at all? the world of professional money management is forced, by clients and consultants, to be destructive in its self-imposed restrictions. "Out" is a rarely considered valid alternative. Clients—whether a pension fund, a mutual fund, a wealthy individual, or the like—hire a professional to manage their money. Accordingly, it is directed to be invested. For example, pension fund clients insist they are hiring professionals to be "in" the stock market, and will frequently and gloweringly say, "If I wanted to be in Treasury bills I could do that myself," or "I already have others managing my fixed-income assets; you're hired to be in stocks." Such clients "manage" their money by dispersing it among managers who have had some success specializing: this amount for small stocks, that much to someone who is good at emerging growth, another amount to a manager whose style is the big cap names, and so on. They've learned how to, and computerized systems make it easy to, switch instantly into Treasury bills if that becomes their choice. To avoid losing funds, the manager has a built-in incentive to stay invested. He keeps trying because that's what he is paid to do, while going to the office every day to watch the blinking numbers on the tape makes him feel like there is always something to do, if only he could find it. Thus *being in the market* is a requirement of the professional that others are not burdened with.

Although the public investor doesn't realize it, and is surely counting on the professional to get him out in time, he's riding in the same boat. The money invested in a mutual fund is supposed to be invested . . . even if, and when, the manager of that fund perceptively thinks a bear market is imminent. The unwritten rule is that it is the investor's decision to take his money away and put it under the mattress; if it stays in the fund, he is presumed to want it invested. The innocent public client, of course, doesn't know this, but assumes that the professional has been "hired" to be aware of when to sell as he would not be. Again, this is the thesis of lessening responsibility instead of lessening risk.

Accordingly, there is widespread belief in that magic word *diversification*. Diversification is designed to "spread the risk." "The prudence of not putting all of one's eggs into one basket," the *New York Times* stated unquestioningly while praising the three professors who won the 1990 Nobel prize for economics, "has been understood intuitively for centuries." The professors did, as the *Times* headlined it, produce "Ideas That Changed Wall Street and Fathered Mutual Funds." But while they made investing large sums of money easier, by providing a style and formula that became socially acceptable, the diversification they champion reduces reward in up markets while failing to adequately reduce risk during bear markets. If their approach were successful, would so many money managers so consistently underperform the averages year after year, and most glaringly in bearish years?

To actualize their theories, brokerage firm strategists provide a *de rigeur* diversified model based on the manner in which the S&P Index itself is structured. If oil components account for 17 percent of the index, a "market weighting" would be 17 percent, and the alleged strategists can then tinker with that percentage, raising it to 19 percent, for example, as an "overweighting," as if that 2 percent tidbit will make all the difference in helping the portfolio manager overachieve. (Actually, it *does*, if the comparison is with a rival manager who is market-weighted rather than with our pocketbooks.) Nor does underweighting by 1, 2, or even 3 percent do much for reducing risk if that's all the manager does even though he has accurately perceived something wrong. Ultimately, because there are so many different market sectors to have an opinion about, and to weigh, any manager in this imperfect game is bound to make mistakes. At best, realignments might offset each other; at worst, picture having to hop around frantically trying to decide whether to be over- or underweighted in energy during the wild Kuwaiti war crude-oil price gyrations of up to $40 and down to $18 a barrel. Decisions made to avoid risk can turn out to be loaded with emotional risk-taking.

Having "all your eggs in one basket" is allegedly a dreadfully dangerous idea. You are given no credence for being smart enough to put those eggs in a sensible basket. When it is put in that manner, can you see that diversification is designed to protect the dumb? Don't you have a better chance of being right if you concentrate on picking the best of 20 stocks than if you have to list them in order of weight?

◈◈◈◈ Let's compare two points of view—"their" diversification and "our" charting. Diversification is designed to reduce risk because it believes in the dangers of risk. It attempts to protect by "spreading the risk." But that, of course, assumes a different, unrecognized, risk. Underperformance, continuing vulnerability to undesirable positions, and the passive comfort of behaving properly are its traits.

On the other hand, charting apparently flies in the face of

safety. The effort that it entails to *find* the best places *requires* actually stepping forward and taking a risk. And while doing so, it requires going against what is known in the news world; works best when it defies bad economic news; gloats in opposing the consensus viewpoint heard everywhere, including the *Wall Street Journal* and *New York Times*; and proceeds with a noticeable absence of a comforting reason why. Its main negative is that it is far from perfect, while its main positive is that it helps identify, at reduced-risk prices, which stocks, any and all of which we don't know enough about, ought to work well.

Diversification—whether it is the portfolio manager's stock selection, or the typical public investor buying several different mutual funds—is designed to protect. It makes the risk greater by seeming to reduce it. It is the equivalent in tennis of pushing the ball back over the net so as to make sure it goes in, regardless of what your opponent can then do back to you. Technical work is designed to lessen the risk by actually taking it. It is the investment equivalent of hitting out on all shots, from the first point to the last.

But the risk of listening to the market's language, instead of conventional wisdom, is clear. Like the "bad" boy whose acting up is actually saying "Hug me" even though it looks like "I hate you," market behavior provides no comforting reasons—even, to the contrary, reminds one of continuing reasons to stay away or, at tops, most dangerously and yet most comfortably, in. But underneath that surface are messages that can "tell" us when it is okay to take the risk. In this way, diversification can be a matter of "when"—when to act, when to be patient, when to rise up again—thus diversifying by timing rather than weightings.

◇◆◇◆◇ This reminds me of a professional racetrack bettor I met long ago while I had a job cashing tickets for win, place, show, previous races, and previous days. He supervised the tellers, produced a morning line for bookies, but only occasionally bet his own money—when the odds were in his favor, which happened two or three times a *week*. Among his rules was

"Never bet when there is more than one possible winner of the race, or when the odds on the one standout are too low for the risk of the horse not being perfect either." Thus when he did bet, it was the very definition of putting all his money on one race.

What happens when you diversify is that you inevitably must underperform. As a bull market progresses, it narrows. The history of bull markets involves a slow aging, a deterioration not unlike human aging, in which fewer and fewer stocks actually keep up with the averages. Some aging processes end with a speculative flurry—hot dogs and cats become the market equivalent of an old farmer running off with a honky-tonk waitress, while others end with a flight to the wheelchair of blue chips. Diversification inevitably results in the portfolio owning stagnant positions: stocks and groups that may have participated during the early stages of the rise, when breadth is best. But in the late stages too many stocks have begun to lag, and you'll own them, waiting in vain for them to participate again. In order to be diversified, you'll have a smidgin of aerospace— at the wrong time in its cycle; you'll own an "underweighting in technology," but what you do own is still getting clobbered along with the whole group; you'll have a "market weighting" in the consumer groups, when cyclicals are all the rage. And so on. *Diversification requires you by its very nature to own some stocks that are not doing very well, relative to the averages.* Thus you must underperform those averages.

How do you beat the averages? By taking the risk of your own perceptions. By betting that you are smart enough, clever enough, experienced enough, to perceive which few groups— perhaps even which one basket to put all your eggs into—will do better than the rest. Rather than trying to cushion your portfolio with the market equivalent of working for a pension instead of a partnership, you try to load up on what looks like a winner or two or three.

But the wisdom of the ages is against you. Everyone says: "Diversify." So let me ask the question again. "How can you win if you diversify?" Has there ever been a market in which everything was terrific? And if there has not, then what diversifying calls for

Chart 15
MODEL EQUITY PORTFOLIO*

	S&P Market Weightings	Current Portfolio Weighting		S&P Market Weightings	Current Portfolio Weighting
Building—Credit Cyclicals	.86%	.5%	**Capital Goods—Technology**	10.52%	13%
Building Materials	.50		Electronics—Semiconductors	.81	=
Mobile Homes	.03	=	Electronics—Instrumentation	.08	=
Home Builders	.03	=	Information Processing: Systems	5.14	+
Savings & Loans	.17	=	Personal Computer/Workstations	.00	+
Hardware & Tools	.14		Telecommunications	1.02	+
Financial	8.44%	4.5%	Aerospace/Defense	2.16	-
Life Insurance	.25	-	Electronic Equipment	.41	+
Casualty Insurance	.45	=	Misc Capital Goods—Tech.	.90	=
Multi-Line Insurance/Misc.	2.01	-	**Capital Goods—Industrial**	6.89%	8.0%
Banks—Money Center	.81	=	Major Electrical Equipment	3.02	= ↓
Banks—Ex New York City	1.56	=	Machine Tools	.02	+
Finance Services	.18	=	Machinery—Agricultural	.18	+
Misc. Finance	1.19	=	Machinery—Constr. Contract/Mat. Handling	.42	=
REIT and Related	.00	-	Machinery—Inds/Specialty	.66	=
Consumer Growth Staples	18.61%	11.5%	Heavy Duty Truck & Auto Parts	.21	+
Drugs	6.82	=	Pollution Control	1.16	+
Medical Products & Supplies	2.70	+	Conglomerates	1.17	=
Hospital Management	.46	+	Misc. Cap Goods	.05	+
Managed Health Care	.00	+	**Energy**	15.09%	19.0%
Restaurants	.53	+	Oil Well Equipment & Services	1.36	+
Retail—Drug Stores	.25	-	Oil—International Integrated	8.18	+
Retail Specialty	1.16	=	Oil—Domestic Integrated	4.62	+
Cosmetics	.59	-	Oil & Gas Products	.12	+
Soft Drinks	2.25	-	Natural Gas Diversified	.66	+
Entertainment	.96	-	Coal	.08	+
Broadcasting—Radio & TV	.73	-	Misc Energy	.05	+
Publishing—Newspapers	.75	+	**Basic Industries**	6.88%	6.5%
Publishing & Printing	1.07	+	Paper & Forest Products	1.60	-
Consumer Defensive Staples	10.57%	10.0%	Cement	.00	=
Household Products	2.34	+	Containers	.10	=
Tobacco	2.68	+	Chemicals	2.22	-
Food Retailers	.91	=	Specialty Chemicals	1.12	=
Foods	3.62	=	Fertilizers	.07	+
Beverages—Brewers & Distillers	.97	=	Aluminum	.59	-
Consumer Cyclicals	7.13%	4.0%	Non-Ferrous Metals (ex. Aluminum)	.54	+
Durables			Steel	.22	=
Auto	1.87	-	Gold Mining	.32	=
Auto Parts—After Market	.27	=	**Transportation**	1.66%	2.0%
Appliances/Furnishings	.33	-	Air Transport	.43	=
Photography	.69	-	Railroads	.99	+
Leisure Time	.06	-	Truckers	.12	+
Misc. Consumer Cyclical	.27	-	Misc. Transportation	.13	+
Non-Durable			**Utilities**	15.34%	21.0%
Retail—Dept. Stores	.59	=	Communication	9.00	+
Retail—Mass Merchandising Stores	2.55	-	Electric	5.51	+
Textile—Apparel & Products	.21	-	Gas Pipeline	.83	+
Lodging	.12	-			
Footwear	.17	-			

Note: Market Weightings as of 10/31/90.   ↑↓ Indicates all weighting changes since last published Model Equity Portfolio.

Industry rankings denoted as 0.0 (ex. REIT and PC/Workstations) are non-S&P categories. Industry totals do not equal 100% due to the exclusion of miscellaneous categories. Cement, a non-S&P industry for which we have a model was added to Basic Industries. Copper and Misc. Metals have been consolidated into one category called Non-Ferrous Metals (ex Aluminum).

*Courtesy Merrill Lynch

is owning something less than terrific, and perhaps merely luke-warm. Will its time come? if so, let me own it then, not now. Has it already been strong? then let me admit that I've missed it, and look elsewhere. "Where is the best place for my money to be?"—which sounds like a perfectly sensible question—shows how fraudulent the policy of diversification is.

There is nothing wrong with being a different kind of player, one geared to being slow and steady rather than aggressive. Our argument is not with the tortoise but with the fool. To willingly hold positions in stocks that are not going up, are going up less than other stocks, or are even going down while others are going up, all in the name of "diversification," is to deliberately try to lose.

◈◈◈◈ Should I own something different, as a hedge? Might I not at least be able to index market swings? Such other questions should be considered in this pursuit of trying to ameliorate risk. After all, one does buy insurance in real life, not to prevent the accident but to make its occurrence less monetarily painful.

One might, for example, own some gold "just in case." I don't know what that case might be, though. If I thought I was capable enough of identifying the oils, when they were ready to be bought, then I ought to be capable of similarly identifying a change in trend for gold. If that "just in case" implies something might go wrong with the market, well, it has, without benefiting gold—see the crash of 1987. If that "just in case" means inflation, surely that is no overnight development. So I'm not convinced that a gold hedge is anything more than a diversification device, couched in the scary terms that gold invokes. It is when gold itself is the egg that belongs in the basket that you buy it.

What about buying puts along the way, or, more intensely, buying puts when one gets into a seemingly vulnerable market climate? Well, there are two problems: (1) By buying puts, you need never consider selling stocks that should be sold in that acknowledged vulnerable climate. If it is a "just in case" alternative, it isn't a hedge, it's a guess. If the market moment isn't magnified enough to warrant selling stocks, then puts, which are so time-oriented that imminence is needed for them to work, are the wrong choice. Sell stop orders would be a sounder strategy. (2) The buyer of puts—as described in chapter 16—is increasingly thrilled that he has hedged his portfolio so cleverly that when the market sell-off is nearing its end he is at his most boastful. Thus it never occurs to him to cash in the puts for the profit—because he planned on them as a hedge rather than a trade—with the result that the market then rallies, while the time problem of his puts goes against him; they expire worthless and the entire hedge, as right as he was, has done him no good whatsoever, except for having been able to boast to his buddies. Owning puts, in fact, encourages such an investor to ignore what the market is doing because he is "hedged."

Derivative products *can* be helpful, if used aggressively on a day-by-day trading basis to offset the difficulties of buying and selling big individual stock positions and, of course, to help atone for unwieldy positions during serious declines. But the very people who could benefit the most from trading such products are those who are locked into longer-term mind-sets. Perhaps the only practical answer for those who describe their portfolio problems as "it takes so long to turn the Queen Mary around" is to use options and indexes as tugs—instead of remaining dead in the water.

How about writing calls against one's position? As a style, this strategy has the virtue of producing an increased return on one's investment. But as a risk-reduction vehicle in which one doesn't expect to get called, it has the flaw of locking in one's equity position at precisely those times when serious selling might be the much wiser course. Better to be out entirely than to hold a declining stock so as to profit by having written calls that expire worthless, enabling you to pocket the entire premium. It works, *until the period of greatest market risk.*

More usefully, it is worth noting that professionals who manage options money don't play the game that way. They write calls against positions as *a strategy that works best* not when the call expires worthless but *the sooner the stock is called away from them.* They have thus sold the stock at a higher price (including the premium written); the sooner that happens, the greater their annualized return on the investment, and the sooner another call can be written. A premium expiring worthless is less desirable because of the stock's vulnerability while waiting. It may seem to work when the stock has remained in a limited trading range, but sooner or later a fluctuation is going to go against you. Thus these managers also have to concern themselves with market trends. Writing calls in a bear trend is *not* capital enhancing.

In that same vein, the great personal disasters of the 1987 crash came to naive investors whose brokers persuaded them that writing puts was a surefire way to make easy money. The puts were supposed to expire worthless because the bull market was going to take stocks up another 1000 points or more. They had the 1000 points right, but not the direction, so that anyone who had written a put, for example, on a stock at 40, so as to pocket the $2 or $3 premium, suddenly found the stock selling at 18, the put being exercised, and his loss being $2,200—less, of course, the $200 or $300 he'd "earned." Of course, that's a lesson in thinking easy money can be found on Wall Street, as well as about writing naked options in the belief that the trend will never change.

The concept of shorting stocks against the box is so futile that it warrants only the comment that if you even think of doing so as a means of reducing risk, you should simply sell the stock outright.

Does the defensive positioning of battered stocks work? If one buys down-and-out stocks, can it pay off as a means of reducing risk? not really. A defensive posture is little more than guessing at the bottom. "Hasn't the stock come down far enough?" they ask. "Isn't this where the stock held before?" Yes; maybe; possibly; perhaps. Even if the bargain-hunting guess is right, a considerable amount of patience is then required. And even if *that* is tolerable, it is unnecessary. That commonly heard brokerage recommendation, "We love it long term, but over the short term it is likely to go down," exposes how foolish it is not to test your patience on the sidelines rather than, painfully, after you buy it. Even for longer-term investors, a sense of imminence is vital.

It is possible to buy bad news—indeed, it's a great style, but *not by guessing* when the stock is down enough. There is no such price as "enough"; market language speaks of "excesses" instead. *The market itself is capable of reporting when a stock is no longer weak, and it is no crime to pay up for that proof.* What we are proposing—a style of buying stocks that confronts the risk positively—is not much different . . . *except that* our interest *requires waiting* until the stock has not only ceased declining but has also proven to us that it can actually go up. That this happens *before* corporate news overtly improves means that although we won't be buying at the bottom eighth, applying this approach will be early enough.

One rule of thumb in the market is the same as the old cliché about life: the rich get richer and the poor get poorer. In the stock market, the rule is that strong stocks get stronger, while the weak get weaker. In a bear market, of course, even strong stocks go down, but they should go down less than the market. In a bull market, weak stocks continue to go down (or at best go nowhere) because something is basically wrong. Weak can be revealed in various ways: the stock was easy to buy at a better price than you expected to have to pay; that it fails to rise on days when the DJIA is going up; that it is recommended all over the Street, but still doesn't go up; that it pays an alluring dividend, but one so high it has to be questioned as to the company's ability to maintain it. All the known virtues provide ready-made excuses, yet the stock limps upward. Will it get livelier tomorrow? perhaps, but the market's message is telling you the stock is "weak." All this may seem petty, but remember that *the infinite god of the details of the surface is the technician's god.*

Compare two computer stocks: Compaq went to a new high in the spring and summer of 1990, while during the same period, although the market, too, raced to its own new high, Unisys broke badly to another new low. Had you bought Compaq in April or May around 50 because of its strength, you'd have had a loss of about 30 percent the following October at the Middle East crisis bottom. The "war" rally in early 1991 took Compaq back up to 74, and you'd have been well ahead for a while. (CPQ then proceeded to make one of the great "easy-to-see" tops in charting history, but that's another story.) Had you bought Unisys that spring instead, because it had been trading at around 15 (at less than half its peak it seemed like a bargain), you'd have ridden it down to under 3, and waited in vain for it ever to come back. Thus the danger is that even in a roaring bull market buying a stock that has been relatively weak does not necessarily mean that it can't, or won't, go down even further. *Weak action is a risk-increaser*, not a bargain-producer.

Go back and review the pages in chapter 2 describing the sequence of Travelers Insurance. Compare that action with the way Unisys—despite the announcements of similar dire news—tumbled and then did *not* rebound. *That* is why it is preferable to wait for the test of the low rather than to try to guess at the bottom itself. You learn—the market tells you— that Travelers was okay to buy, but that Unisys wasn't. Sometimes the market tells you even more: the same week as the Travelers writeoff also produced dire-sounding announcements by General Motors and Monsanto—each followed by the stock going up, not down. These were the first instances of stocks holding in the face of bad news since the entire 550-point downtrend had begun. Thus their resistant/rising action served as a subtle market indicator, too, reporting on a change in the underlying tone after three months of relentless decline—call it soldoutness, if you will, or belief reborn, but this sort of resistance to bad news is a necessary ingredient to identifying important bottoms.

If we want to buy down-and-out stocks we must wait for the market to tell us the risk has gone out of the stock, and the way we learn that is when the stock refuses to go down any more on bad news. You don't guess, estimate, daydream; you don't need to rely on faith, hope, or charity; you can *wait* for the market to tell you. It is worth repeating yet again, that for those with patience, *this is the least risky long-term style of buying stocks.*

You see, there *are* things you do know. When your broker phones with a recommendation, and you ask, "If it's so good, why isn't it up already?" you are expressing something *you* *know* about the market/stock—its lack—that the broker doesn't seem to know, or if known, doesn't seem to understand, or wants to deny. And if the stock is already up, the question must be, "Why should it go up any more? Who is left to buy it but me?" What you do know isn't everything; it isn't clear; it doesn't make the decision easy. It may only be knowing which questions to ask. But it helps. So how come you think you don't know anything compared to the broker?

There are, of course, examples of how even those who understand nothing of the workings of the stock market know something useful—the employee who can see how the loading dock has begun to bustle after a long period of workers sitting around idly; or who sees all those U.S. Steel airplanes landing at the little Marathon, Ohio, airfield. It's fascinating to hear of people who know about "one plus one" but who didn't add it up to "do." And then there are the innocent. To be so naive as to buy stock in a gold mine peddled by a salesman they've never met, via phone from thousands of miles away—and then to equate this with investing—is the market equivalent of blithely leaping on a grenade because they've been brought up to believe it is the American thing to do. It is not heroic to be a fool.

❖❖❖❖ On the other hand, what would happen if you did know everything? It would be perfect. But that is no more true of life than of the stock market. *Both are tests that never end.* Not even fortune tellers can help, or fortunes. Ask the Hunt brothers; you cannot win by trying to buy out the risk. You cannot win by tempering the risk, dodging the risk, laying off the risk. What's scary about confronting risk is having to depend on what you do know. The more "normal" response is to back off, to accept, to say, "The market can't be timed" or "Who knows what the market is going to do?" And yet, the outcome of doing is much more likely to reward than the shrug style—it turns out that, although scary, there is actually less risk in being decisive. *Making the strong, rather than the careful, decision is risk-reducing.*

But it is not, you see, that the risk is reduced in your mind beforehand. When you are confronting the decision—whether it is to buy a stock or a house, whether it is to stay with the same job or to leap out on one's own—the risk looms. Let's pick on the market again for an example, although the accumulation of lists of all the reasons why, and why not, occur in those daily life circumstances as well. Here we are with several head and shoulders bottoms, let's say; they've appeared, to your surprise, while every day's front page has become a succession of gloomy economic details. Today's headline reads: "No Hope for Any Rebound Soon." But there are those stocks that in this environment aren't supposed to but do qualify as buyable; they don't go down any more while the DJIA does; don't go down even though they've reported lower earnings. You want to buy but you feel as if you should wait and watch some more, just to be sure. Then, whoops, the market is up 40 points one day, 55 points the next. *You should have bought*, you think, but now emotions rule: the price is running, you're frantic, but . . . so you decide to wait for a pullback because you can't bear to pay such high prices when you could've bought them so well. Or you can't stand it anymore, so you buy and make the top tick.

Consider how big that risk of waiting proved to be, how treacherous making decisions under the emotional pressure of rising prices. Compare it with the risk of acting "too soon." You buy, knowing—*because* you're scared—that this is a fragile moment. So you pay closer attention; you are more sensitive to the possibility that your stocks may do something wrong; you won't tolerate their failures the way you might if you had a huge gain and had gotten overconfident. In sum, you are alert, *alive*, as you step forward. By proceeding in a freeing, rather than constricting, manner, you have actually reduced the risk twice: as to a better "price," and then, by having avoided getting caught up in "under the gun" emotions. You *do* what you yearn to believe in. I use the word *freedom*, but others would say: *if you go for the reward* rather than protecting yourself against the risk.

Oddly enough, you have learned to do this already when crossing the street. Unless you are being careless (or unless you are the fool who rushes thoughtlessly to the other side because

you thought you saw a piece of green paper in the gutter there),
you factor in all the available information—and do not hesitate
or wait for more before proceeding. When you are at the corner,
you know enough to adhere to the traffic-light messages because they reduce the risk of crossing at *that* juncture. Even so,
you instinctively look to make sure, but that glance does not
slow you up—unless, of course, you sense or catch a glimpse of
danger coming around the corner. And then, when you cross,
you proceed with the freedom that experience and knowledge
of crossing with the light have given you.

And if there is no traffic light, if you are crossing in the middle of the block . . . you also know (while understanding that
the risk has increased) how to proceed. You've seen enough nervous nellies get stuck, panic-stricken, out in the road to know
that decisiveness is less risky. You may even have to make the
"strong" effort (running across) if—*because*—the goal is that
important to reach or, of course, to correct a miscalculation, or
to flee from unexpected danger. In sum, you have learned how
to reduce the risk by acting with the reward of the other side in
sight, even though the danger of crossing is always there.

Somehow, growing up, you've gotten free enough to cross the
street. This "freedom" can be abused by trying to dash across
ahead of an oncoming ten-wheeler; it can be denied, especially
as one reaches retirement age, by timidly proceeding. It can be
used unnecessarily, when there is no rush to be somewhere else
or real need to get across. But in its most positive form, it enables you to take that risk because you are in control. In control
of what? of yourself. *That* freedom produces reward.

· 18 ·

Listening

THE way to get the market to do what you want it to do is simple. You listen to what the market is telling you it wants to do—and then announce that *that* is what you expect the market to do. Jiggles, tinkering, diversions, and deceptions aside, you'll be amazed at how close you'll come (especially after those deceptions have led you to give up expecting it to happen).

There's a Sesame Street skit in which Big Bird leans over Ernestine's baby carriage and carries on a conversation with her goo-goos and walla-wallas. When asked if he really can understand Ernestine's baby talk, Big Bird admits that he can't; what he's doing, he explains, is figuring out what she *would* ask and answering those questions. When a toddler whines, is it hunger, or tiredness, or discomfort? but always something we aren't quite sure of. When a child fusses for attention, isn't that "language" because he or she *needs* attention? although we may not know why. Are we therefore to stubbornly refuse to listen, just because we feel the child shouldn't be hungry, or should have eaten its spinach so it wouldn't be hungry, or has no right to interrupt what we're doing just because of a selfish craving for attention?

A similar simple example is the dog that, having been trained, scratches at the front door to be let out, or pulls the leash down with its teeth and drags it over to you. You respond, as if the leash is a "stop loss" signal, because *you've* learned the consequences of ignoring such a message! Sense of risk stems from how we view, how we listen, how we respond—to whatever is presented to us in whatever language form of communication it takes.

Thus, a herd of 20-wheelers thundering by can make crossing the street a big risk to those who wouldn't dream of parachuting as a Sunday afternoon sport. But if they had to bail out of a plane on fire, that leap would suddenly become an acceptable risk.

◇•◇•◇•◇ With that in mind, let's see what the market tells us . . . and what it doesn't.

Despite constant flare-ups into emotional patterns, our primary function is thinking, and our language is as rational as possible, so as to express those thoughts. Then along comes the market, seemingly perverse, contradictory, complex, "talking" in a manner designed to fool us. The market, more than any of the old, stale jokes about women, is allowed to change its mind. We've already discussed how the market tells us, in its own more sensory, less clear language, when a change in trend is developing. Its "words" are often so contrary to what we expect, or want to believe, that it is accused—by professors and public alike—of being unfathomable. And yet it is precisely *when* market language is reporting on change, on failures, on patterns that contradict the consensus, that it is most important to listen.

Maybe humans and the market are thinking and talking about different things. That is, it might be argued that what the market is actually reporting on, in its *sensory* manner, is an accumulation of what are, indeed, *rational* (that is, human) decisions to buy and sell. For example, when everyone has become bullish, everyone has already bought—and thus the market's language is accurately reporting "bullishness" in its own way, which is that "no more buyers are left, so sell," precisely when investors are intellectually convinced that their decisions, on the evidence, are correct. Similarly, when everyone has already sold, a vacuum of sellers has been left overhead virtually simultaneously with an extreme of bearishness, so that the mere beginnings of buying can start a reversal, unimpeded, to the up-side. In this way, the market's language is of those extremes, while the "thinking" stock market player has become imbued with this bullish or that bearish point of view, so much so that such an investor is too convinced to think anymore at all. Rational decisions (collectively) have taken the market to the point at which the investor becomes locked in emotionally. If you have lately sold, a couch-analyst would say, you are inclined to view everything negatively. Hence the wall of worry that arises during the early phases of a new bull market.

This can perhaps best be understood by looking at an oddity of the commodity markets. In March, for example, they are already trading the December corn or soybeans contract—before anything has been planted! The contract is pure . . . nothing can affect it, not drought or rain, or insects, or over- or underplantings, *because nothing has happened yet.* Thus the price action is a pure intellectual/emotional exercise. Indeed, this seemingly abstract price action actually affects the very things that are supposed to affect price: whether to plant more or less, whether to buy a new tractor or not.

Think what that means: both the buyer and the seller of the December contract must base their decisions on what they know about things they don't know. They take the risk based not on information but on opinions based on what has already happened. It is the market language that speaks to them about what to do, even though they might call it "news" so as not to be tarred with the technician's application of what has already happened. In the market, everything is risk, not because disaster lies ahead at the very next minute (or euphoria, for that matter), but because change can begin at any time. Thus we are not talking about interpreting the news, or being surprised by it—because we are not dealing with the news itself—but *believing* what the market is saying *when* it says it. Put that way, market risk is not risk at all, but choice.

◆◆◆◆ *The market speaks in ticks.* That makes what it says seem extremely short term in nature, but that's not really the case. Everything is short term in the marketplace *when* it takes place. The portfolio manager who insists he is a long-term investor, with a three-to-five-year outlook, nevertheless needs to understand what is going on each day, and eventually needs to narrow down to a day at a time any changes the market might begin to tell him to make. His so-called long-term point of view means he should require much more evidence of change before acting than the in-and-out trader, but it doesn't mean letting market life pass him by.

Since the market is always "talking," it is important to understand that the anticipatory aspect is ours, not the market's, our conclusions from the ticks. We can watch all the active corn contracts to see what the market is telling us might be the best thing to do about the December contract (or about whether to buy that tractor), but what we are watching is current behavior. Someone's ticks cumulatively form tops or bottoms, and thus can be "read"—again, cumulatively—as anticipating falls or rises. And we can anticipate that an individual stock "should" rise to 40, or fall to 25, and then, if the stock doesn't, or can't, or exceeds, we "learn" that there's been a change of message. In one way or another, the language of the message is "failure." The stock gets to 38, and then has a normal pullback; when it comes on again, we would expect it to achieve our 40 target— but while we wait and watch it gets only to 37, struggles, turns down again. Another example might be spotting the development of a very potent-looking head and shoulders bottom. The stock comes riproaring up across the neckline and we grin—but then we notice that the volume has been mediocre at best, that the stock does go up a point at first, but closes the day up only half a point, and there's no follow-through the next morning. The message has changed from potent to fizzling. To continue the analogy with the December "intellectual" contract, the news can't affect judgment because there is no news; it is the market behavior of other contracts that is the message. The only way "why?" can be answered is in relation to the market's language of "what?" Sometimes the language is what is happening, at other times it is akin to the Sherlock Holmes story about the dog that didn't bark—what doesn't happen is significant, even though, eventually, it isn't until after it doesn't happen that you learn it hasn't happened. Again, dear Watsons, understanding the market is a matter of *believing.*

◇◈◇◈◇ How are you going to have an opinion about the December contract, unless you know the message of the marketplace? When nothing has happened yet, no seed planted, when the Fed meets tomorrow, OPEC meets next week, and there's a G7 meeting next month, what do you know except what the market knows? No wonder fundamental analysts want to see two more "real" quarterly earnings reports before believing in what the market is "saying" will happen. Ticks— that is, the trades as they occur—are the heartbeats of any market's trend. We can dance around other aspects of market analysis all we want—trying to measure sentiment, for example, or trying to figure out whether the Fed is going to tighten—but the net is that anyone, everyone, who has an opinion, who knows something, who has analyzed, usefully or foolishly, a company, or who is influenced by someone who has, or who is simply following the trend of the moment, must act in the marketplace in order to attempt to benefit by that knowledge/opinion. In the stock market, that act—the buy or sell order—is reported as a transaction on the tape (now consolidated to encompass other markets as well as what happens on the floor of the NYSE), or via similar reporting messages for the Amex and NASDAQ marketplaces. This "tick" may indeed be as minuscule as the grain of sand on the beach, may, indeed, get washed away to be replaced by others, but, similarly, the grains have their cumulative effect: they make a beach. That "tick" may be initiated by a clever trader, an experienced investor—or a simpleton. Some are "right," others "wrong." There can be beginner's luck; a seasoned pro can blow one badly. No wonder it isn't easy.

So we have to keep the contradictions and inconsistencies in mind even as we begin by trying to "hear" the message of the ticks. Obviously, that doesn't mean watching the tape all day every day. Even professional traders from the good old days

don't need to do that (although watching the opening and closing is useful, while lunchtime is the least important and most
likely to be deceptive). The day's ticks are summarized in the
newspaper tables of high, low, and closing price. Volume, an
important part of the message, comes with the day's price
range. Thus the newspaper's listing, and the chart you can make
of it, is an *objective and accurate* summary of the day's market
action.

(In this regard, don't try to chart too many individual stocks
at once, or you'll get frustratingly behind. Try to use semiloga-
rithmic [rather than arithmetic] paper if you can, because the
patterns and trend lines are more reliable and consistent when
percentage moves are being recorded, and if you have a software
program that can recall for you the high, low, close, and volume
of the stocks you are charting, it'll speed things up immensely.
It should take you no more than three or four weeks to get the
rhythm of doing it quickly and easily, and you can add names
thereafter. Start with several of the market leaders and most
active stocks: General Motors, IBM, Merck, Fannie Mae, Phillip
Morris, Deere, Dow, and the like, so you will get market messages from key stocks as well as individual buy and sell signals.
Don't worry about being brilliant at first; it takes several
months for a chart to become readable, while you are learning
the language of what your pencil is feeling.)

This graphic representation of the stock's (or the market's)
ticks is the core of the market's language. To cite the cliché, *it is
what people are doing, not what they are saying.* In this modern age, the message can be presented to us in several different
ways: (1) You can ask a machine, because certain software programs are capable, with varying degrees of sophistication, of
putting a chart up on the screen for you to analyze. To utilize
this, you have to know, of course, which stock (or average) you
want to ask about. That therefore excludes all the potentially
profitable things going on in all other stocks, and provides no
means of discovering which ones they are or what they are saying that might be different from the chart you asked about. You
have imposed your own limited human knowledge at precisely

the moment when you want an expansively conversational market to talk to you. (Indeed, many software programs admit that what they are showing you is insufficient because at the bottom of the screen they also supply additional readings of such abstractions as RSI and/or Stochastics—trying to define *momentary* swings with mathematical (read magical) formulas.

(2) You can subscribe to, and scrutinize, the various chart services that supply entire books of charts. In this way you have the useful universe in front of you. Browsing through such chart books can provide a sense of what the general run of stock looks like at that particular time, as well as identifying this or that particular stock that you hadn't noticed before. Keep in mind that skimming is superficial; peruse slowly and thoughtfully, not casually; otherwise you will come to believe you know enough, and then blame the charts.

However, (3) once you have developed a more than cursory approach to chart reading, it is certainly helpful to have a subscription to such chart services (for example, *Daily Graphs, Mansfield, Trendline*). None of us can keep our own charts of every stock, so a service available to look up any stock (such as one which has just appeared on the new high list) is handy to have. But *there is no substitute for doing your own charts.*

You may not believe this, or want to accept it in this computerized era, but once you start to keep even a handful of charts yourself you'll see (and feel) the difference. The very nature of how the stock is behaving rises to the surface via your pencil's posting the volume and the pattern. Of course, it's not perfect; it isn't even close to perfect. Sort of like Churchill's backhanded compliment about capitalism, *it's just better than anything else, and certainly better than nothing.* What happens is that the market "talks" to you as the language of its ticks becomes recordable on your chart paper. Keeping your own charts is the way the market's language can be heard most directly. To paraphrase a more important statement: All the rest of technical analysis is commentary.

Charts do *not* reduce risk. They turn what seems like risk into the reality of choices. This can be applied most directly to the stock market, but something similar ought to help identify consistent behavioral patterns: what you eat and when you eat it, for example, or how TV might be affecting your child's bedtime behavior, or how you cross the street. Charts are simply a way to accumulate and express, and perhaps act on, perceivable information. Women keep track of their menstrual cycles for baby or not-baby opportunities. Dieters would recognize a pattern of excessive calories at particular times. If you saw how often you crossed in the middle of the block every day, and noted blips at the start and end of the business day showing on the "chart" that you raced across, it might then occur to you that your risks were increased at those times, and you'd wonder whether such sprinting was necessary.

Stock charts provide the same sort of message—they plot the sequences of activity to see if/when patterns will emerge. Not every stock "speaks" at the same time, although those rare times when an increasing number do reveal similar patterns are treats for a chartist, for that accumulation of similarities has its own message of an important development in the market's *overall* trend. You've probably heard many of the personalized names attached to what we identify as patterns—the head and shoulders, for example—but *all useful bar-chart patterns have at their root something as simple as a trend line.*

For example, a head and shoulders top breaks down into a trend line drawn from the head to the top of the right shoulder, for a downtrend line. The neckline of the pattern is an obvious trend line. Putting the two together would identify what otherwise would be called a decending triangle within the overall head and shoulders top. In November 1990, a bottoming pattern developed in the Dow Industrials that within a reverse head and shoulders could be seen a symmetrical triangle. No matter what you call it, breaking one or the other of those trend lines becomes the message of a changing trend.

It is not the purpose here to discuss in craftsman's terms the details of this or other identifiable chart patterns. Our point is the message of the trends. Some lines have no pattern associated with them, but depict a sequence of higher lows—an uptrend line—or lower highs—a downtrend line—and it just so happens that the sequence is often so neat that one line connects those sequences. Use as a rule that two points make the line; a third point touching validates the line and establishes its importance. Trends mean exactly that—a definition of direction. The lines themselves become undeniable behavioral messages—that the kid is crying must mean "something." The market, like life itself, is never so simple as to present black and white patterns, so listening to its messages requires an objective ear. One cannot—should not—damn well better not—deny in ostrichlike fashion the existence of, and then the breaking of, a trend line . . . because such a trend line is the objective factor of the moment. It is denial that increases risk. And *it is objectivity that keeps risk from being its dictionary definition of danger and turns it into choice* instead.

The market is capable of "talking" to you in either direction—it has no emotional prejudices, couldn't care less about up or down. The useful indicators—internal (advance/decline and highs/lows); sentiment (put/call ratio and bull/bear numbers); monetary (bond and dollar charts)—combine with the chart patterns of individual stocks to provide messages of important market turns in *either* direction. We are not here just talking about loss. The denial of the message may mean missing a profitable opportunity as well.

Bottoms can be identified by almost everyone when they consist of an extensive, prolonged sideways movement after a steep fall. But sheer sidewaysness is not sufficient. They are *not* bases when seen in the context of a stock that has gone sideways (read "nowhere") while the rest of the market has been rising, although after the market has been rising for a long time, such laggards are easy to believe in. Bucket shop stories of how the innocent are seduced are rooted in such climates—a fast-talking salesman can make such a story sound safe as well as super. Interestingly, however, the great bottoms are always denied; even the most perceptive broker can't get an order.

Bases, like our daily lives, are best when they are liveliest. Dynamic swings forecast dynamic moves thereafter. What's more, the best stocks bottom first, ahead of the crowd, ahead of the averages, so that although the market is whispering to us that they have begun to show relative strength, *such bases are obviously much harder to believe in.* The laggard is "buyable" because the already-rising market has confirmed the safeness; the precursor is "dangerous" because the still-falling market makes its improvement incredible.

Examples abound as I write this. Consider the simple triangular base that developed in Digital Equipment during the fall of 1990—the period of buildup for the Persian Gulf war. There were some terrific stocks that actually made their lows in August, but DEC didn't reach its low until October, along with the Dow Jones Industrial Average itself. It never went lower— forming a triangle rather than a head and shoulders pattern— and broke out on the upside of that triangle in early December. Scoffed at, disbelieved, when it had a "normal" pullback to the breakout level in early January, fundamentalists became convinced that bad news was mounting. Actually, Digital was doing well in the face of whatever negative announcements it made; overall, the stock showed three successively higher lows. Thus it was in great shape to soar, as soon as the market did.

Compare this to the chart of the DJIA itself. You can see the persistent disbelief as a major head and shoulders bottom formed. (See Chart 16.) Short selling increased, to the point where mainstream articles were being written about staid institutions turning to the short side—in December, at right-shoulder time! The emotional content of the marketplace was aversion to stocks. Thus when the upside breakout came with such dynamic and persistent strength, it took many days and a few hundred points before the bearishness was converted. As the Dow neared 3000 again, latecomers were chasing Digital, and stocks like it, up another 15 to 20 percent, while the previously hated stocks, such as the New York City banks, were up 50 percent.

Since human nature prefers to be bullish, once stocks have risen long enough and far enough to tear down "the wall of worry," then optimism begins to intensify; it becomes increas-

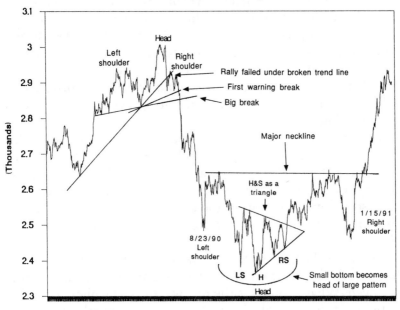

Chart 16
DJIA HOURLY
April 1990—February 1991

ingly easy to believe. Thus when a toppy formation appears, investors don't want to believe in it, partly out of fear of going contrary to the apparent evidence (as is also the case at bottoms), but even more so because a top is too "awful" to accept, much like the denial of a wife who has been told—with increasing evidence—that her husband has not been "working late at the office" after all.

◇◆◇◆◇ In *When to Sell*, I wrote about an "ideal" time to sell. This consists of a top formation followed by the breakdown that announces that the top has been completed and that the trend has *officially* changed from up to down. Such a top needs to be big enough to affect the long-term moving average line as the lower prices cause it to start rolling over and also head downward. As part of the market's characteristic fluctuations, there is then a rebound up toward the level at which the breakdown occurred. Since, by then, the long-term moving average line has had sufficient time to also head down, the pull-back runs into two roadblocks virtually simultaneously: the resistance at the top (at the neckline of the pattern, if you will) and the now downtrending moving average line, which is also formidable resistance. *That* juncture proves to be the "ideal" time to sell. Why? *because it is believable!* you've seen the breakdown, you are getting the bounce-back opportunity to sell, the twin resistance roadblocks tell you where. So why don't people believe?

The chart itself is objective. That's all it is: just a graphic record of the day's, or week's, trading. Successful businessmen who have their aides prepare all sorts of audiovisual displays when they give a presentation at a meeting never connect what they so willingly rely on in their own work with what depicts the same sort of thing for the stock market. So why can't they believe?

The same lack of belief occurs at bottoms as at tops. The bigger—the longer it takes—the more important—*the less it is believed.* What happens is the renewal of risk: while the market is trending downward, the acceptance that something's wrong gradually grows; similarly, the more the market trends upward, the more the wall of worry comes down and the rise is accepted. That environment of lessening risk then becomes what is familiar. What is the "norm"? To consider a change of trend is not much different from considering a change in one's own body: it goes on and on familiarly, so much so we scarcely consider it at all, so that when there is a change in "trend," bleeding in a stool, lump in the breast, *there is an enormous rejection of that revelation.* The danger comes from not listening.

And yet the risk has become greater.

· 19 ·

The Nature of Risk II

WH E N we say someone is "lifeless," when we remark of certain kinds of work that it is "boring" or "dull," one meaning is an absence of risk. The presence of risk often equals feeling alive—midlife crises as an out-of-control way to revive life, or the moment-to-moment excitement of pulling the handle on a slot machine. It may even be that when we discover something potentially life-threatening, the risk of facing such a fact can lead to a paunchy puffing defiant "I'll show 'em that I can live." Training, practice, and growing up are efforts along the way to understand what risk is. Conventional classroom teaching is often an attempt to control potentially risky behavior, while manners, for example, or laws, are attempts to define behavior as *justifiable* risk.

But the word *justifiable* throws the notion of risk awry. Once risk is justified rationally, it has gone past some level of risk itself. Justifiable risk is the explanation for the failure: "I did this dumb thing, but it seemed to make sense at the time." But sometimes one takes the tennis shot because there is no other shot available. In advance, risk cannot be justified, because we can't know enough.

Risk has its own life form. To some, it is actually the desire for danger; to others, the risk stems from their fear of danger. Even though one can teach defining and controlling risk, "risk-taking" itself is not so much taught as absorbed through experience.

1. How do we raise children? *no one is ever trained to be free.* Much, if not most, of a child's upbringing is coercive: to be careful, to be proper, to be nice; how to eat, how to speak, how to "be seen and not heard." Children are trained to do our bidding, which then becomes a coercion. The "shoulds" are imposed right from the beginning. Discipline is different from "Behave yourself." You can't train children by saying "Whatever you want to do is all right"; that lacks discipline. But you *can* tolerate children expanding the limits of their own turf in ways that are annoying or make babysitting more difficult, instead of saying "Don't." Now think: if you can understand that saying "Don't," or "You can't," is inhibiting to children—why are you saying "Don't," or "You can't," to yourself?

Children intuitively do things that involve a risk we are afraid for them to take. Sometimes that's because they don't know the danger, while we do (touching a hot stove, for example); at other times, they can learn from taking the risk, either some self-discipline (self–toilet training), or some sense that what was ventured was gained (discovery). But when we educate coercively, we take away; we defraud children of their own interests. If *we* look terrified because the toddler might topple as he takes his first step, we increase his sense of danger, diminish his chance to learn how to handle risk. We dominate with the power of being parents what children instinctively know *and* do better—love, trust—turning *those interests* of growing and achieving and flourishing inevitably into taking risks we don't approve of or reserve only for grown-ups (including, to be mild about it, nicotine and alcohol).

2. Even more coercive is the way we train a dog or horse. "Heel" is the equivalent of "should." How do we ever train an animal to use its imagination, its own senses? Typically, stories of brilliant animal behavior are of the "Lassie shut up" variety, a dog doing something the trainer couldn't understand, tried to stop. Riders who have a lot of stories about incurably crazy horses, says Vicki Hearne (*Adam's Task*, Alfred A. Knopf, New York, 1986), tend to find that many of the horses they ride are crazy. The visions—the risk-taking—that leads to genuine horsemanship are *visions that "come from artistic rather than psychological thinking."* Craziness is the risk: the attempt to go beyond, to be/do more, a "more" that scares the observer but not the tryer.

Indeed, we learn from the horse what it is that makes us think he's crazy. That is, while the horse evidently sees the barrier as something that *can* be leapt, *we aren't sure enough of what we see.* This is as true in explaining why we involuntarily hesitate before crossing an empty or one-way street as it is about the stock market. The horse acts on its vision because *that* is its primary sense. Truly, what it sees is what it knows. Because we, on the other hand, think our primary sense is thinking, we pause to contemplate the risk in some rational way, relying not on what we've intuitively seen, but on what comes later—the after-the-leap "justifiable" risk. Beforehand, before the rhythm, before the grace, the horse's leap can seem crazy.

3. Riding a jumper in the ring in Madison Square Garden not being something I've ever done, let's translate this into tennis. For now we have the human being—on occasion—like a horse: responding to what is seen as a primary vision. There's the ball! there are the boundaries of the court, and the net, there's the opponent standing in the way. Just like, I suppose, the way the fence rails look as they loom up in the center of the ring.

Is this not similar to that absurd stock market cliché of "the risk/reward ratio"? If an analyst proudly pronounces that the stock has a chance of going up 3 points, but could fall only 1, he believes he is identifying a positive risk/reward of 3 to 1. But that begs the question, because the choice—the what-to-do-ness—is still based on our ability to perceive which way it ought to go. If the stock is more likely to back off, what good does the better theoretical reward do a buyer? One looks at the stock as the horse looks at the rails: can it do it, or not? The reward comes from being right, not from a ratio. The horse intuits the leap as it leaps.

4. Tennis experience tells of two opposite patterns. If one, in that less than a twinkling, *thinks* of hitting the ball here, or there, or how, the *thinking* creates a bad shot, all too typically flubbed. The rational minisecond interferes with the stroke itself, delaying, disrupting; the "thought" that might seem to help analyze the situation, and come up with an "answer" that reduces the risk, actually increases the chance of failure. At the other extreme is the untranslatable notion of "zoning," a sports word used to describe playing beyond oneself. One scarcely remembers hitting the ball, can't recall the point, but knows, afterward, that he was playing as if the court was infinitely roomy enough for any stroke. To play like that at match point against, to win that point, to keep playing like that until the match is won, is to understand how the risk can be taken freely, *as a matter of life itself.*

5. Such "zoning"—winning games by relaxing and just hitting the ball—until having to deal with being ahead causes a locked elbow and iron forearm, also can be identified in revolutionary politics. A dictator, having won the power, goes rigid, actually *becomes* the dictator instead of the hero of the people, because of the winning, and turns that power into destruction in an attempt to avoid any further risk. But the path *toward* that power had been of risk-taking, typically with the ability, because at first it is perceived as freeing, to carry the public along.

6. In this way risk becomes not danger but a positive, motivating force toward doing.

◆◆◆◆ How does any of this happen? How does the horse leap? the child venture? the tennis player or cellist intuitively let go with all he's learned? the practice, the experience, the skill, and yes, the confidence, that comes from putting all this together successfully often enough to believe in it. Many people learn the beginnings, the venturing forth. "To venture causes anxiety," my favorite trader quotes Kierkegaard, "but not to venture is to lose one's self."

Let me remind you of the bright-eyed look and delighted chortling of that toddler as he toddles, lurches, lunges—even as he loses it—toward your arms? *That*'s the venturing. And then up and trying again. Not to venture can cost that child his self.

But—we're talking about 20 and 30 years later—it is not enough just to be a smart guy. Ego reward (and even the first promotion or two) may seem sufficient, but it is as momentary as being patted on the head like a puppy by one's mother; it is never quite believed. You've got to be free enough to protect the tangible, because not to take what is there is a form of losing. (That's the nonsense of "No one ever gets hurt taking a profit.") Venturing is just a beginning, can be cut short by fear—and worse: by the settling for the ego satisfaction of having tried. This "aborted reward"—the inability to carry to fruition, even if begun well—is as if to avoid death by tiptoeing away.

Ah! there's the lurking danger. There's *the* fear that if you're too assertive—step out of bounds, fight city hall, insist on more—everything could be taken away from you tomorrow. Crisis, peril, danger—all those dictionary-definition words relate to our mortalness. Life or money—'tis the same—becomes too dangerous to risk, and so, as in "Appointment in Samara," becomes the risk anyhow.

◆◆◆◆ What happens in the stock market is instructive. Even when a particular transaction is over—bought and sold—it isn't over. The money has a continuing appetite; the market is billed as a "continuous auction." The reward is truly momentary. As a result, although it may be triumphant, it is never satisfactory. You are getting "paid" for what you do, but only if you continue doing it well, sort of the way "You're only as good as your next picture" has become a denial of ability in Hollywood. As long as it continues momentary, *it is always a risk.* No wonder the fear, the anxiety. No wonder the movie actor, or the husband, feels he has to keep performing or he's done for; the investor is terrified that his proxy performance— the transaction—is about to turn into a loss. But since the fluctuating stock market will always have this characteristic of "continuous momentary," we have to learn to live with that anxiety without letting it turn the investment into danger. The way to do that is to play the entire game, to accept the momentary by creating a whole out of each game.

In the stock market's equivalent of life, one assumes the responsibility not only for venturing but for the sell side, too . . . the totality. Satisfaction comes from assuming the entire risk *and* thus overcoming the dangers of the incomplete. Just as the cellist has to be free enough to take that note where no one ever has gone before, the stock market player has to let the totality of the transaction evolve. *To feel whole you've got to play the whole game for the whole move.* Reward is not so much the profit or loss, reward is not the opposite side of the risk ratio, *reward is the balance.*

◇•◇•◇•◇ *The risk doesn't go away.* It doesn't need to. We make of it the danger that we want, we feel of it the out-of-controlness that excites, we give it those awesome powers over us because we otherwise would have to be responsible. Much of our behavior is nonresponsible or, more accurately, aresponsible (as in *amoral*). Risk as danger, risk as excitement—even if the risk is as corny and common as an affair, or as defiant as Sunday afternoon hang gliding—turns a free man into the man who believes in falling on a grenade if need be.

But when we make of our risks an everyday unfolding, it means we have assumed the responsibility for ourselves: adultness might be defined that way. In the midst of risk, being responsible—the risk being balanced with reward—makes sense of the situation. Hence dealing with risk can be defined as *the assumption of responsibility. It is the manner in which risk passes beyond danger and is absorbed into the choices of everyday life.*

Responsibility has its own requirements of courage, discipline, intuition, trust, and doing. And *that's* scary. Perhaps that's why so many prefer the risk-taking of adolescents, because it is at that age when *not* knowing enough is unimportant; teenagers are sure at all times that they know all they need to know when they don't even pay attention to what is knowable.

The adolescence of midlife—the discovery of sexual vitality all over again as if it is an ocean of feeling instead of just a geyser of emotion—involves what can be identified as emotional risk. Emotion is misleading; like other forms of craziness, it can be a fleeing rather than a freeing. While those who are caught up in this midlife-crisis stuff believe passionately that they know what they are doing, what they have done instead is to confuse their emotion with the "feel" of intuition when they are not the same. They insist that they "feel" love when it is, rather, an emotional risk-taking, a plunging into an affair with the fever of being young again when they are not. They would tell you, with the experience of middle age, that love grows on one, and didn't grow in their first marriage—and then plunge all over again. They claim to be long-term investors, but play each minute as emotionally as currency traders.

This period of life can be readily, although perhaps simplistically, explained as the panicky risk-taking that arises when mortality as a fact finally penetrates. It is the same kind of anxiety stock market players feel in the midst of a transaction. "Stop the trade—I want to get off" becomes the theme song. Trading green pieces of paper for the risk? trading the risk back in for greenbacks, and being glad to get off whole plus one. There is the relief of "I'm still alive."

This fear of mortality is cousin to the safety risk, the bureaucratic approach to handling the risk of growing old by trying to turn it into no risk at all. Pensions become the palliative, relieving without curing. Rather than the work itself, the goal of being able to retire becomes the goal of going to work every day. And while the husband leaves home every morning for his post-office–style job, so that he won't ever have to assume the responsibility of crossing the street again, his spouse has beaten him to it; by marrying into housewifeliness she has hedged all risk as if simultaneously owning puts and calls (maybe a calendar spread, perhaps a butterfly) on the same human commodity.

In stock market life we see both of these forms of risk: the one speculates, using the market as a surrogate, avoiding the responsibility of sound investing for the emotional. Others, searching for safety, never change their portfolio through the market's ups and downs because of the bureaucratic belief that when they are done, when they are ready to withdraw into retirement, all will be there waiting for them as their due for avoiding the fluctuations of life. Although the stock market provides a day-by-day opportunity to take a *genuine* risk, it as if both extremes believe the market (as life) is too risky to try to play well!

◇•◇•◇•◇ We aren't all like bureaucrats craving pensions rather than taking a chance on old age. But even if we venture, even if we succeed, there is a letdown after the glamour of winning, because the game is over. Professional athletes cease to play well—a form of dying—after signing multimillion multiyear contracts; tennis players cease to play well on becoming number one. And isn't that what postpartum depression is? the letdown after the success of birthing because there is now a responsibility to raise that baby. These seemingly monumental risks cause breakdowns, as if one has reached the top and can now only, however slowly, die.

Remember that money becomes a measure of being. Losing money, therefore, seems to many people to be symbolic of death. Thus the money risk becomes a substitute for other risks. The purpose of speculation, as Richard Russell has perceptively pointed out, is "to beat time." We want action, which perhaps explains why we cross a traffic-filled street to save 15 seconds. Or are we trying to save our lives by doing something lively? to make even crossing the street more defiant or to retire? because loss, *any form of loss, can mean the loss of all possibility of trust.*

In our personal lives, we phrase this as "I took a chance in loving you, in marrying you, in trusting you, and you let me down." That marriage, to woman, stock, employer, doctor, system, currency contract, and so on, turns out to be "dead" wrong.

What an expression! Death, as the ultimate and complete failure, has gotten into our being, and nothing, not even a successful trade, can get it out again. *Death is the extreme of risk.*

◇◆◇◆◇ But if you have the patience to go for the reward, rather than getting tied up in risk-anxiety, when the reward is achieved, the game, the goal, isn't over after all because *you are free to do more games.* The lesson of the stock market, as symbolic of life's risks as well as being its own reality, is that because of its "continuous momentary," reward isn't the end-all and be-all: indeed, to keep your money alive you *need* to keep investing. Thus the fear of achievement as a form of death is a false fear connected with fear of risk. If you lose, that fear whispers, you can make excuses, rationalize, and try again; if you win—it's over. *There's a subconscious fear that if you do get the reward, you'll never be able to do it again, which thus requires you never to try again, which instills the fear of the reward at the outset.*

If death is the end of success, then the nature of risk is the terror of losing all that we've gained. Our defiances, from smoking to speculating, are dances of fear. *We must risk death*—to achieve the reward of living. The acceptance of responsibility accepts loss as acceptable. All others panic.

· 2 0 ·

The Freedom of
Not Knowing:
A Modern Know-Nothing Theory

H O W can freedom emerge from—proceed from—expand from—*not knowing enough?*

There exists in physics nowadays an attempt to develop a "theory of everything" (TOE). Such a TOE "would bring new depths of understanding to every basic process in nature." (I am here relating to, and arguing with, not the book itself—*The Emperor's New Mind*, by Roger Penrose—but to a review of that book by Timothy Ferris [as published in the *New York Times Book Review*], because I'm one of those Ferris refers to when he writes that "readers lacking at least a graduate student's comprehension of physics will find parts of it rough going.")

Penrose differs with the artificial-intelligence crew who believe it will be possible to build computers capable of equaling or exceeding "the thought processes of the human mind." Those proponents of the "strong A.I." strain "argue that the brain is a computer." Penrose responds that "computers have inherent limits which . . . are not necessarily imposed on human thought." One is that the machine deals with computable numbers. Yet there are "noncomputable" numbers that "ought in principle to be inaccessible to computers." Penrose writes: "Perhaps our minds are qualities rooted in some strange and wonderful feature of those physical laws which actually govern the world we inhabit, rather than being just features of some algorithm."

In quantum physics it is "observation that matters." Only in observation do probabilities become essential to the calculations. "Chance, therefore, rules the quantum world." It is here, of course, that the stock market enters the discussion. The stock market must be dealt with by these folks: it is supposedly ruled by chance, but of course that's not true; observation and probabilities—observation *of* probabilities—are the ways technicians try to overcome the apparent chance. It is a separate, yet observable, world, with its own language that can be interpreted, but is nevertheless still alien. What we perceive as chance is the almost infinite number of subsequent significant possibilities that derive from each millisecond's change. *What the hell does it mean next?* derives both from the shifting grain of sand thesis and the market's anthropomorphic brain. (The notion of "chaos," which became so popular on Wall Street after the 1987 crash, denies the ease with which that particular top could have been seen beforehand and relies only on making the major aspect what was simply the proverbial straw.)

The review goes on to point out Penrose's belief that one might be able to link quantum phenomena to the operation of the brain. Quantum effects "may explain intuition, judgment, esthetic taste and the other qualities that Penrose views as attributes of human thought and not of computers." He is here trying to come to grips with—isn't he?—two different aspects: the one hand of *thinking*, and the other hand of *intuition*. The thinking, of course, requires inputs, knowledge, quanta if you will. But the stock market, as well as tennis, and babies, raises the question: Does the brain function as a "thinking" machine all the time, or is intuition, and its skills, derived either from the brain as an entirely different suborgan or from an entirely different "place" itself?

◇◆◇◆◇ The brain. Intuition. Imagination and inference. Thinking. *How do we know something we don't know?* Unexpectedly—intuition working again—I found an answer in my barn where I came across an old and mildewed philosophy textbook that hadn't been opened since my college days. It was entitled *The Nature of Thought*, by Brand Blanshard (George

Allen & Unwin, London, 1939), and there, in my own school-boy's scrawl, were some remarkable notes and underlinings.

"Perception," Professor Blanshard wrote, is "the simplest activity that aims at truth directly and may conceivably yield it." Not realizing I would ever apply his words to the stock market, I had underlined: "Direct intuitive understanding of an occurrence or a thought or an universal or a meaning is the only level at which truth can be arrived at—if it is intuitive, it is the truth, if only for that single moment. . . . " In the margin of another page I had scribbled, "The power to see in things the universal." And *"The end we are seeking reveals itself only as the seeking goes on."* (Emphasis added, due to stock market experiences.)

Because it is when events are changing that we know the least, there's a "shock to the system of thought already present when a new idea is presented. . . . The first step in reflection," my prof had written, "is the appearance of disunity that intelligence cannot abide." Is not that "disunity"—old inputs tangling with new—how a stock market trend changes? Forty years ago I had underlined: "Tension goads"; but *"anxiety inhibits."* "Men tend to see what they expect or hope or fear to see . . . " but the [successful stock market forecaster] has "an intuitive perception of the similarity in dissimilars, and the power to grasp and develop a system."

A system? so *that's* the understanding we've been striving for! But what can go wrong? "when we observe the wrong things; fasten on the irrelevant; select relevant but too exclusive things; manufacture the data for ourselves"; and, I hasten to add now, not believe. "Truth consists in *coherent* system," Professor Blanshard concluded, "absolute truth in a system from which nothing is excluded, *relative truth in those comparatively chaotic and fragmentary systems to which a narrow capacity limits us."* "Coherence must be a test of reality," I wrote at the bottom of the page, "even if we don't know everything that might or ought to be included."

❖❖❖❖ As a college sophomore, I was pleased with the notion that we didn't have to know everything in order to sound off about anything. Now, look how words from that philosophical tome apply to the stock market! With its "chaotic and fragmentary messages wrapped in a system," the stock market provides for its own correction faster, and more unlike, any other scientific system that comes readily to mind. It is its constant change that makes trying to perceive coherence in the stock market so challenging. It is the constant change, too, that makes the stock market seem so risky. And it is the constant change that, ironically, makes it possible to forecast; the fluctuations are needed in order to grow the patterns that become discernible. "A proposition can be true precisely to the extent to which it is necessary, and necessary to the extent that it is true. Since necessity and truth are never quite attained"—we are back to never knowing enough—"no truth will be quite true, nor will any false proposition be completely absolutely false." And so, Professor Blanshard wrote, "construe the world we live in as to make escape from it conceivable." When we understand what we don't know, we can prepare for anything.

❖❖❖❖ So look where we have come to: skilled, competent, grown-up. We have even developed some confidence that what we do we do well; we have even assumed some responsibilities in life. So why don't we trust ourselves? we lay our risks off on other people—doctors, lawyers, brokers, and, for that matter, interior decorators—so unsure that we hedge our bets, sell calls against our confidence, buy puts in case we're "wrong again." *What are we afraid of?* becomes the nature of risking ourselves.

Most people really do think of risk in its dictionary definition terms: danger, peril. They take that belief to the one extreme or the other of defiantly daring all or doing nothing at all, whether at home or at play, at work, or in the stock market. For those of us who want to confront risk so as to turn that anxiety into a positive, what *are* we afraid of?

Requiring thinking, dependent on knowing, *we aren't intuitively sure enough of what we intuitively see.* We proceed through decisions like the child who "knows" 2 + 2 = 4, but has to check it out by putting up two fingers on one hand, and two fingers on the other, and adding them up together.

This is, of course, another way of stating that *we don't trust our own intuition.* The lack of faith in doubt, and the quest for an absolute answer, produces a rejection of imperfect techniques—without accepting what we do know: that it is an imperfect world. The belief that science will carry the day leads to the misconstrued notion in the stock market that corporate fundamentals will provide an answer, that "value" will win out, if only the right numbers are plugged in. As a result of being rejected, an increasing number of technicians—like journeymen baseball players wanting to use aluminum bats—have also set out in search of the right numbers to plug in.

Scientimorphism is what does in not only technicians but all investors who believe that because they can't know all, they can't know enough. No one would trust what cartoonlike gurus up on a cloud-shrouded mountain said the market was saying because the market world's almost hieroglyphic language wasn't rational—until scientimorphism came along. But science has proven to be a concentrated form of coercion, taking the place of religions, and becoming but another expression of the Western world's need for absolute answers. In the manner of Communist party leaders throughout Eastern Europe, who were secure in their faith in the party, there is an underlying belief, particularly in fundamental analysis, that "the market can be coerced into behaving" in a sensible fashion.

It can't be.

Nor, of course, and no matter how many administrations pass through Washington or party leaders through Prague, can we coerce the nature of life around us. *Taking a risk is an attempt to deal with the coercions of life.* It is the knowing of not knowing enough that frees the investor from the anxiety of losing what he has and, instead, lets him proceed toward the reward. A wrong note, a missed shot, a losing transaction, is all part of the passage. You can't be a better player without accepting that risk along the way—indeed, without having experienced loss along the way.

One needs the confidence that comes from bringing risk into every moment of life, so that it is not risk as danger, but risk as the positive that makes every day worth getting up for in the morning. If reward is the balance, then shorting oneself on reward creates a disharmony that breaks fibers down all along the way, including one's health and wealth. The fear of death as loss is turned into a positive only by the ongoing.

This is the informed risk—relying on the assumption of responsibility rather than the laying off of the test on external factors. As with horse racing, "the essential comparison is between the horse and itself." And thus, between the stock and itself, between one's own life which *is* itself and one's personal "wall of worry" put up in the way of potential reward.

The remaining question, then, is, Why don't we trust ourselves? Our relationship to risk—that risk which has fear of death at its core—can best be understood by using the stock market's life as metaphor for real life. Speculative trading functions as if none of the market's action or its losses are real, the way teenagers gleefully watch heads blown off in horror movies because, knowing none of it is real, their fear of death is expiated. But the responsible investor relates to what *is* known—what the market is telling him—while knowing that he doesn't, and never will, know enough. But he can know dimensions, proportions: whether there is a top overhead, or a bottom forming, or a trend in existence, or, in some cases, such a blurred message that he must step aside. In this way the degree of risk—its potential danger—can be tempered and even brought under control so that one can focus on the potential reward. *There is enough out there to know that one need do nothing foolish.* As for what is not yet known, *that becomes intuition's responsibility.* Intuition is perceiving the "relation between what is actually given in sense and what is only thought or judged." Answers come from not knowing, and yet "knowing." It is our own intuition we have to trust: Buying, Selling— Doing!